INFORMATION TECHNOLOGY

INFORMATION TECHNOLOGY
A Scientific Revolution

ARUN BABEJA

ISHA BOOKS
New Delhi - 1100 09

Information Technology : A Scientific Revolution

Rs. ´790

ISBN: 81-8205-399-4

Published in 2007 in India by
ISHA Books
1st Floor New Gupta Colony,
Near DDA Market,
Delhi-110009

Lasser Type Setting by: Rudra Computer Graphics, Delhi
Printed at : Salasar Imaging System, Delhi

Contents

Preface

Information Technology (IT) considered by a number of people as revolutionary has marred rapid development and diffusion in an increasing number of sectors particularly in the developed market economy countries. The services sector, which with few exceptions lagged behind other sectors in adopting technological innovations, has emerged as a major IT users. The characteristics of IT are especially attractive. It cuts the cost of information processing, speeds up data transmission, decreases size and increases reliability of equipment while enhancing the importance of software. The progress in mobility, interactivity and networking capabilities of IT have led to a number of advantages in the production and export of goods and services. More specifically, economies of scope, flexible production lines and greater customization of products are made possible through the application of the technology.

Information Technology systems also allow for interactivity, a time-and-labour saving procedure for tasks formerly rendered by human operators.

Enhancing efficiency has been the main objective behind the application of Information Technology. In addition to labour and time-saving, such applications have the potential to reduce stock lend and wastage, ensuring better coordination and flexibility in production along with adaptation of the quantity and quality of products of market trends.

The spread of information technology in industry has taken place more so in the production of engineering design services rather than construction implementation, although some progress has been made in automating construction methods that involve the traditional labour-intensive tasks of cutting and bending as well as electrical wiring a piping.

Information Technology together with the development of expert systems and innovation in construction material is changing the profile of the industry. Firms competing in the international market place are making more use of the technology weapon to maintain or enhance their competitiveness.

The spread of IT may have also influenced the institutional location of production.

The advent of Micro-electronics and Information Technology has lowered energy consumption and harmful emissions especially in the transportation sector. The role of Information Technology and learning in the shaping the competitive advantage of construction and engineering services forms is also significant.

Information Technology has also brought a fundamental changes in the military C4 I environment. Without information research and industry would decline. To know-how to obtain information in the minimum time is indisputable factor in competitiveness. Databases and databanks (DB), accessible on-line from a microcomputer or a video text station can provide this decisive factor. Nowadays, these are thousands of millions of references stored in thousands of databases, this represents an enormous wealth of information, really a supermarket of information, that is still largely underused. The mention of growth and coverage of databases and databanks have been significantly discussed. Importance of the digital communication networks has also been mentioned.

Identification of some very implications of Information Revolution for both the military and civilian sector has been discussed in this book with greater significance.

The creation of Electronic Library, computerized front-ends and implications for developing countries, simulated man-machine system as training supervision and computerized tools for self-learning, Human-centred approach to designing information systems, designing Interactive Systems and theories of Human Mind Process information all have really revolutionized the world.

Today a question generally stands before us how best to produce and provide the information being needed by all sorts of users. Hypertext and hypermedia have been introduced as situation to this question.

Multimedia Interface Design, System of ayachive Translation, the SUB-Language CONCEPT, MITI'S New Programme in the context of Real-world computing and flexible information Access, Systems Management Approach, Information Technology and Institutional Cooperation all are of greater importance.

The most advanced countries have indeed already entered the Information Age—a creature of information technology that itself results from the marriage of computers and tele-communications, hardware and software, information systems and services. By the year 2000, as it is told, to all intents and purposes, information technology will be able to create a nearly information-transparent world, while fiber optics will carry libraries of information to any one-anywhere, who pushes a button. It appears that three revolutionary technological changes will be required to bring about affordable individual access to global on-line information, efficient large-scale database construction and maintenance, high speed digital transmission networks and highly precise intelligent searchware. "As these technological revolutions appear over the next several decades, they will result in a worldwide information system that will have a major impact on the entire information industry."

In Tokyo a conference was convened to explore the role of information technology in facilitating access the potential of scientific and technological developments for enhancing the capacity to handle, transfer, exchange and access information.

As far as the inter-governmental organizations of the UN system is concerned, most of the organizations within the UN system have developed information systems to support their internal needs and international information systems in their fields oriented towards members states. The United Nations Bibliographic Information System (UNBIS) of the Dag Hammarskyold library is online bibliographic and factual information system covering the publications and documents of the United Nations. The United Nations Centre on Transnational Corporations (UNCTC) had developed the Corporate Profile System (CPS) dealing with the activities of transnational corporations in developing countries and the issue of technology development. The Economic Commission for Africa (ECA) operates a regional multi-disciplinary bibliographic information system called the pan-African Documentation and Information System (PADIS) containing references to information on African economic, social, scientific and technological development.

At the most obvious level, the information revolution offers militaries potentially dramatic improvements in force effectiveness. The military must now look towards procurement of commercial off-the-shelf, duatuse equipments and open systems architectures instead of relying on the classic but autarchic military R and D and acquisition systems which produced highly optimized and cutting-edge systems but at high-cost-usually with proprietary technologies.

The technological component of what we call the information revolution is the outcome of a set of related technical innovations, together yielding substantial enhancements or even the revolutionary change that the term itself implies.

1

Advent of Micro-electronics and Information Technology

Introduction

In the access to information there are big gaps in the world. For example, in 1986 the developed countries had approximately 1000 radio receivers per 1000 citizens, followed by Latin America and Caribbean with 327, the Arab States with 247, Asia with 162, and Africa with 142. The distribution of the several telephone main lines in service is even more uneven. In 1987, Europe had 154.4 million main lines in service, followed by North America with 136.8 million, Asia with 126.2 million, Latin America with 21.7 million, Australia with 8.4 million, and Africa with 6.5 million. On a per 1000 residents basis, the U.S. has 10 times more telephone lines than Latin America, 12 times more than Asia, and 48 times more than Africa. In 1990 the U.S. market for the transmission of telegraphic and telex messages and data was calculated to be 60 times bigger than the African market and 30 times larger than the Latin American market. The evolution of information technologies has shown an explosive improvement in their performance ratio. This has induced further expansion of the micro-electronics and informatics industry. In the OECD countries, only an estimated 10 to 20 per cent of the profits derived from information-technology-based innovation has so far been reaped; the rest will be received in the next decade. Similar trends are observed in applications of information technologies, such as the automation of telecommunications and the connections of computers by data transmission. These applications, together with word processing and computerization of management systems, have changed finance, banking, business management, and public administration. Information systems developments are continually being applied by private and public sectors to enhance the productivity, quality, and efficiency. Currently large companies have begun to use information systems to transmit technical and economic information among numerous computer systems at various geographical locations. In manufacturing and to some extent in agriculture, several processes have been automated, some requiring highly flexible, self-regulating machines, or robots. The engineering industry has been transformed by computer-assisted design (CAD) and three-dimensional, computerized screen displays.

In the 1990s more technical advances are expected in automation. Examples are programmable automation, or computer-integrated manufacturing that has the capability of integrating information processing with physical tasks done by programmable robots

The development of the computer and telecommunication industries is still rapid and pervasive. As proxied by selected industrial categories, the world postulation for telecommunication equipment has been growing at an annual rate of 8 per cent during the 1980s. World demand for computer equipment and services is estimated to grow more speedily than telecommunication equipment and services for the period 1985-1990, with the U.S. share standing at about 45 pr cent. Even speedy growth has been recorded for the semiconductor industry, which produces the basic components used in all computerized applications. This sector may account for 4 per cent of whole world manufacturing output by the year 2000 (equivalent to $200 billion in 1980 prices).

The world production of information technology systems is expected to grow from $390 billion in 1986 to $1200 billion in 1995, with software achieving the highest annual growth rate of 20 per cent during 1986-1995. Production of hardware in 1995 will account for 52 per cent, software 36 per cent, and telecommunications and computing services 12 per cent. Until 1995, in the U.S. alone, expenditure on computers, data processing equipment, and telephone and telegraph systems is projected to grow at an average rate of 20 per cent.

The world market for telecommunications and broadcasting satellites in the 1990s will be dominated by developed countries; Latin America, for instance, will account for only 2 per cent. The world market will be about 7 billion in 1986 U.S. dollars in the late 1990s, but it will rise less rapidly in the late 1990s than in the 1980s and early 1990s. The diffusion of informatics in developing countries is still in an embryonic stage. They accounted for only 5.7 per cent of the total number of computers in the world in 1985. The developing countries have so far used the computers chiefly for standard functions of inventory control, accounting, and payroll. Currently, however, some activities in microelectronics such as assembly of mature components and final testing have relocated from Hong Kong, Singapore, and Taiwan province of China to new locations in the Caribbean, China, Indonesia, the Philippines, Sri Lanka and Thailand. The semiconductor market in the South-East Asia has expanded rapidly; South Korea, Hong Kong, and Singapore are projected to raise their semiconductor sales from $2 billion in 1986 to $5.4 billion in 1990. During 1981-1986, the Brazilian electronics market rose to about $8 billion, thus becoming the tenth largest in the world and slightly larger than that of the Republic of Korea; Brazilian-controlled firms have rapidly expanded their production of computers. India has been particularly successful in software. It has created a niche in the international software market through its government policies of tax breaks and liberal foreign exchange regulations for this sector. India increases its software exports each year by about 40 per cent and plans to produce $100 million worth of software annually by the year 1990s.

Telecommunications technologies and micro computers offer potential opportunities of fulfilling the developing countries' needs, comprising above all access to information and telephone services. Also, telecommunications technologies may be very factor in improving the market mechanisms for small businesses and developing the rural sectors and underdeveloped regions in developing countries. Microcomputers have found several applications in small and medium-scale enterprises and in education in developing countries due to their rapid improvement in cost/performance ratio and the widespread availability of First Generation

Babbage's work relied mainly on mechanics and physical machinery. It was not until the twentieth century invention of the electrical vacuum tube and then the transistor that computers became a possible means to solving problems.

War ha been a remarkable factor in the development of the computer. In 1943, during World War II, the British and Americans developed electronic computers. Colossus, a British effort, was specifically developed to crack the German coding cipher Lorenz whilst an American effort, Harward Mark I, was developed as a more general purpose electromechanical programmable computer.

Regarded as early 'first generation' computers, these machines primarily consisted of wired circuits and vacuum valves. Punched cars were employed as the input, output and main storage systems.

Following on from initial developments, INIAC (Electronic Numerical Integrator and Computer) was completed in 1946 by the Americans, Capable of carrying out 100,000 calculations a second, it was significant for its day. Like all first generation machines, ENIAC was very big and power hungry (weighing 30 tonnes and consuming 25 kilowatts of electricity).

Second Generation

Similar to light bulbs, valves were prone to failure, requiring tedious checks to sort out problems (ENLAC alone comprised 18,000 vacuum valves). In '947 the transistor was invented. Performing the same role as a vacuum valve, but less prone to failure, smaller and more efficient, the transistor allowed smaller 'second generation' computers to be developed throughout the 1950s and early 1960s.

Computers remained the province of government and universities due to their scale of cost of size. There use was remarkable in nuclear weapon and power generation research and development—one field drove the other.

Third Generation

In 1958 Jack St Claire Kilby produced the first integrated circuit, a 'micro-chip'. A micro-chip is comprised of a huge number of transistors and other components bonded to a single substrate—typically a wafer of silicon, interconnected by a surface film of conductive material ratherthan by wires. By subsiding distance between components, savings are made in both size and electricity. In 1963 the first 'third generation' computers based on 'micro-chip' technology appeared.

Fourth Generation

In 1971 Intel produced the first 'microprocessor' heralding a 'fourth generation' of computers. The Intel 4004 (capable of 60,000 instructions per second) grouped much of the processing functions onto a single microchip. Around the same time Intel invented the RAM (random access memory) chip which grouped phenomenal amounts of memory onto a single chip. Intl remain today as a leading chip manufacturer. Successive microprocessors had every-increasing calculating ability while the capacity of RAM increased also. Super computers and mainframes utilizing scores of microprocessors had terrific power in the order of 150 million instructions per second.

The power of the computer has significantly increased as science has scaled down the size and electrical consumption of the core component (the transistor) from thumb size to far smaller than the thickness of a human hair, allowing a greater density and thus increasing the total power of the computer. Developments such as multiple-layer circuits and the use of copper instead of gold continue to yield gains in size and performance through miniaturization.

The microprocessor made easy the advent of very powerful supercomputers and also allowed small and affordable micro or personal computers. Early micro computers included the Altair 8800 in 1974, the Apple I & II, Commodore PET through to the IBM PC based on Intel's 8086 in 1981. The 8086 chip began a dynasty of hugely successful microprocessors for Intel that continues today with the Pentium III range.

IBM's original PC set a standard which was effectively wrestled from IBM by companies making clones or copies of the IBM design. IBM prepared the initial PC only to see other companies take the lion's share of the market. The operating system supplier Microsoft made thousands of times more money out of the IBM PC than IBM ever did.

In the mid 1980s Apple Computer rejected its highly successful Apple II computer range to generate the Apple Lisa and Apple Macintosh computers utilizing the Motorola 68000 processor. Being the first widely available commercial computers with a graphical mouse/pointer driven interface they were comparatively expensive compared to the command line (text only) operated IBM PC clones. The Lisa was abandoned but the Apple Macintosh today ranks as the second largest personal computer system.

In the early 1990s RISC (reduced instruction set computing) became common. Compared with conventional CISC (complex instruction set computing) chips, a RISC processor uses a small set of highly able instruction types in combinations to get the same result as one CISC instruction. Because of performance optimization the RISC chip can often do some tasks more rapidly than a CISC chip.

The first RISC chips were installed in UNIX servers and workstations. In the mid-1990s Apple Computer teamed up with IBM and Motorola to produce the PowerPC chip. Apple stopped shipping personal computes with the aging 68040 CISC chip and instead utilized the PowerPC chip. Around that time Intel started shipping the Pentium CISC chip. Successive releases have produced ever faster versions of the Power PC and Intel chip sets. For instance, from an initial speed of 66 MHz in the mid-1990s, the PowerPC chip was released at 1,000 MHz in 2000.

Next Generation

Most modern computers are still regarded as 'fourth generation' as they use necessarily the same technology, albeit highly miniaturized. The future of computer technology is widely thought to be dependent on the physics of light. Already used widely in the computer industry for high speed communications, laser light offers feasibilities for both calculation and storage.

As has been seen, there is huge diversity in the field of computer science and processor types are no exception—there have been literally hundreds of design families and thousands of processor models, and constraints of space preclude discussion of them all here.

Programming Languages

A multitude of programming languages have been devised with the common view of devising a programme of instructions for computers to follow to achieve a task. Programming languages are categorized by generation:

IGL or first-generation language is the machine language that the processor chips execute. Instructions and arguments are in binary form(strings of zeros and ones). For the very early computers machine language was sole choice as there was often insufficient resources to support assembly language or even an operating system. Machine language tends to be highly specific to a specific processor or processor family.

2GL or second-generation language. Assembly language is a human-understandable language insofar as uses names instead of numbers. An assembler program takes assembly language and turns it into a machine code program. Very common on early systems where resources (speed, storage) were at a premium, it is typically only used today as an output from 3GL and higher systems. It is rare for the assembly language of two separate processor families to be identical but they all share similar syntax. Assembly language programs do not lend themselves to being used on different hardware platforms.

3GL or third-generation language is a 'high-level' programming language. Typically more readable and concise than assembly language, 3GL programs are charged by a compiler program into either machine or assembly language for later execution. 3GL languages allow programs to be converted or ported from one operating system or hardware platform to another (with varying degrees of effort) and allow more complicated data structures and program flows than 2GLs, 4GL or fourth-generation language is designed to be nearer to natural language than a 3GL language. Languages for accessing databases are often described as 4GLs.

5GL or fifth-generation language programming uses graphical development environments to create source language to be compiled with a 3GL or 4GL language compiler. Generally, 5GLs are used to develop prototype applications which have the look and feel of a final application but often without the underlying power provided by a 3GL or 4GL. Often a mix of generations is used, with a high level language (4 or 5GL) used to produce interface elements and a lower level language used to give the processing power.

Operating Systems

An operating system (OS) is a set of utility programs that acts as the liaison between the computer user, the computer hardware (processor unit, memory) and its peripherals (hard disk, mouse, display, printer, network etc.) and the program that a user is running (e.g. a spreadsheet).

The first computers had no operating system, and each program had to directly control the hardware on its own adding greatly to be burden of programming a computer. Initial input was by setting dials and switches (or even plugging cables), with calculation outcomes shown on dials. The input was in the form of elementary machine language encoded in binary.

The early code-breaking systems utilized teletype paper tape. Then came punched cards—where instructions were laboriously encoded onto cardboard cards that were fed through the machine telling it both what to do and giving it the information or data to compute. The consequence was either produced onto further punched cards or output on to rudimentary display panels.

The use of punched cards allowed some routine components or programs to be reused (by re-using routines on sets of cards). Subsequently, development of memory chips, magnetic tape and hard disks have allowed more extensive programs and information to be stored, executed and re-executed.

Early OS were hardware and vendor-specific with assembly language or machine code the programming language. Each computer model or series tended to have its own particular operating system.

In 1969 a major mainstream operating systems UNIX, was first released. Originated at Bell Labs in the USA, it was based on 'Multics', an earlier time-sharing system. UNIX was one of the first operating systems that could be ported (converted) to a variety of system hardware. This ability was made mainly through the use of the 'C' programming language which was first defined and developed around the same time.

UNIX has evolved into many different versions or 'strains' due in part to the fact that the source code is largely free and written in C. UNIX systems were keystones in the development of the Internet and a large proportion of Internet servers today are UNIX-driven. UNIX is available on more hardware platforms than any other OS, although there is no dominant version of UNIX with a dozen or so large versions.

In 1979 Digital Equipment Corporation (DEC) released VMS (Virtual Memory System) as the operating system for the DEC VAX mini-computer. The main features of VMS was the embracing of a 32-bit virtual memory system that allowed use of hard disk as virtual memory in place of actual RAM chips. Thee have been several operating systems devised and rejected over the years.

Personal Computer Operating Systems

Throughout the 1990s the personal computer world has been dominated by two main players – Microsoft and Apple Computer. Although not important manufacturer of computer equipment itself, Microsoft Corporation has built on its market share secured in the 1980s with MS-DOS to become the market leading operating system provider. Microsoft's MS Windows range of personal computer operating systems are setup on more computers than any other commercial operating system. Concern over the market dominance of Microsoft has led to legislatures in the US and European Union bringing anti-trust (anti-monopoly) lawsuits against the company. Success or failure for Microsoft in such litigation is likely to remarkable shape the future of computing over the first decade of the new millennium.

Microsoft's main rival is Apple Computer. Established in the 1970s, Apple became very successful with its Apple I, II and III range of personal computers and is one of the few of a flock of personal computer companies from that time who have continued to manufacture both their own operating system and hardware to run upon it.

Unlike Microsoft, Apple's strategy has been to control both the hardware and software of their systems. The Apple Macintosh operating system (MacOS) can only be run on Apple Macintosh hardware. This has resulted in a benefit that is also a curse—the Macintosh is a quality product but quality tends to cost. Microsoft profited from the production of a large volume of less expensive PCs, while Apple sells on quality and features. Both have significant advantages and downfalls. Several other operating systems exist but tend to be brand-or hardware-specific.

'The Net'

Prior to the Internet or 'the Net' as it is known colloquially, computers tended to be connected together by hardware and protocols that were peculiar to each particular connection. Typically, links were point-to-point (a link had to be directly and physically established between the two computers).

As in other areas of computing, the military had significant influence on the development of what was to become 'the Net'. In 1969 ARPANET was formed by the US Department of Defence. A main concern was to establish a way for the compute capability of the military to be dispersed so that no one centre was critical to the operation of the network as a whole. This was achieved by interconnecting computers both directly and by way of other intermediary computers; thus if one link or 'node' computer was hit by a nuclear bomb, other pathways of communication could be set up. The interconnections, when drawn, appeared as a mesh or net or web.

ARPANET was extended to non-military users such as universities early in the 1970s, with initial international links appearing in 1972. Early network research lead to the protocol of request for comments (RFC) whereby ideas in development can be followed and studied by other computer users, who will comment on it, expand it and improve on it allowing a de facto standard to quickly evolve. The collaboration ethos instilled in the RFC protocol has fuelled development of the Internet and related computer spheres. RFC number 1 was written in 1969 and there are well over 2,000 today.

Early Internet was merely a means for computers rather than people to communicate and was side-effect of research into networking. It was not 'the Web' and web pages and e-mail as we know it did not exist—these were the days of command line, text-only green screens (if not Teletype printer/keyboards).

The application of domain names (e.g. ditdit.co.uk) in 1984 offered an easier means of using the Web. Prior to domain names one had to remember IP numbers (e.g. 192.168.1.100) for accessing destination computers. The use of e-mail increased and implementations improved as various RFCs were adopted as standards; however, the Internet was primarily limited to government agencies, the military, academic and research organizations and some big businesses.

In 1989 what most people perceive as 'the Net' was born. It was effectively invented at CERN (the European Particle Physics Laboratory) by Tim Berners-Lee as a way for scientists to share information by placing it in a prescribed format (defined in an RFC) on a server. Initially text only, development of computer capability allowed insertion of images through use of a program called NCSA Mosaic—the first graphical'browser' (see glossary).

By 1993 a whole new industry of ISPs (Internet Service Providers) had started, allowing computer users to dial up via a modem and access the Internet and to view the Web through their browser of choice. The leading two browsers today, Netscape and Microsoft Explorer, were both based on the open source code of NCSA Mosaic.

In the mid 1990s the term 'information superhighway' was coined to refer to the Internet. Sadly, the Internet is not a superhighway—it suffers from rush hours, traffic jams and link closures in spite of the fact that new connections are added at a frantic pace.

Developments of the late 1990s have allowed music, video, games, text, graphics and even telephone conversations to co-exist on the same

Internet. The core technologies underpinning the Internet are TCP/IP, routers and domain names (see glossary).

The future of the Internet is likely to see the majority of telephone calls and probably video being transmitted over the Internet for at least part of its journey. Expansion of fibre-optic cable networks to homes and business will underpin this. The introduction of high-capacity mobile phone will also facilitate and demand expansion of the Internet.

Simple but successful virus attacks like the 'love bug' computer virus of early 2000 show how much the world relies on and is affected by Internet technology. With no central governing body or legal jurisdiction the legal implications of the Internet will continue to puzzle for years to come.

2

Information Technology and Computer Science

It can be said that there have been three marvels of the twentieth century: modern medicine, nuclear fusion and the computer. It can be further said that modern medicine and nuclear fusion might not have so advanced were it not for the invention of the computer.

So speedy has the pace of the computer's development been and so broad the sphere of computer science that no article of such brevity can be wholly accurate or complete.

Ancestry

The ancestors to the modern century computer are the Difference Engine and Analytical Engine devised by mathematician Charles Babbage. Designed in 1820 to automatically compute mathematical table, construction of his mechanical, clockwork-like Difference Engine was left by Babbage in the 1840s due to financial problems, personal tragedy and a disagreement with head engineer Joseph Clement.

In 1834 Babbage started work on his Analytical Engine. Unlike the Difference Engine, the Analytical Engine was designed as a general purpose tool with a store to hold information and a mill to take information input on punched cards and translate it into outcomes, or output, on similar punched cards.

Following the financial problems with the incomplete Difference Engine Project, Babbage was unable to secure further government funding for his Analytical Engine and it was not until 1991 that an actual engine was built by a group of historical enthusiasts.

First Generation

Babbage's work relied mainly on mechanics and physical machinery. It was not until the twentieth century invention of the electrical vacuum tube and then the transistor that computers became a possible means to solving problems.

War has been a remarkable factor in the development of the computer. In 1943, during World War II, the British and Americans developed electronic computers. Colossus, a British effort, was specifically developed to crack the German coding as cipher Lorenz whilst an American effort, Harward Mark I, was developed as a more general purpose electromechanical programmable computer.

Regarded as early 'first generation' computers, these machines primarily consisted of wired circuits and vacuum valves. Punched cars were employed as the input, output and main storage systems.

Following on from initial developments, INIAC (Electronic Numerical Integrator and Computer) was completed in 1946 by the Americans, Capable of carrying out 100,000 calculations a second, it was significant for its day. Like all first generation machines, ENIAC was very big and power hungry (weighing 30 tonnes and consuming 25 kilowatts of electricity).

Second Generation

Similar to light bulbs, valves were prone to failure, requiring tedious checks to sort out problems (ENLAC alone comprised 18,000 vacuum valves). In 1947 the transistor was invented. Performing the same role as a vacuum valve but less prone to failure, smaller and more efficient, the transistor allowed smaller 'second generation' computers to be developed throughout the 1950s and early 1960s.

Computers remained the province of government and universities due to their scale of cost of size. There use was remarkable in nuclear weapon and power generation research and development—one field drove the other.

Third Generation

In 1958 Jack St Claire Kilby produced the first integrated circuit, a 'micro-chip'. A micro-chip is comprised of a huge number of transistors and other components bonded to a single substrate—typically a wafer of silicon, interconnected by a surface film of conductive material rather than by wires. By subsiding distance between components, savings are made in both size and electricity. In 1963 the first 'third generation' computers based on 'micro-chip' technology appeared.

Fourth Generation

In 1971 Intel produced the first 'microprocessor' heralding a 'fourth generation' of computers. The Intel 4004 (capable of 60,000 instructions per second) grouped much of the processing functions onto a single micro-chip. Around the same time Intel invented the RAM (random access memory) chip which grouped phenomenal amounts of memory onto a single chip. Intl remain today as a leading chip manufacturer. Successive microprocessors had every-increasing calculating ability while the capacity of RAM increased also. Super computers and mainframes utilizing scores of microprocessors had terrific power in the order of 150 million instructions per second.

The power of the computer has significantly increased as science has scaled down the size and electrical consumption of the core component (the transistor) from thumb size to far smaller than the thickness of a human hair, allowing a greater density and thus increasing the total power of the computer. Developments such as multiple-layer circuits and the use of copper instead of gold continue to yield gains in size and performance through miniaturization.

The microprocessor made easy the advent of very powerful supercomputers and also allowed small and affordable micro or personal computers. Early microcomputers included the Altair 8800 in 1974, the Apple I and II, Commodore PET through to the IBM PC based on Intel's 8086 in 1981. The 8086 chip began a dynasty of hugely successful microprocessors for Intel that continues today with the Pentium III range.

IBM's original PC set a standard which was effectively wrestled from IBM by companies making clones or copies of the IBM design. IBM prepared the initial PC only to see other companies take the lion's share of the market. The operating system supplier Microsoft made thousands of times more money out of the IBM PC than IBM ever did.

In the mid-1980s Apple Computer rejected its highly successful Apple II computer range to generate the Apple Lisa and Apple Macintosh computers utilizing the Motorola 68000 processor. Being the first widely available commercial computers with a graphical mouse/pointer driven interface they were comparatively expensive compared to the command line (text only) operated IBM PC clones. The Lisa was abandoned but the Apple Macintosh today ranks as the second largest personal computer system.

In the early 1990s RISC (reduced instruction set computing) became common. Compared with conventional CISC (complex instruction set computing) chips, a RISC processor uses a small set of highly able instruction types in combinations to get the same result as one CISC instruction. Because of performance optimization the RISC chip can often do some tasks more rapidly than a CISC chip.

The first RISC chips were installed in UNIX servers and workstations. In the mid-1990s Apple Computer teamed up with IBM and Motorola to produce the Power PC chip. Apple stopped shipping personal computes with the aging 68040 CISC chip and instead utilized the Power PC chip. Around that time Intel started shipping the Pentium CISC chip. Successive releases have produced ever faster versions of the Power PC and Intel chip sets. For instance, from an initial speed of 66 MHz in the mid-1990s, the Power PC chip was released at 1,000 MHz in 2000.

Next Generation

Most modern computers are still regarded as 'fourth generation' as they use necessarily the same technology, albeit highly miniaturized. The future of computer technology is widely thought to be dependent on the physics of light. Already used widely in the computer industry for high speed communications, laser light offers feasibilities for both calculation and storage.

As has been seen, there is huge diversity in the field of computer science and processor types are no exception—there have been literally hundreds of design families and thousands of processor models, and constraints of space preclude discussion of them all here.

Programming Languages

A multitude of programming languages have been devised with the common view of devising a programme of instructions for computers to follow to achieve a task. Programming languages are categorized by generation:

IGL or first-generation language is the machine language that the processor chips execute. Instructions and arguments are in binary form (strings of zeros and ones). For the very early computers machine language was sole choice as there was often insufficient resources to support assembly language or even an operating system. Machine language tends to be highly specific to a specific processor or processor family.

2GL or second-generation language. Assembly language is a human-understandable language insofar as uses names instead of numbers. An assembler program takes assembly language and turns it into a machine code programme. Very common on early systems where resources (speed, storage) were at a premium, it is typically only used today as an output from 3GL and higher systems. It is rare for the assembly language of two separate processor families to be identical but they all share similar syntax. Assembly language programmes do not lend themselves to being used on different hardware platforms.

3GL or third-generation language is a 'high-level' programming language. Typically more readable and concise than assembly language, 3GL programs are charged by a compiler program into either machine or assembly language for later execution. 3GL languages allow programmmes to be converted or ported from one operating system or hardware platform to another (with varying degrees of effort) and allow more complicated data structures and programme flows than 2GLs, 4GL or fourth-generation language is designed to be nearer to natural language than a 3GL language. Languages for accessing databases are often described as 4GLs.

5GL or fifth-generation language programming uses graphical development environments to create source language to be compiled with a 3GL or 4GL language compiler. Generally, 5GLs are used to develop prototype applications which have the look and feel of a final application but often without the underlying power provided by a 3GL or 4GL. Often a mix of generations is used, with a high level language (4 or 5GL) used to produce interface elements and a lower level language used to give the processing power.

Operating Systems

An operating system (OS) is a set of utility programs that acts as the liaison between the computer user, the computer hardware (processor unit, memory) and its peripherals (hard disk, mouse, display, printer, network etc.) and the program that a user is running (e.g. a spreadsheet).

The first computers had no operating system, and each program had to directly control the hardware on its own adding greatly to be burden of programming a computer. Initial input was by setting dials and switches (or even plugging cables), with calculation outcomes shown on dials. The input was in the form of elementary machine language encoded in binary.

The early code-breaking systems utilized teletype paper tape. Then came punched cards—where instructions were laboriously encoded onto cardboard cards that were fed through the machine telling it both what to do and giving it the information or data to compute. The consequence was either produced onto further punched cards or output on to rudimentary display panels.

The use of punched cards allowed some routine components or programs to be reused (by reusing routines on sets of cards). Subsequently, development of memory chips, magnetic tape and hard disks have allowed more extensive programs and information to be stored, executed and re-executed.

Early OS were hardware and vendor-specific with assembly language or machine code the programming language. Each computer model or series tended to have its own particular operating system.

In 1969 a major mainstream operating systems UNIX, was first released. Originated at Bell Labs in the USA, it was based on 'Multics', an earlier time-sharing system. UNIX was one of the first operating systems that could be ported (converted) to a variety of system hardware. This ability was made mainly through the use of the 'C' programming language which was first defined and developed around the same time.

UNIX has evolved into many different versions or 'strains' due in part to the fact that the source code is largely free and written in C. UNIX systems were keystones in the development of the Internet and a large proportion of Internet servers today are UNIX-driven. UNIX is available on more hardware platforms than any other OS, although there is no dominant version of UNIX with a dozen or so large versions.

In 1979 Digital Equipment Corporation (DEC) released VMS (Virtual Memory System) as the operating system for the DEC VAX mini-computer. The main features of VMS was the embracing of a 32-bit virtual memory system that allowed use of hard disk as virtual memory in place of actual RAM chips. Thee have been several operating systems devised and rejected over the years.

Personal Computer Operating Systems

Throughout the 1990s the personal computer world has been dominated by two main players – Microsoft and Apple Computer. Although not important manufacturer of computer equipment itself, Microsoft Corporation has built on its market share secured in the 1980s with MS-DOS to become the market leading operating system provider. Microsoft's MS Windows range of personal computer operating systems are setup on more computers than any other commercial operating system. Concern over the market dominance of Microsoft has led to legislatures in the US and European Union bringing anti-trust (anti-monopoly) lawsuits against the company. Success or failure for Microsoft in such litigation is likely to remarkable shape the future of computing over the first decade of the new millennium.

Microsoft's main rival is Apple Computer. Established in the 1970s, Apple became very successful with its Apple I, II and III range of personal computers and is one of the few of a flock of personal computer companies from that time who have continued to manufacture both their own operating system and hardware to run upon it.

Unlike Microsoft, Apple's strategy has been to control both the hardware and software of their systems. The Apple Macintosh operating system (MacOS) can only be run on Apple Macintosh hardware. This has resulted in a benefit that is also a curse—the Macintosh is a quality product but quality tends to cost. Microsoft profited from the production of a large volume of less expensive PCs, while Apple sells on quality and features. Both have significant advantages and downfalls. Several other operating systems exist but tend to be brand or hardware-specific.

'The Net'

Prior to the Internet or 'the Net' as it is known colloquially, computers tended to be connected together by hardware and protocols that were peculiar to each particular connection. Typically, links were point-to-point (a link had to be directly and physically established between the two computers).

As in other areas of computing, the military had significant influence on the development of what was to become 'the Net'. In 1969 ARPANET was formed by the US Department of Defence. A main concern was to establish a way for the compute capability of the military to be dispersed so that no one centre was critical to the operation of the network as a whole. This was achieved by interconnecting computers both directly and by way of other intermediary computers; thus if one link or 'node' computer was hit by a nuclear bomb, other pathways of communication could be set up. The interconnections, when drawn, appeared as a mesh or net or web.

ARPANET was extended to non-military users such as universities early in the 1970s, with initial international links appearing in 1972. Early network research lead to the protocol of request for comments (RFC) whereby ideas in development can be followed and studied by other computer users, who will comment on it, expand it and improve on it allowing a de facto standard to quickly evolve. The collaboration ethos instilled in the RFC protocol has fuelled development of the Internet and related computer spheres. RFC number 1 was written in 1969 and there are well over 2,000 today.

Early Internet was merely a means for computers rather than people to communicate and was side-effect of research into networking. It was not 'the Web' and web pages and e-mail as we know it did not exist—these were the days of command line, text-only green screens (if not Teletype printer/keyboards).

The application of domain names (e.g. ditdit.co.uk) in 1984 offered an easier means of using the Web. Prior to domain names one had to remember IP numbers (e.g. 192.168.1.100) for accessing destination computers. The use of e-mail increased and implementations improved as various RFCs were adopted as standards; however, the Internet was primarily limited to government agencies, the military, academic and research organizations and some big businesses.

In 1989 what most people perceive as 'the Net' was born. It was effectively invented at CERN (the European Particle Physics Laboratory) by Tim Berners-Lee as a way for scientists to share information by placing it in a prescribed format (defined in an RFC) on a server. Initially text only, development of computer capability allowed insertion of images through use of a program called NCSA Mosaic—the first graphical'browser' (see glossary).

By 1993 a whole new industry of ISPs (Internet Service Providers) had started, allowing computer users to dial up via a modem and access the Internet and to view the Web through their browser of choice. The leading two browsers today, Netscape and Microsoft Explorer, were both based on the open source code of NCSA Mosaic.

In the mid 1990s the term 'information superhighway' was coined to refer to the Internet. Sadly, the Internet is not a superhighway—it suffers from rush hours, traffic jams and link closures in spite of the fact that new connections are added at a frantic pace.

Developments of the late 1990s have allowed music, video, games, text, graphics and even telephone conversations to co-exist on the same Internet. The core technologies underpinning the Internet are TCP/IP, routers and domain names (see glossary).

The future of the Internet is likely to see the majority of telephone calls and probably video being transmitted over the Internet for at least part of its journey. Expansion of fibre-optic cable networks to homes and business will underpin this. The introduction of high-capacity mobile phone will also facilitate and demand expansion of the Internet.

Simple but successful virus attacks like the 'love bug' computer virus of early 2000 show how much the world relies on and is affected by Internet technology. With no central governing body or legal jurisdiction the legal implications of the Internet will continue to puzzle for years to come.

3

Impacts of the Information Revolution

Here is the identification of some key implications of Information Revolution for both the military and civilian sectors. However, one of these impacts will dominate all others—the intermingling of civilian and military technologies and users that will be not possible to disentangle; and this impact will require dramatic changes in how we think about potential controls over the diffusion of these new information technologies.

Beyond this overriding impact, there are a small number of potential essence that deserve specific mention. First, this revolution presages a flood of previously unavailable information that now will be widely distributed near-instantaneously to interested users located anywhere. Much of this information is derived from a kind of advanced sensors that are owned and operated by civil or commercial entities. Second, this information will be supplied in quantities and at speeds that were earlier unattainable, yielding totally new functionality in its use. Masses of data previously unusable or uninteresting in their discrete, atomistic form will be merged, correlated and interpreted into useful information and knowledge. These new capabilities will raise remarkable economic, legal and societal issues about privacy, data security and integrity, intellectual property rights, and other appropriable advantages resulting from these activities. Third, this revolution provides remarkable increased utility from previously available processed information by synthesizing, integrating, customizing, indexing and compressing it—changing the nature and role of data storage and archives, libraries and

Encyclopaedias, movies and videos. Fourth, this revolution in communications technologies gives the capability to transmit vast volumes of information certainly on demand, with high assurance and low costs; this degree of portability and mobility for information and information users is unprecedented. Fifth, together these capabilities permit coordination of diverse individuals and activities in ways never before feasible. How these "virtual" organizations, communities and teams will alter existing work processes cannot yet be conditioned. Finally, real-time encryption gives privacy and security never before available but, at the same time, concern over vulnerability of our information systems, and about those systems dependent on them, has never been higher.

Background

For the American military, as for militaries throughout the world, the emergence of the Information Revolution portends a range of changes that will ultimately reshape underlying assumptions and transform not only the operations (including both the character and the execution) but the very organizations themselves. Throughout the Cold War, the American military believed that its information, command, control and communications requirements were exceptional, if not unprecedented, unmatched in the civilian or commercial worlds—views probably held by most other advanced militaries. Therefore, they believed their requirements demanded the most advanced sensors, the most real-time data collection capabilities, the most advanced computers, and the widest bandwidths, thereby permitting the military to set the nation's R&D agenda and control the rate of technological change, at least in this crucial arena. However, while military users may continue to have particular needs, they have now lost the vanguard position so currently held because these demands are no longer exceptional, either in quality or timing.

Fundamental Changes in the Military CI Environment

At the most conspicuous level, the information revolution offers militaries potentially dramatic improvements in force effectiveness from three types of potential applications. First, as foretold during the Gulf War, seamless "sensor-to-shooter" links offer the ability for not just smart but "brilliant" weapons launched from survivable stand-off ranges.

Second, these same technologies can give military commanders and decision-makers with real-time information and insights enabled by Dominant Battlespace Awareness. Finally, these technologies can permit seamless real-time integration of air, sea and land forces in a common tactical operating environment.

Less conspicuous are four key structural developments wrought by the Information Revolution to the intelligence and communications environment to which the military had become long-habitual also demand acceptance:

- The opening of that long-closed CI environment;
- The military's loss of technological leadership to the commercial sector;
- Reversal of several of the long-standing technical and cost relationships; and
- The military's need to accommodate itself to the commercial sector's pace of change.

(a) Opening the Closed Communications Society

For most of the post-Second World War period, the military constituted a closed, autarchic society in the communications domain. This was appropriate for the particular circumstances of the nuclear confrontation between the United States and the Soviet Union. But the military moved quickly from the highly secure, closed system that even five years before it controlled end-to-end (from R&D through acquisition to operational use) to today's increasingly open system. In such new environment, core military C4I functions are highly embedded, if not inextricably entangled, within a web stretching from the Defence Information Infrastructure (GII). Today, completely 95% of day-to-day American defence communications are carried by commercial channels, mostly through the public switched network (PSN).

(b) Losing Technological Leadership

Even if the dramatic reductions in defence expenditures since the depths of the Cold War had not occurred, the civilian commercial sector might still have taken the lead in developing several of the new technologies as the opportunities for economic efficiency and advantage became evident with commercial exploitation of these technologies. Esoteric technologies that earlier appeared to have few civil applications are now being rapidly applied across a wide range of civilian activities, both for commercial and domestic purposes. These consist of widespread adoption of advanced telecommunications systems on a global basis, incorporation the new digital technologies in everyday appliances, application of GPS-based navigation systems to personal use, and employment of extremely advanced sensors to support real-time production and control systems. These changes have substantially changed the direction of technology development in computers and semiconductors. For instances, Silicon Graphics, Inc. (SGI) now lists commercial customers, particularly in the entertainment industry, as its key "Lighthouse Partners" for defining leading-edge technology requirements.

(c) Reversal of Key Relationships

The military must now look towards procurement of commercial off-the-shelf, dual-use equipment, and open systems architectures instead of depending on the classic but autarchic military R&D and acquisition systems which produced highly optimized and cutting-edge systems but at high cost—usually with proprietary technologies. Hardware is now cheap, special objective proprietary software is expensive—but maintenance of "legacy" systems, both hardware and software, is now prohibitively precious.

(d) Rapid Pace in Commercial Sector

The military has found itself spurred into adopting more quick acquisition processes—both to keep up the pace with a rate of technological advance set by the commercial sector employing a common digital technology base that the military no longer dominates or drives, and to subside the costs of its outdated, autarchic legacy system.

The proliferation of new telecommunications services such as data, cellular and personal communication systems created several new companies not only to serve these markets but also as new competitors for existing services and new spurs for advanced, competitive-advantage producing technologies. These four changes result in the military becoming only one among several users (and in most cases, not even primus inter pares), buyer of systems rather than a developer, an adopter of technology rather than an advancer of the state-of-knowledge, and a buyer of services rather than an operator. These will demand important cultural adjustments, not only by militaries but also by the arms control community as well.

A Constellation of Advanced Information Technologies

The technological component of what we call the information revolution is the outcome of a set of related technical innovations, together yielding substantial enhancements or even the drastic change that the term itself implies. What we are witnessing does not seem to be a case of inexorable technology creep but rather an explosive technology rush. Every two yeas the speed of silicon processors doubles and storage costs decline by half; every five years compression efficiency is squeezing data to 1/30 its size; and laser diode speeds, critical for fibre optics, are doubling every three and a half years.

These capabilities support a full panoply of advanced sensors that gather more and different data, new communications architectures comprising "untethered" mobile systems that change basic cost relationships for information storage and dissemination and mobile "supercomputer" capabilities married with seamless integration that multiplies individual component functionality and effectiveness—all based on continued development in digital microelectronic technologies.

The Digital Revolution

Probably the dominant contributor to this shining constellation of new technological capabilities is digital technology itself. With the increasing introduction of computer and semiconductor technologies into almost all facets of our existence, there is increasing convergence of commercial telecommunications, entertainment, home electronics, and computers; as Nick Negroponte, the high priest of the digital age has said, "Bits is bits."

Digital technologies give rise to two key implications that require important changes of the information user's frame of reference. First, information in digital form can be replicated at will, without degradation or change from generation to generation; second, digital data streams are inherently encrypted by the system of converting data into streams of binary digits. Because real-time algorithmic manipulation is possible, extremely high security ("strong") coding schemes are possible at low cost; indeed, they allow real-time on line encryption that allows secure synchronous communications. Moreover, these capabilities can be applied not only to written or data communications, but to voice and video as well. At the same time, these digital technologies are raising fundamental questions related to ownership and control of intellectual property, privacy and security of valuable data, and equities contested between law enforcement and national security communities on the one hand and commercial interests on the other. Not only for the military, but for the national security community as a whole, these complex changes must be incorporated at the same time they are still adjusting to the important structural changes produced by the end of the Cold War.

Ubiquitous Computing

The second key contributor to the Information Revolution is the continuing advance in computing power. Computers are now 10 5 faster and 10 3 less costly than during the 1950s, with even greater enhancements in functionality following the graphical user interfaces, modern software, networking and platform integration. There is little indication that Moore's Law, predicting doubling of memory capacity every eighteen months, is slacking off very much from its historic rates of advance and will perhaps continue for at least the next decade. Increases in computational speeds, in fact, appear to be speeding up, with current improvements averaging about 55% per year compared with 35% in 1985; recent computational power has outpaced earlier predictions made in the early 1980s by over a factor of 100.

(a) "Supercomputers" for Everyman

As a result, the use of cutting-edge machines available only a few years ago only to select military and other national security users is now sternly appended in everyday commercial use and best practices.

(b) Embedded Computers

The same solid-state technologies—semiconductor microprocessors and memories—that permit desktop supercomputers also enable the computational heart of these instruments to be appended in other machines and systems, thereby fundamentally changing effectiveness and usability of commonly available tools, appliances and even complex systems.

(c) Cheap, Random Access Mass Storage

A critical complementary technology breakthrough is the availability of high-capacity, random access mass storage, now measured in giga to terabytes of instantaneously accessible data. Portable archives of this size permit complete map and geographic databases to be locally resident, requiring only change functions to bring them instantaneously up-to-date.

(d). "Highly Cognitive Displays" and User-Configurable Interfaces

Probably the next frontier that technological advances in semiconductors, computation, storage and software will address is effective processing, individuation and display of complex information with a view to allow it to be easily and properly assimilated by the user. Increasingly large-scale integration of networks and synthesis of useful information from massive, complicated data archives for commercial customers are giving the driving forces for advanced representation and display systems. Virtual reality technology (VR) is creating new ways of exhibiting information rather than as static data sets.

"Infinite" Bandwidth

A third key element in the information revolution is cheap, "near-infinite" bandwidth transmission capacity that generates an entirely new communications environment. Progress in this area is largely the fruit of continued advances in the same solid-state digital technologies that have fuelled computational and storage abilities—here embodied as signal processors, amplifiers, transmitters and receivers—they have continued to press usable frequencies ever higher. Ka-Band (20-36 GHz) satellite transmission capability and similarly wide band capacities in advanced fibre-optic cables represent fundamental advances in information transmission capabilities that do not seem to be slowing down. Indeed, existing laboratory work has experimentally demonstrated terabit transmission capacity using advanced laser diodes and optical fibres. In generating these systems to meet civil and personal requirements, the commercial sector is constructing a global information infrastructure that meets many of the military's demands, and in some cases, meets latent needs that have not yet even been recognized.

"Untethered" Communications

Historically there were some users, other than the military community and steamship companies, who expressed a need for mobile (as opposed to relocatable) communications capabilities—either to supply orders to moving units whose location was not certain or to obtain situation reports from those units. However, the unbelievable speed with which the civil society, not only in the United States and the rest of the developed world, has followed cellular telecommunications and now personal communications systems (PCS) services testifies to a widespread latent demand for "anywhere, anytime" communications.

In 1955, wireless communications created more than $22 billion in revenues; and this growth, with 20 million domestic users, outstripped predictions made less than a decade ago by more than a factor of 100. By 2001, it was forecast that five hundred million people worldwide will use mobile communicators such as cellular or PCS (whether linked through terrestrial or satellite networks); radio modems will link laptops and other mobile information processors and distributors back into the entire national or global information infrastructure. To meet these demands, at least seven major space-based terrestrial mobile-user communications systems are now planned, covering a number of service features and price points.

Sophisticated Sensors and Discrimination Algorithms

Many critical military needs can now be met by commercially available systems. Space, once the sole province of the two super-powers' military establishments, is quickly becoming an important adjunct to day-to-day civil society, and not only for developed nations. Sensors increase the reach, decrease the time for measurement and perception, and extend the spectrum well beyond direct human senses and experience; they can make real what was not even before received. Civil society has find out the value of increasingly sophisticated information-related capabilities. Commercial entities are inventing ways to transform these demands into benefits by employing the most advanced sensors for data collection, earlier only available to the national security community, across an extraordinarily wide range of applications. The Russians are recently selling less than 1 metre resolution, formerly top secret compartment data, from reconnaissance satellites.

For several uses, high resolution data is essential. For instance, formerly secret data and classified techniques and systems are in huge demand by oceanographers and oil companies. Civil or commercial systems employing extraordinarily sophisticated sensors contain advanced air traffic control (ATC) systems, Doppler weather radars for wind shear and storm warnings, space-based environmental monitoring systems, and supervisory control and data acquisition (SCADA) systems for monitoring and control of large-scale telecommunications, energy transmission, and continental and regional transportation networks that affect millions of people in their daily lives.

(a) Precise Navigation

The Global Positioning System (GPS) was developed by the American military to allow military units to condition their location with extreme precision by comparing the time taken by radio signals from several different satellites to reach them. Today the civilian GPS industry and civilian users now dwarf those of the military.

(b) Mapping and Monitoring

The rapid development of sophisticated geographic information systems (GIS) enabled by high resolution maps is being employed widely across a wide range of civil and commercial applications: crop management, store locations, flood control, emergency response, etc.

Implications of Advanced Information Technologies

1. Conclusions

Probably the greatest effect from the new information technologies is the breaking down, across several dimensions, of traditional distinctions and boundaries between the different information-related elements—comprising those that distinguished and separated the military and civilian sectors in their demands and uses of advanced information technologies. This convergence is occurring in the technological dimension, underwritten by a common technical base of solid-state digital microelectronics. It is occurring in the user dimension, as individuals no longer want to differentiate among information sources and providers, nor employ various instruments to tap them. It is occurring at the system level as network architectures must be prepared to supply seamlessly integrated multi-media products. It is originating in the geographical dimension, as physical and political national security dimension as the traditional differentiation between raw information and processed intelligence is fat disappearing both following the widespread availability of relevant open source information and as operationally oriented users demand usable real-time actionable knowledge. And it is occurring in the legal and regulatory communities as the old differences and barriers between various information forms and regimes collapse.

Three overall results flow from this revolution in information technologies, capabilities and employment. The first is that the widespread adoption of these merged, cutting-edge information technologies has created a vast commercial and consumer constituency that dwarfs the national security community, both in the United States and abroad. As a consequence, the previous priority and obeisance accorded to national security interests is not likely to continue, and a lot of "equities" that would have previously been settled on terms favourable to the national security community can now be expected to be decided for commercial and civil interests.

As a second important result, these new information and telecommunications capabilities are creating a truly global information infrastructure and environment in which traditional notions of geography and spatial separation no longer exist; geographic distance no longer means time delays in communication between any two points. The increasingly intertwined nature of the "infosphere" also means that there are no impenetrable boundaries between nations or even domestic domains—this loss of geographic reality has exposed the formerly "safe" rear spheres of the nation's domestic infrastructure. Thus, there are no sanctuaries. Even formerly secure rear areas are now as exposed as front-line forces to information attacks by opponents. Moreover, differences between military and commercial functions are increasingly meaningless when greater than 95 per cent of defence messages move over the public switched network, when just-in-time logistics for forces engaged in combat "reach back" into contractor facilities, and when commercial contractors are giving real-time communications and analysis services in support of ongoing military operations.

A third important consequences that results from our Faustian acceptance of the information revolution is the occurrence of a collective national infrastructure (electricity, telecommunications, oil and natural gas, freight, air traffic control, etc.) that is increasingly reliant on real-time scheduling and process, and is fully integrated with a global information infrastructure. Besides, these systems are generally monitored and controlled remotely through system control and automated data acquisition (SCADA) systems that are themselves networked telecommunications systems tied into the same potentially sensitive infrastructures. These trends are generally a system that is increasingly efficient, but it is stable only in its dynamic configuration and may not degrade gracefully.

Efforts to create a new arms control regime—to impose old-style to be either feasible or effective. Worse, because it is starkly not relevant to this new environment, this attempt would merely serve to imply progress and disguise the futility of the underlying approach.

2. Some Other Implications for Information Security

For several key reasons, these changes portend important implications for effective concepts of information security and protection. First, the shift from a national security-dominated to a commercially-dominated information environment means that the national security community will no longer drive the rate and direction of innovative activity, the kinds of systems produced, nor the set up of formal or de facto standards. Second, the widespread adoption by both military and civil/commercial users of common, COTS [commercial off-the-shelf] equipment, systems and practices eases the difficulty that potential hackers or attackers will have in recognizing entry points or finding vulnerabilities. At the same time, military communications carried over shared dual-use systems or in common frequency regimes with standardized protocols may find decreased vulnerability both from being "lost in the noise" of a massive redundancy resulting from the complex network of alternate service providers in the commercial domain. Third, while the military and intelligence communities have been traditionally more related to system security and survivability than commercial users, the growth of new commercial and civil uses that are real-time and "mission critical" means that commercial users may be just as related in the future about privacy and security. Widespread adoption of real-time, online transaction services and SCADA for critical infrastructure systems generates a fundamentally new demand for security, privacy and verifiability, particularly where the flows involve billions of dollars daily or the lives of millions are at risk. Fourth, widespread access by news media and others to advanced real-time sensor and communications systems may generate an completely different set of security and information protection concerns. With increasingly "free access" up and worldwide direct satellite broadcast down, the content and timing of television and radio news coverage will greatly be outside of government control over. The availability of small, direct up-link high capacity systems capable of supporting real-time video together with demands from news organizations for proper time information, unfiltered or uncensored by governments, are likely to produce substantial discomfort as security interests clash with claims of press freedom.

References

1. Jaffrey R. Cooper is Director of the Center for Information Strategy and Policy at Science Applications International Corporation in McLean, Virginia, United States of America.
2. With the addition of computers, the C3I environment became known as the C4I environment.
3. UNIDIR 1997, *The Transfer of Sensitive Technologies and the Future of Control Regimes*, Alves, P.G & Hoffman K. (edts), New York.

4

Growth and Coverage of Databases and Data Banks

Introduction

Here the application of bibliometric methods to the analysis and evaluation of databases is described. The potentials for Hypertext and Multimedia are outlined. Economic aspects of the sphere are investigated and problems of ownership and copyright are raised.

Without information, research and industry would not flourish. To know how to get information in the minimum time is an indisputable factor in competitiveness. Databases and data banks (DB), accessible online from a microcomputer or a videotext station (Minitel in France), can give this decisive factor. Today there are thousands of millions of references stored in thousands of databases; this represents an enormous wealth of information, really a supermarket of information, that is still largely underused.

Although the first databases had surfaced at the beginning of the century, online databases only saw light of day in the 1960s. These early databases were often in-house, or otherwise not openly available. They included the large limited-access on-line database systems built under contract by Lockheed, (e.g. the Nasa-Recon system) and by SDC, (e.g. the National Library of Medicine's AIM-TWX system). It is right to say that no sizeable public access systems were available until about 1972. Growth thereafter was quick.

Some Figures and Definitions

The terms database and data bank are generally used interchangeably and in somewhat different senses on different sides of the Atlantic. I will try in this document to standardize these terms, a task becoming more and more problematic with the development of mixed products, and will use the acronym DB as the general term. In the library sense, an "online bibliographic database" is often understood to mean a collection of records held online in rapid-access computer store.

This concept has become remarkably diversified nowadays and DB differ not only in the content of each entity described, but more and more in the media used. Bibliographic databases can be distinguished by their different contents: simple bibliographic citations, citations accompanied by index terms, or complete references consisting of citation, abstract, and index terms. The abstracts can contain or be accompanied by factual or numeric data, evaluated or not. Full text DB are now quickly expanding. DB also differ by the media in which they are available (diskettes, magnetic tapes, etc.); we can see also a dramatic development of CD-ROM and a diversification of access methods (ASCII or videotext). Nomenclature and description become so complicated that increasingly sophisticated DB catalogues have become best sellers.

As for the number of databases available, the latest figures are 5,200 issued by 2,200 producers and available on nearly 800 hosts. If we compare these figures to those of 1980, the growth has been significant. In 1979/1980, the Cuadra Directory of Online Databases listed 400 DB, 220 producers, and 59 hosts, while today it lists 6,414 DB.

We must also note the current appearance of a new kind of database that mixes textual or numeric marks, logos, or illustrations. These graphics DB require special equipment for their use. The Information Market Observatory (IMO) of the European Community recorded in 1989 1,048 different DB produced in the Community and 2,214 produced in the United States. This figure comprising only DB accessible in ASCII up to the end of 1989, and thus excludes DB that are only produced in videotext. In accordance with the IMO, the United States produces nearly twice as many ASCII DB as Europe, but the European Community has a higher growth rate: 101 new DB, representing 11 per cent growth, in Europe and 151 (7 per cent) in the United States. In Europe, Great Britain dominates with 34 per cent of the production.

It has been estimated that there are some 25,000 videotext services within the EEC. Half of them are located in France, which is the largest installed base of videotext terminals (about 6 million).

The CD-ROM market is also growing very rapidly: the number of titles published doubles each year. It is expected that the number of titles (about 750 in 1989) will increase to more than 6,000 worldwide in 1992.

As for the typology of DB, production of ASCII DB is dominated by bibliographic data in Europe (62 per cent of new DB) and by full text and factual DB in the United States (76 per cent of new DB). There is no very much difference between the United States and Europe regarding the target markets: the sector with the most products is that of services (especially banking, finance, and insurance). In the industrial sphere, chemistry is one of the most important subjects. The total turnover of the DB industry in 1989 increased to 35 billion francs (US $6.5 billion), of which 10 per cent was from videotext DB. For Europe, it is near to 14 billion francs (nearly US $3 billion). In 1993, these figures should reach 72 billion francs (plus minus US $12 billion) and 28 billion francs (US $6 billion).

The United States dominates the market with 56 per cent. English is confirmed as the pre-eminent language for documentation, three-quarters of the DB being accessible in it. Japan imports more electronic information than it exports; this is one of the few spheres where its trade balance is negative.

Typology of World Databases and Data Banks

This typological study, which is only indicative, has been carried out by analysing information in the Cuadra Directory, mentioned above. The percentages have been calculated from the 6,414 bases in the Cuadra Directory, except for the percentages for the main fields covered, which were obtained by extrapolation from 877 references selected randomly. The percentages given can only indicate the distribution of the total. They are in fact false because the same base can be mentioned several times, under various headings. Thus, from the 877 references selected for fields covered, we obtained a total of 1,296 by adding the number of bases by field. In other words, a base is listed an average of 1.5 times. However, in this case the distribution of bases is expressed as a percentage of the number of bases studied (877) and instead of function of the number of bases obtained (1,296).

This is the reason, although a significant number of fields have not been listed, having few references (less than 1 per cent, e.g. urban planning, biotechnology, contracts and awards, etc.), the total exceeds 100 per cent. In the process of search, 275 different fields were encountered. The principal areas covered have thus had to be grouped together.

Principal fields covered	
Finance, economics	29.0%
Business, industry, trade	25.0%
Law, justice	9.0%
Energy, environment	10.8%
Government, defence	4.8%
Chemistry	3.7%
Medicine, toxicology, nutrition, agriculture	5.6%
Science and technology	3.4%
Social sciences, humanities, administration, human resources management	5.6%
Research, innovation	2.6%
Computer, engineering, communications, telecommunications	7.3%
Miscellaneous	16.7%

Principal producer countries	
United States	62.4%
England	7.6%
Canada	6.4%
France	5.8%
Germany	4.7%
Australia	2.3%
Spain	2.0%
Italy	1.9%
Japan	1.4%
Sweden	1.3%
Netherlands	1.2%

Principal distributing countries	
United States	66.8%
England	13.4%

Canada	7.7%
Germany	6.0%
France	6.0%
Italy	3.3%
Australia	2.2%
Spain	2.0%
Japan	1.5%
Sweden	1.4%
Netherlands	0.9%

Principal Types of databases

Reference databases	
bibliographic	18.8%
referral	16.4%
Source databases	
numeric	17.5%
textual numeric	6.7%
full text	28.2%
images	4.2%

Principal languages used

English	72.0%
French	9.3%
German	5.2%
Spanish	3.5%
Italian	2.3%
Swedish	1.4%
Dutch	1.1%

Cooperation among Database Producers

We have to go far back in time if we want to find out onte aghin the whole history of cooperation between information services. Indeed, it was in 1896 that the Royal Society organized the first Conference for the Joint Production of the International Catalog of Scientific Literature, a complete abstracting and indexing service that was to last 25 years. In 1948-1949, Unesco organized a number of conferences on abstracting and indexing in biology and medicine and on scientific document analysis. These conferences led to the creation of the ICSU-AB, which was the forerunner of today's ICSTI. The Royal Society Organized the Conference on Scientific Information organized in 1948 and the International Conference on Scientific Information held in Washington, D.C., in 1958 are two other instances of this will to cope with the new communication needs that scientific information organizations had to face in the science and technology context of the time. These issues were formalized for the first time on an international basis when the proposals of a three-year (1968-1970) UNESCO-ICSU possibility study were considered at the UNISIST intergovernmental conference convened by UNESCO (1971) to prepare the ground for a worldwide scientific information system. In 1971, the keywords, so to say, were enhancement of scientific information as a basic means and promotion of international cooperation.

It was very felt that this resource should become more accessible and easier to use, so that as a global wealth, it could best contribute to the scientific, educational, social, cultural, and economic development of all countries of the world.

During this period, different approaches to international cooperation were discussed. Ron Smith, from BIOSIS presented in one of the Miles Conrad Memorial lectures a review of the various panoramas of the situation.

The first view grew out of some of the work of the International Council of Scientific Unions Abstracting Board (ICSU-AB) and was largely based on bilateral agreements that followed discussions by all member services in a special discipline. This type of international cooperation is still pursued. An instance of this concerns an interaction that developed in an experimental way among three abstracting journals in the area of physics: the English-language journal Physics Abstracts (PA) the French-language journal Bulletin Signaletique (BS), and the German-language journal Physiklische Berichte (PB). ICSU-AB conducted a survey of the journal literature of physics as covered by these three abstracting services.

The second view to international cooperation was undertaken by the ICSU/UNESCO (International Council of Scientific Unions/United Nations Educational, Scientific and Cultural Organization) Committee (UNISIST), in the framework of assessing the possibility of the previously mentioned World Science Information System. The study was based on the concept that this World Science Information System would be a flexible network based on the voluntary cooperation of existing and future information services, which was not attributable to any one organization but which has been fairly widely discussed in Europe, was that of setting up one information service in each of the disciplines into which the existing services would all feed; it was first assumed that the information services set up would be in English and that services in other languages would agree to feed material into the system. It was then propose that instead of having the same information processed number of times in different languages it would be processed only once in one language and later made available by translation if necessary.

The fourth view—the mission-oriented concept—is well-known and a few international systems of this kind are operating. One is INIS, of the International Atomic Energy Agency, another is AGRIS, of the FAO; still others are less well-known but probably equally effective.

Today, the problems of international cooperation are viewed in rather separate way, since networks or other technologies that allow efficient exchanges of information have rendered obsolete the exchange methods envisaged 20 years ago. Collections of data bases are created above all at the level of the hosts, who provide the important interfaces with the users and eliminate duplication where necessary.

Database Production

Database production has developed dramatically in the last 30 years. From the totally manual production in the 1960s of references on paper worksheets, of which sections were cut-off and sorted manually (slips the size of a postage stamp for authors and slips a little bigger for index terms), to the quasi-automatic production of data distributed online, many generations of systems have come and gone. I will not dwell on the past and will try in this chapter to look at the stages of modern database production, although the processes used are still very.

It will aim at a description of the traditional functions and the way in which they are most handled.

Bibliographic Description

Bibliographic description is the first operation in the processing of each document. Very brief rules exist for compiling bibliographic references. National and international standards permit producers to process this information in consistent ways, thus allowing exchange.

The elements treated are the title and its variants, author names, their affiliations, the titles of the publications from which the references have been taken, their type, editors' names, publication language, etc.

Conceptual Processing of Documents

Document Abstracts

The addition of abstracts to bibliographic references enormously enhances a database. For several years, these abstracts have been written by information scientists according to rules learnt in schools of librarianship or information science. So many types can be distinguished, analytic or indicative, objective, or oriented towards a specific type of user. The relative qualities of one or the other have been the subject of different discussions, even polemics. Nowadays most texts are accompanied by author abstracts, and the use of these is becoming more and more common. However, there are two kinds of use: author abstracts used unmodified and in full, or author abstracts edited and/or shortened. In the case where the database producer decides to his own abstracts according to the editorial policy of the DB, this work is often subcontracted to outside workers.

Indexing

Indexing is inevitable to enable retrieval of the stored documents. The operation varies greatly from one database to another. The quality of retrieval depends largely on the specificity of the indexing. Existing systems vary from simple assignment of a limited number of unstructured terms to multi-level hierarchical indexing from sophisticated controlled vocabularies. Indexing consistency is an important factor for DB quality. Indexing is an expensive operation because it requires substantial number of qualified staff. This is the reason most of the organizations are looking towards indexing methods, aided or not by expert systems, that will allow the introduction of completely automatic indexing.

Indexing Systems

First, we must define the terms before discussing indexing systems. Indexing is an operation that consists of describing and characterizing a document with the help of representations of concepts contained in the document. In other words, the concepts are transformed into documentary language after extracting them from the document by analysis.

Indexing must permit effective searching for information in document sources. It leads to the recording of concepts contained in documents in an organized and easily accessible form, i.e., to the production of documentary search tools (catalogues, indexes, files, etc.).

Indexing is a documentary concept that is still of recent interest. However, today a new qualifier more and more frequently accompanies it: "automatic" indexing, or more exactly "computer-assisted" indexing. In fact, the large and ever-growing volume of document to process with a view to make information available to the user as fast as possible makes it necessary to look for ways to speed up the processing.

Documentary Languages

Documentary languages are indexing tools that permit the transcription, in a concise and standardized form, of the concepts contained in the documents to be analysed. They provide a bridge between the natural language in the documents forming the documentary means and that of the users' questions.

Indexing tools fall into two main types:

- Languages with a hierarchical structure, called classificatory (classification, etc.).
- Languages with a combinatory structure (lexicons, thesauri, etc.).

Classification is historically the first kind of indexing tool to have been used in documentary systems. These classificatory languages are based on the prior coordination of ides to express a concept and on the interlocking of classes of concepts. They go from the general to the specific, each class including the previous one and the whole can be represented as a hierarchical tree.

Classifications in general use employ codes or indices (numeric, alphabetic, for alphanumeric) to represent concepts. Instances are the Dewey Decimal Classification, the Universal Decimal classification or the Library Decimal classification or the Library of Congress classification. Classifications have the advantage of offering a general logical framework and the feasibility of enlarging or restricting the subject at will by using the hierarchy of classes and subclasses. However, they are awkward to update, complex ideas can only be expressed with problem, and their rigid structure requires a formalized approach towards the concept searched for.

Data Formats and Capture

Processing formats of databases were the subject of much work and discussion in the 1960s and 1970s; the format most generally used is that recommended by the ISO-2709 standard. This offers a general structure, a framework designed particularly for communication between systems. Although it was not designed as an internal format for systems, it has strongly influenced them. It gives a structure for data exchange formats such as Unimarc and its derivatives, the UNESCO common communication format (CCF), or other formats less generally accepted but used. Recently there is a move towards the replacement of this type of format by one more suitable for electronic publishing, such as the SGML format (ISO 8879-1986 standard).

Use of Databases

Paper Products

Not very long ago, the principal product produced from databases was in printed form. Bibliographic bulletins, under different names, contained the whole or part of the database. Their manufacture and distribution did not demand any special advanced technology, and the revenue from the subscriptions, received in advance, represented a financial guarantee for the producers. The products, still widely disseminated, are nevertheless being replaced little by little by other methods of accessing the stored information. Miro-forms, for which a short-term fashion led to the thought that they might replace paper products, have not gone beyond the status of storage media. If they do not disappear completely, they will instead become an adjunct to paper products.

Online Access

On-line distribution of databases began at the end of the 1960s as part of time-sharing systems. The 1970s saw the beginning of their growth. The first search systems such as STAIRS, RCON, and ELHILL/ORBIT are still recognized names.

The National Library of Medicine and NASA were pioneers in the field. The systems were at the time strained by poor telecommunications and by prohibitive storage costs. Nevertheless, the market stared to emerge, as did the idea of hosts, organizations that take liability for the distribution of databases produced by others. These hosts provide search systems, storage media, networks, and user training, in general in collaboration with the producers. The hosts can be classified either as supermarkets or as specialists. Some producers are at the same time hosts.

CD-ROM

The CD-ROM (compact disc read-only memory) is a database distribution medium that was applied few years ago for the storage of texts and graphics. It exhibits much the same advantages is the mirofiche stores of earlier decades of texts. The disks are comparatively easy to produce and to duplicate; they are also easy to ship from place to place, and can therefore be used for local storage of databases and for local retrieval activities. CD-ROMs also provide high-density storage for both text and graphics. A standard disk will store up to 600 million bytes of information.

Floppy Disks

The floppy disk information delivery medium is emerging as an option for personal computers. Disks are not difficult to manufacture and can be produced in-house. They can be produced for a kind of operating systems.

New Methods of Access to Information

Most attempts to improve access to information contained in databases are aimed at moving from documentation to information. In fact, online information is little used by companies despite their needs. According to recent figures, databases provide only 7 per cent of the total information processed by companies.

Bibliometry Applied to STI or Scientometry

Definitions

Bibliometry was defined by A. Pritchard in 1969 as "the application of mathematics and statistical methods to books, articles, and other source of communication." "Scientometry" is specialized bibliometry applied to the STI field. A third term, "infometry," was adopted by the FID in 1987 to designate the group of metric activities appropriate to information (thus covering both bibliometry and scientometry).

The Functions of Scientometry

The functions of scientometry are the analysis, evaluation, and graphic representation of STI by the way of statistical methods, mathematics, and data analysis. The analysis has the purpose of answering the question, "Who is doing what, and where?" from STI. The evaluation that can be done on STI is of two kinds, one being "metric evaluation" of information flow (articles and journals), the other being "quality evaluation" of information processed in databases. As for graphic representation, this intends to present STI in the form of maps consisting of both research fields and the participants (researchers, institutions, countries). The end is to provide a representation of the structure of information at any given time of its development.

Documentation and Information

We know that the amount of stored documentation is increasing exponentially, but its informational content is only growing linearly. Remember that documents and information are not the same thing. By asking the question of the analysis of information and its representation, what we are endeavouring to do is to map the knowledge structures of this information, and not simply to count the documents. It is important, however, to present the information in the framework of a relevant cognitive structure. This is the reason it is necessary to be able to represent, with the aid of bibliometric techniques, such a framework based on the knowledge contained in the scientific literature. This is the reason it is necessary to be able to represent, with the aid of bibliometric techniques, such a framework based on the knowledge contained in the scientific literature.

Analysis Techniques

The technique used for this objective is the method of formation of keyword clusters; this allows the structuring of the information and allows its processing in hypertext form, in that, because each cluster (or group of interlinked keywords) indexes a particular number of bibliographic references, this is a means of organizing the information thematically, and thus represents a knowledge structure. Instead of looking through a body of information in sequential order, a simple list of references, a series of bibliographic citations, we have here a method of following a thematic order that can be constructed from the bibliographic data themselves.

The Contribution of Linguistics

Several researchers are working incessantly on the construction of a new generation of knowledge bases, with the view of using them in documentary computing. Others are applying themselves to improving access to full-text databases with a view to allow multilingual searching, or to showing that it is feasible to apply artificial intelligence techniques to database searching.

Hypertext

Ted Nelson proposed in 1967 the term hypertext as non-sequential writing that it would be not convenient to produce or represent on paper. The structure of a hypertext database does seem to provide the flexibility that is important to create a database that would help researchers to search for information, to follow associations in ways that reflect their normal information-seeking activities. However, the implementation of such a data-base would also need adequate and guidance facilities and more powerful text retrieval capacities.

Multimedia

Databases nowadays cannot be discussed without mentioning multimedia. This concept is so wide that it is nearly not possible to fix its limits. Multimedia systems, which should in due course permit combined manipulation, from a single workstation, of text, sound, and images, should bring together several of different technologies. The market for this type of product is still unknown. Documentary searching, which in 1989 was almost the only sector concerned with these technologies, should reach a global turnover of US$4 billion by 1994. Nevertheless, it seems that the tools recently available are not sufficient for large applications. We know how to navigate in small graphs held in memory but not in multimedia databases of several gigabytes.

Economic Problems

The Position in the Economy

Activities concerned to database production and distribution were for a long time considered as scientific activities managed by an exchange system, but the existing situation is very different. The explosion of information technologies and their rapid distribution into every aspect of economic life ha put back onto the agenda a thought already raised in the 1960s. The emergence of new skills, generating many jobs in the database field, has kindled research and discussions. An American researcher, M.V. Porat, carried out a significant statistical study in 1977 in which he estimated that by 1967, 46 per cent of the American GNP was already related to information activities. Using Porat's method, J. Voge estimated that in 1984, information workers represented between 40 and 47 per cent of the workforce of the major industrialized countries. It is fact that information production includes not only activities of design and transmission, but also of recognition and integration by the user. It is at the same time process and product. Database production and distribution are integral parts of these analysis. Several studies have been carried out on the value of information and its important features since it is considered to be an economic connection.

The Costs

Regardless of the discussions and studies on the place of databases and data banks in the economy, their production and distribution represent a remarkable cost. DB production costs an be divided into four categories: direct production costs, manufacturing costs, indirect costs, and administrative costs.

Production costs include very large staff costs for the library-related and conceptual processing of documents. Analysis and indexing are operations requiring scarce, highly qualified staff that create high costs. It is in these areas that producers are trying to achieve savings by using author abstracts and by encouraging studies on assisted or automatic indexing techniques.

Manufacturing costs inevitably include magnetic tape production and the operation required to put them into the different formats of the hosts, the production of derivative products, such as publications consisting all or part of the DB, CD-ROM, and diskettes.

Indirect costs include the development costs of new methods and products, promotional costs, marketing, user training and assistance, staff training, and user documentation.

Overhead, as for other activities, varies in accordance with the facilities offered.

Pricing

Although most of the participants in the information world agree in considering information as a resource, a product, pricing problems are still treated outside real economic considerations. One of the proofs of this is that most database producers, except for business databases, are not-for-profit organizations, and several of these databases are government-subsidized. Pricing problems are also treated differently depending on the products produced from the databases. In fact, what tends to be called the "market price" still plays an important role in fixing prices.

Online pricing is most often fixed by the hosts, whose own pricing policies are also developing. For some years the division or revenue between database producers and hosts has been the subject of controversy, sometimes acrimonious, and has led to confrontation between the major participants of the two professions.

It is not the object of this paper to enter into the details of pricing, which are extremely complicated. It can simply be noted that one of the critical points for database producers is the set up of a sales and pricing strategy.

Ownership, Legislation, and Copyright Problems

Because of the late recognition by countries and even by producers of the economic value of databases, they are not at present explicitly protected by current legislation.

The legislation that does exist is varied and in some instances can even feeble the establishment and operation of a real market. Moreover, new technologies and the increasingly widespread availability of localized equipment permit pirating, which, even if not organized in most cases, is very dangerous for database producers. Some could even disappear for this reason.

Conclusion

In this paper I have attempted to show the role and the importance of databases as a component of the economy and as a tool for research and industry. However, this field is in continual technological development and in its spectacular growth cannot live in isolation. Firstly there must be thought on how to organize production and development, with a view to be always up to date with the technologies. This means a continual monitoring of the quality and security of the data that are produced. DB operation must then be organized in an environment where the actors frequently change their roles. Database production depends heavily on the availability of sources, which means managing the relationship with publishers. DB distribution relies on hosts and users. Relations with hosts must be closely monitored, although they are generally without particular problems. The user is the person who justifies the existence of the database. He also develops, from the experienced professional tot the end user, who has neither the time nor the inclination to experiment with systems that are too sophisticated. It therefore seems that in future attention be directed towards him.

5

A Digital Communication Networks

The Multimedia Communication is being widely expanded and promoted by a fully digitized communication network and the Integrated Services Digital Network.

Introduction

ISDN is a wholly digitized communication network that is expected gradually to take over the telephone network. ISDN was standardized comprehensively by the International Telegraph and Telephone Consultative Committee (CCITT), and thus the worldwide connection of ISDN should be easy.

In Japan, ISDN was made available commercially by Nippon Telegraph and Telephone Corporation (NTT) in 1988. Since then, ISDN has been growing and is now available almost across the country. Multimedia computing is a popular topic among people engaged with personal computers and workstations. Multimedia computers are believed to take full benefit of ISDN. In other words, ISDN will promote multimedia communication.

ISDN is relied on synchronous transfer mode (STM) technology. To improve multimedia communication features, novel technology, called the asynchronous transfer mode (ATM), is being developed in various countries. CCITT has been standardizing the broad-band ISDN (B-ISDN) on the basis of ATM. One of the most potent parts of B-ISDN is the "fibre-to-the-home" (FITH) concept.

In FTTH, optical fibre cables are extended to customer premises; specifically, optical fibres will remove the metallic twisted pairs now being utilized for subscribe loops. B-ISDN is expected to push telecommunications strongly toward multimedia services, covering up to high-definition TV (HDTV).

This paper mentions the state of the art in ISDN and future trends relevant to B-ISDN.

The Narrow-band ISDN

User-Network Interface

The present ISDN is often referred to as "narrow-band ISDN" (N-ISDN) to distinguish it from B-ISDN has two types of user-network interface (UNI): the basic-rate interface (BRI) and the primary rate interface (PRI). BRI has two 64 Kb/s channels, called B, and one D channel, and thus it is repeatedly called the 2B+D interface. PRI has the bitrate 1.536 Mb/s, and can be classified into B (64 Kb/s), Ho (384 Kb/s), and D(64 Kb/s). Typical division is 23B+D, and thus it is frequently called the 23B+D interface. However, when high bitrate is necessary, the whole bitrate 1.536 Mb/s can be utilized as one channel, and it is called Hii channel.

The D channel is chiefly used for control between user terminals and the network. All information is "packetized" in D channel. A customer can utilize D channel as a packet communication channel; in this case, control information and customer information are packet-multiplexed in D channel. The packet switching service is also provide through B channel. In this case, the total bitrate (64 Kb/s) in B channel can be assigned to customer packets.

In the long-run, ISDN provides switched 64 Kb/s service, comprising telephone, switched 384 Kb/s service, switched 1.536 Mb/s service, and switched packet service, through both B and D channels. Furthermore, ISDN has several features suitable to multimedia communication.

Multimedia Communication Features

One of the biggest differences between ISDN and the telephone network is that ISDN is receptive to different communication media, while the telephone network is strongly biased to the telephone service. ISDN is equipped with universal communication protocols according to the standard OSI reference model. The layer 1 interface of ISDN consists of BRI and PRI. The layer 2 and layer 3 protocols go through D channel. The layer 2 protocol mainly establishes the data connection between a terminal and the network. The layer 3 protocol is very important to multimedia communication. Among different commands in the layer 3 protocol, bearer capability, low layer compatibility, and high-layer compatibility commands are closely concerned to multimedia communication. Using the bearer-capability command, a terminal requests to the network the kind of channel that is important; namely, the bitrate, B, Ho, or Hii, and speech, audio, or unrestricted 64 Kb/s in the case of B. Low-layer compatibility is used to choose end-to-end transfer capability. High-layer compatibility is used for match-making of terminals at both ends; namely, high-layer compatibility specifies the type of terminals at both ends; namely, high-layer compatibility specifies the type of terminals: telephone, facsimile, telex, teletex, MHS, etc.

In several cases, different kinds of terminals, e.g. telephone, facsimile, and videotex, are connected to a BRI. When a call is developed by a Group 4 facsimile, the transfer bitrate is specified as unrestricted 64 Kb/s and the kind of terminal as a facsimile using the high-layer compatibility. At the receiving side, terminals different from a facsimile do not respond, and thus only a facsimile gives a response.

Thus, different kinds of terminals connected to the same BRI can communicate independently with the same type of terminals at the receiving end. This feature is very valuable to multimedia communication.

ISDN Application to Video Telephone and Video Conferencing

Figure 1 exhibits the standard model of video telephone/video conferencing system. For standardization of video codec, a common interface format (CIF) for TV signals was defined to make-able the interconnection of the 525/60 (North American, Japanese) and 625/50 (European) TV systems, as exhibited in figure 1. The standard codec encodes TV signals with CIF. The inter-change between a national TV standard and the CIF can be done independently in each country. For low-cost video codec, a quarter CIF (OCIF) was also defined.

Table 1 exhibits typical usage of ISDN channels to video-telephone/ video conferencing services. The use of B or 2B is likely appropriate to video telephone, and Ho or Hii to video conferencing. The combination of QCIF, 48 Kb/s video, and 16 Kb/s audio may facilitate offering low-cost video telephone service.

Figure 3 exhibits a one-board video codec developed by NTT. This codec can be used with B and 2B in Table 1. Its works cover NTSC/CIF conversion, video codec, and transmission codec. A 16 Kb/s audio codec can be mounted as a child board on this board.

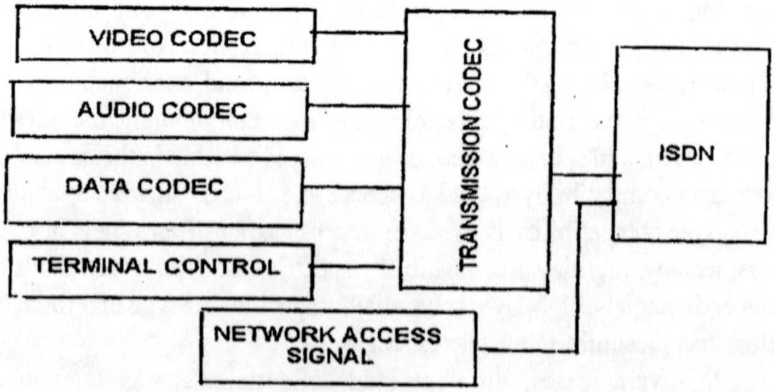

Figure 1
Standard video telephone/video conferencing system

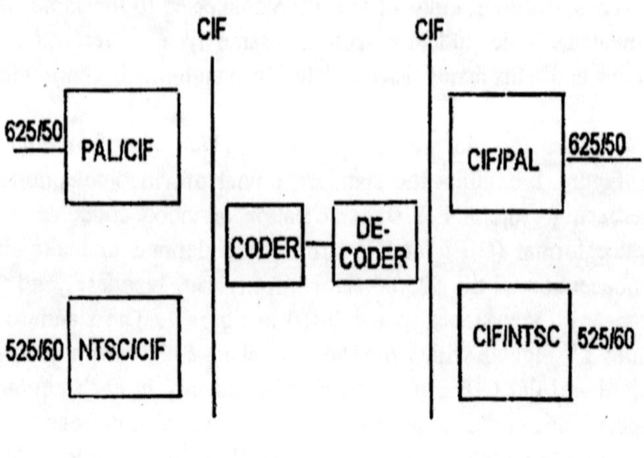

Figure 2
International connection through the Common Interface Format

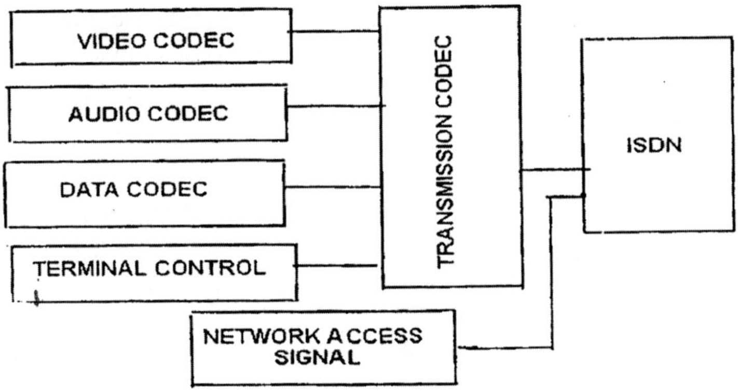

Figure 3

Figure 1 exhibits a codec for 384Kb/s video. Four newly developed DSPs are used in the former and eight in the latter.

TABLE 1
BITRATES FOR VIDEO TELEPHONE/VIDEO CONFERENCING

Channel	*Division*	*Coding*
H_{11}	B (audio) + 23B (Video)	Audio; SB-ADPCM PCM
H_0	B (audio) + 5B (video)	Video: hybrid coding
2B	B (audio) + B (video)	
	16 k (audio) + 112k (video)	Audio: LD-CELP
B	16 k (audio) + 48k (video)	Video: hybrid coding

Colour Picture Transmission and Colour Facsimile

The standard colour picture codec, based on the JPEG standard, was developed as exhibited in Figure 1. This codec has an interface to the VME bus and can encode a picture having maximally 8192 pixels in one direction. By assigning bitrates appropriate to brightness and colour difference signals, the data compression rate ca., come down to 1/20 without noticeable degradation. An optical disk memory and the JPEG codec board are appended to a UNIX workstation to constitute a colour picture filing system, as shown in Figure 1. A colour copier appended to the workstation can be used as an I/O terminal. Colour pictures are transmitted through ISDN. A JPEG codec is useful to save transmission time and storage potential.

The JPEG standard will stimulate the standardization of colour facsimile. Important points of colour facsimile may be as follows :

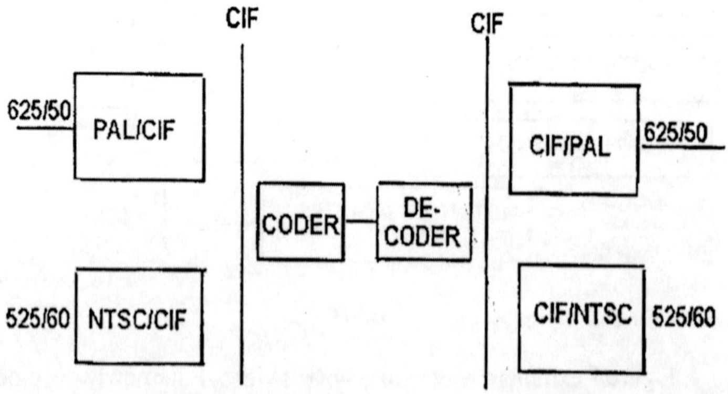

Figure 4

- Interworking with prevailing facsimiles, especially with Group 4 facsimile;
- The same resolution as Group 4 facsimile in the black and white portion;
- Application of JPEG for the full colour portion;

These should be guidelines for standardizing colour facsimile.

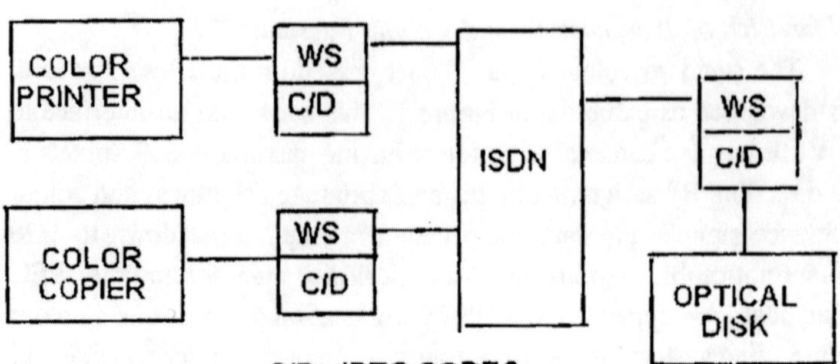

Figure 5

Broad-band ISDN

Outline of Broad-band ISDN

The broad-band ISDN (B-ISDN) being standardized at CCITT can be understood though these keywords like asynchronous transfer mode (ATM), the fibre-to-the-home (FTTH), and a multimedia network covering data up through a high-definition TV (HDTV).

As exhibited in Figure 6, the transmitted data stream is divided into sequences of a little amount of data called a cell. Each cell has a 5 octets header and a 48 octets information field. At the transmission line, cells are packed without any gap, as shown in Figure 1. Various recognizers in the header specify a cell and contain sufficient information to deliver a cell. When a high bitrate is important, more cells are captured. In other words, network customers can define the capacity of a channel at their own will. This is known as a virtual channel. Customers can take as many virtual channels as desired in their subscribers' lines.

B-ISDN is largely believed to be the telecommunication infrastructure for the twenty-first century. On the ground of B-ISDN, NTT announced the Twenty-first century, telecommunication service vision, by the name VI&P, an acronym for visual, intelligent, and personal communications services.

TABLE 2
HDTV DIGITAL TRANSMISSION

Usage	*Bitrate*
Studio grade	624 M b/s
Program distribution grade	100-150 M b/s
High quality entertainment	40-50 M b/s
Application specific	10-20 M b/s

Multimedia Service Example

Visual Telephone

Visual telephone is said to be one of the major terminals for the twenty-first century. Its picture quality will be much better than the CIF-based picture in the N-ISDN environment.

HDTV

Based on the application of high-definition TV (DHTV), necessary bitrates will become versatile, as exhibited in Table 2. FTTH in B-ISDN will make a wide range of HDTV applications easy.

Personal Multimedia Teleconferencing

A desktop workstation (WS) used in the office will become multimedia. Office workers will be able to do different kinds of work at their WSs. Teleconferencing is an instance. In order that office workers with their own WSs will be able to participate in meetings from their desks, multipoint capability is essential. The requirement for participants in a meeting to see one another makes multi-motion-picture-windowing important. It may be desirable to distinguish who is speaking.

Figure 8 exhibits a typical screen image of such a multimedia teleconferencing system developed by NTT. From the WS, a participant can send text, scanned image, and telewriting information; his own voice and image; and stored video in colour. The system has audio-window potential. The voice of a person whose picture window is at the left comes from the left, and the voice at the right from the right. Another feature is private conversation capability. Any two persons can talk with confidence during the meeting; this private conversation voice comes from the extreme right.

Network-casting

Network-casting is an idea that can be positioned somewhere between broadcasting and conventional telecommunication. Broadcast media such as radio or TV are called mass media, by which information is disseminated to many people, e.g. several thousands of people. Conventional telecommunication media such as telephone and fascimile can disseminate information to only a small number of people, e.g. less than 30 people in a certain amount of time, and thus may be called "mini-media." In relation to these, network-casting might be called a midi-medium.

A baseball game in a local stadium may be network cast to people in a big city through B-ISDN. In an ATM switch, an incoming cell could be duplicated to branch into two or more outgoing cells, as exhibited in the upper part of Figure 8. Then information from the visual source could be disseminated to many points. The other method is to branch by using local nodes as shown in the lower part of Figure 9. These two methods could be combined for the economical realization of network-casting.

Different from broadcasting, which is relied on radio waves, network-casting goes through optical fibre cables, whose capacity is unlimited. TV programmes that are represented by terms such as personalized TV and interactive TV can be disseminated through B-ISDN. This is one reason for characterizing network-casting as a mini-medium.

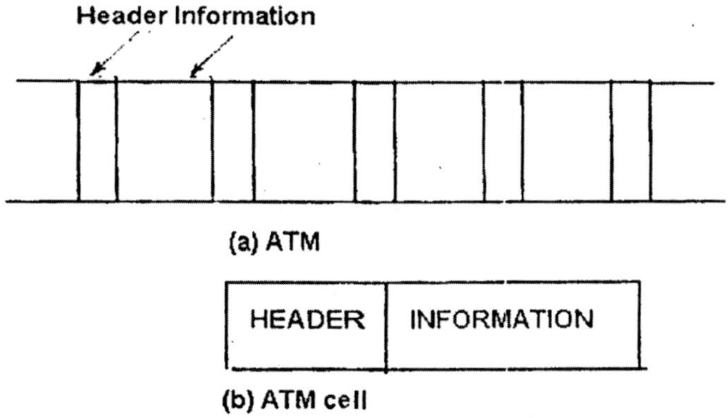

Figure-6
Asynchronous Transfer Mode (ATM)

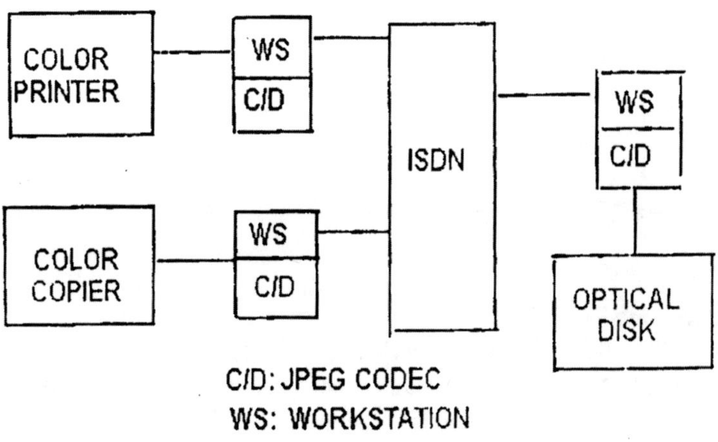

Figure-7

Figure-8

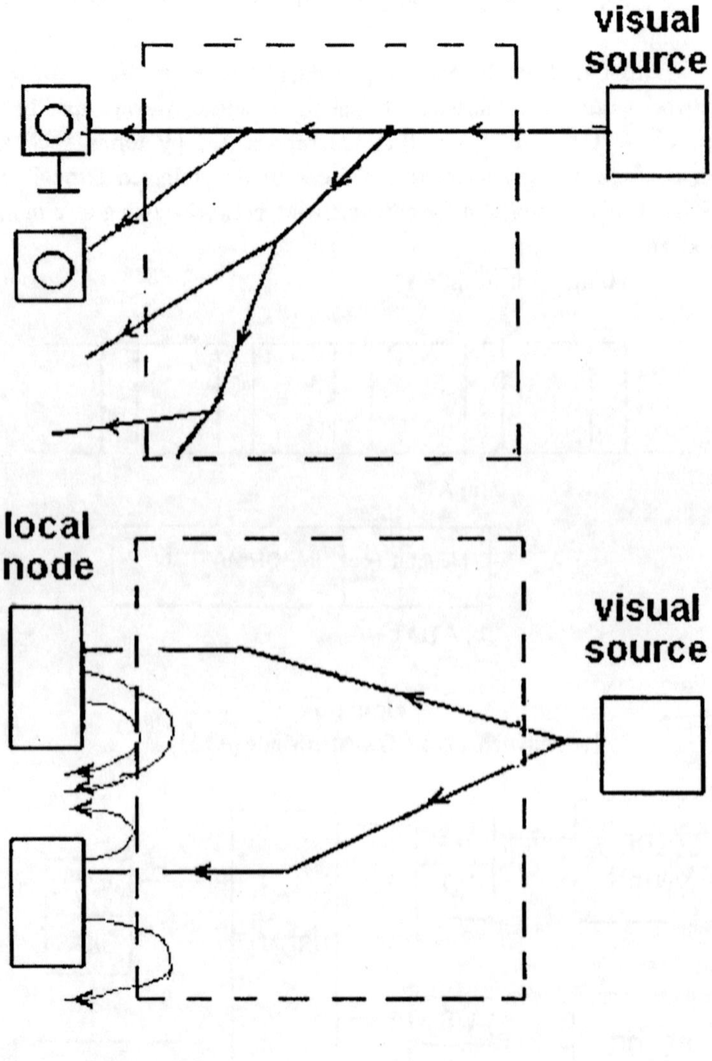

Concluding Remarks

The status of ISDN service and its application have been mentioned. Multimedia communication, heralded by ISDN, will be promoted by B-ISDN. In addition to this, B-ISDN will facilitate providing a new information service, which might be called network-casting.

6

Advantages and Technical Consequences of "Extended Retrieval"

The traditional composition of information retrieval is of a single resource file and single retrieval mechanism.

Introduction

The conventional form of an information retrieval system is composed of two parts: a resource file and a retrieval mechanism. A bibliographic retrieval system or an online library catalogue, for instance, is compose of a file of bibliographic records and a retrieval mechanism designed to perform the most commonly desired searches on that file or records, like a search by author, title, or subject. It is, in effect, a unitary system, a single system formed of one resource file and of one retrieval mechanism. The new information technology is leading to a new computing environment. The cost-effectiveness of computer hardware is increasing, the cost of electronic storage is falling, and connectivity through telecommunications is becoming pervasive and less expansive. In the meanwhile, labour costs and building costs incessantly rising. These changing conditions are resulting in a new environment in which:

- workstations are becoming largely available;
- very large sets of data can be stored economically;
- several thousands of computers are interconnected over local, national, and international networks; and
- the standards and protocols important for effective cooperation are being developed and adopted.

In this situation, we find a fast growing number of databases, an increasing use of databases, and a trend for individuals to use many of heterogeneous databases. The result is increased complexity for the searcher and a greater requirement for expertise to identify what resources exist and how to use them cost effectively. (For a convenient general introduction, see Lynch and Preston [7].) This changed information technology has developed a new information retrieval environment in which the potential for information retrieval now extends far beyond the traditional form of a unitary retrieval system formed of one file and one retrieval mechanism.

I use the term "extended retrieval" to denote this more general form of information retrieval. In this paper, I describe what I mean by extended retrieval and provide instances. Some technical results of the extension of information retrieval from a traditional, unitary form to an extended, network environment will be noted.

Four Information Retrieval "Architectures"

The generalization of information storage and retrieval beyond the traditional, unitary case of one file and one retrieval system to the more general model of multiple files and various retrieval systems can be expressed as four combinations:

1. Traditional, unitary retrieval systems with one file and one retrieval mechanism. An online library catalogue of the nine campuses of the University of California, for instance, retrieves 266 records for books using the combination of subject keywords "science" and "Japan".
2. Multi-stage retrieval from a single file. An example of multi-stage retrieval would be when the outcomes of a search by one retrieval system on a file are subjected to additional retrieval operations by a second retrieval mechanism as "post-processing". For instance, at Berkeley, an experimental system known as OASIS can be used to refine the results of MELVYL searches [5]. For instance, if the results of the previous example, the 266 MELVYL catalogue records for books on "science" and "Japan", are downloaded into OASIS, additional processing can recognize numerous subsets defined by date, by language, and by the libraries where copies are held (see table 1).

TABLE 1

ANALYSIS OF 266 RECORDS BY LANGUAGE, DATE, AND CAMPUS, SEARCH REQUEST: "SCIENCE" AND "JAPAN"

Location	*At Berkeley*			*At UCLA*			*At other campuses*			*Total*
Languages	*Japanese*	*English*	*Other*	*Japanese*	*English*	*Other*	*Japanese*	*English*	*Other*	
1991	3	1	0	0	0	0	1	0	0	5
1987-1990	17	9	1	8	2	0	6	11	0	54
1984-1986	3	8	0	10	4	0	7	8	0	40
1978-1983	3	10	2	7	6	1	10	7	0	46
1972-1977	0	8	1	15	5	0	7	5	0	41
1963-1971	0	7	0	14	7	0	6	4	0	38
1962	1	6	0	19	10	0	3	3	0	42
TOTAL	27	49	4	73	34	1	40	38	0	266

3. A retrieval system that searches many files would be one in which a single retrieval mechanism can search and derive records from two or more files simultaneously. An instance is the "Onesearch" feature of the DIALOG retrieval service.

TABLE2

UNITARYANDEXTENDEDRETRIEVAL

Retrieval Mechanisms	*Number of files*	
	Single file	*Two or more files*
One	(a) Unitary retrieval e.g. online library catalogue	(b) Multiple file searching, e.g. DIALOG Onesearch
Two or more	(b) Single file, Multiple processing, e.g. post processing	(d) Fully extended retrieval

4. Retrieval using multiple files and multiple retrieval mechanisms. The more general case is when multiple files and multiple retrieval mechanisms are used. This is the logical results of the development of the new information technology environment: It is a networked environment in which may varied files of resources and many varied retrieval systems exist and are, in principle, widely accessible over the network.

Illustrations of Extended Retrieval

To illustrate some of the potential of extended retrieval, let us consider two sorts of data: bibliographic data and scientific data.

Bibliographic Data

A record in a library catalogue will comprise author, title, location (call number), and a subject heading (e.g. from the Library of Congress Subject Headings list). A record in a bibliography representing the same document will likewise include author and title, but may also include an abstract and a subject heading perhaps from a different list, such as Medical Subject Headings. A citation index would comprise again, the author and title and the references from the document. These overlapping contents are shown in Figure 1. What we have for the same document is three rather different bibliographic descriptions by various publishers, in different formats, and ordinarily searched on different retrieval systems. These three records include:

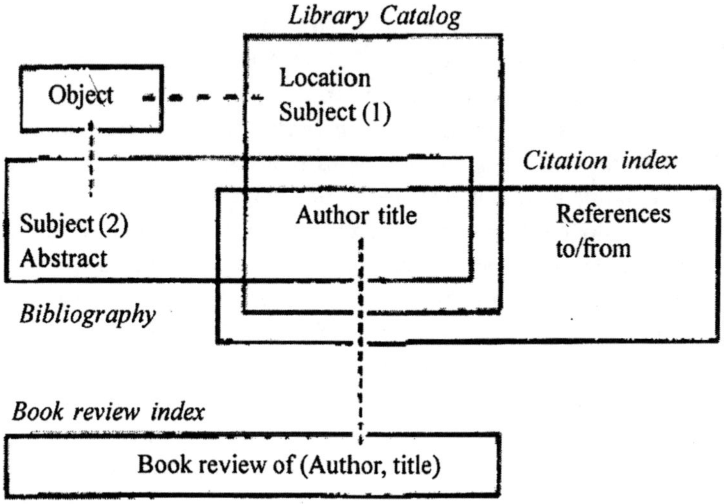

Figure-1
Related bibliographic files

- information that is the same, though probably expressed differently and not essentially recognizable as being the same, and
- some information not provided by the others, e.g. the catalogue has the location of a copy; the bibliography has an abstract; and the citation index reflects references to and from the document.

The relationship between the records retrieved from the various data bases is that they all represent the same document. But this is only one of varied possible relationships. Figure 1 also exhibits two further relationships:

- a book review index may comprise a record for a different but related document, a book review; and
- outside of the bibliography and library catalogue may be some object that the book is about.

In this way, one's knowledge can be importantly increased by extending one's search to two or more heterogeneous databases. However, although the different bibliographies may refer to a single document, there is no assurance that they will do so in a proper way. The form and contents of records in bibliographies (like references at the end of papers) vary considerably. This is not normally a problem for human beings, who can recognize what is meant, but it is a rather serious problem for recognition by a computer.

Differences in subject description can be substantial and significant. Consider, for instance, a searcher interested in coastal pollution. A search on "coastal pollution" in the Library of Congress Subject Headings in the University of California MELVYL online catalogue yielded nothing either as a phrase ("exact subject") or as a pair of subject terms ("subject keyword search"). Nor does either form of search result anything in the MELVYL file (1988 to date) of the MEDLINE bibliography. Nevertheless, material on coastal pollution does survive in the both, and some of it can be found by searching for documents that comprise the words "coastal" and "pollution" in their title. Analysis of these records shows that the subject headings actually assigned to these documents consist of:

LCSH (MELVYL Catalogue)	*MeSH (MELVYL MEDLINE)*
Water—Pollution	Becteria
Marine pollution	Seawater
Coastal zone management	Water pollution
Petroleum industry and trade	Water microbiology
Waste disposal in oceans	Water pollutants

Not merely is the plausible phrase "coastal pollution" not used in either set of subject headings, even as a cross-reference, but there is remarkably little overlap in the terms that are used.

Science Data

Consider the range of different data that could be proper and available for studying a geographical area like Kyoto Prefecture or the Sacramento delta:

Topographic: latitude, longitude, altitude

Satellite image

Political map
Land-use map
Gazetteer: place names
Textual documents
Weather: temperature, precipitation, humidity, wind
Census and socio-economic statistics
Photographs, etc.

Handling the retrieval of such different kinds of data from quite different sources is a major challenge.

Some Technical Issues

We use the phrase "extended retrieval" to refer to the extension of information retrieval to contain search and retrieval in multiple files and/ or using, multiple retrieval mechanisms. In the new environment, a number of interesting problems arise and require to be resolved:

What Resources Exist?

The fact that many electronic resources exist in many places does not mean it easy to recognize or find them. Files stored on computers are just that: files that are stored. There is, as yet, little or no tradition of cataloguing computer files, so that they can be recognized and found, as there is for cataloguing library books and museum objects. The task of developing "directories to the Internet" is not likely to be simple or inexpensive, but it is now receiving increasing attention. The question of recognizing which resources one might wish to search is a bibliographic problem, although the describing of electronic resources is still not developed. However, there is also a question of which retrieval system to choose for any given search if there is a choice. For instance, the catalogue records of the library of the Berkeley School of Library and Information Studies can be searched using four different retrieval systems. Different information retrieval systems have different retrieval capabilities. For a specialized search, one may require to select the retrieval mechanism asmuch as the resource to be searched. This means a knowledge and understanding of the varying characteristics of different retrieval mechanisms available, with which resources they can be used, and how to use them, singly or in combination. This knowledge is inadequately developed, though Belkin and Croft [1] provide a useful review.

Search and Retrieve Protocols

It is now feasible to access databases at remote sites as well as databases at remote sites as well as databases at one's local computer centre. This ordinarily needs establishing a telecommunications connection, a personal account and password, and the use of an unfamiliar command language (as in Figure 2a). This is inconvenient and requires expertise. An important new development is the creation of national (e.g. US NISO Z39:50) and international standards (ISO 10162/10163) for computer-to-computer "search and retrieve" standards. The adoption of these standards will help one to delegate to one's local retrieval system. The Search and Retrieve standards translate searches from one retrieval command language to another [3, 4]. This development began among librarians to support easy access to each other's catalogues, but it has wider application. The effect is shown in figure 2b.

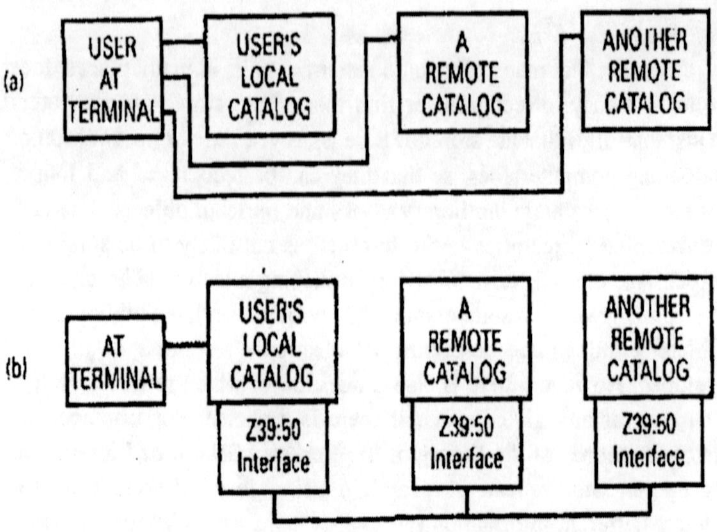

Figure 2

" Search and retrieve" (Z39:50)protocol (a) A user can connect with various online catalogues and must know how to use each. (b) With the "Search and retrieve" (Z39:50) protocol, the user need only know how to use the local catalogue and to instruct it to extend a search to other systems.

Questions of Relatedness

Extended retrieval among heterogeneous resources raises difficult questions of relatedness. If a name found in one database is synonym to a name in another database, are they variant forms of the name of the same person? The same difficulty arises with records in bibliographic databases that may or may not represent the same document [2]. More generally, in extended retrieval in heterogeneous databases, one is related the retrieval of related material but the nature of the relationship may be not easy or to determine.

Anatomy of the Retrieval Process

Retrieval in a unitary retrieval system is easily viewed as an event rather than a process. When considering information retrieval in a networked environment, one might think in terms of local "client" search machines and remote resource "servers," which means a distinction between a search and retrieve mechanism and a resource file. This may exist when a retrieval system is built to retrieve from two or more files. But information retrieval is in practice, a complex process comprising several different components. The question arises concerning how the retrieval process could be optimally divided into various stages on different machines. In fact, when one analyses the individual elements of the retrieval process, considerable complexity and choice emerges. For instance, with bibliographic searches:

- separate bibliographies represent different, more or less overlapping, populations of documents;
- separate bibliographies will have more or less separate descriptions, even for the same document;
- the access points ("indexes") that can be searched vary between systems;
- there can be more or less cross-referencing between various index terms ("see," "see also," and other kinds of syndic relationships);
- different retrieval systems support various types of searching (matching, comparing), even in the same bibliographic files. Some permit searches for keywords and/or composite Boolean search requests and others do not.

So, correspondingly, one can immediately identify five separate classes of causes for extending searches to two or more online bibliographies and/or online catalogues. Depending on the circumstances, different options might be chosen:

1. Because different bibliographies represent different populations of documents, one may with to extend a search to another bibliography or catalogue because what was desired was not found in what had already been searched and it would be desirable to extend the search to a new population of documents.
2. Because different bibliographies contain different descriptions for the same document, one may intend to extend a search to another bibliography or catalogue for a document that has already been found because differing bibliographic descriptions can be used to accumulate extra information. As noted above, a book might be available in a library catalogue, in a subject bibliography, and in a citation index. All three will have more or less varying bibliographic records for the same document: The catalogue will have a standard catalogue record and a note of the location of each copy; the medical bibliography may support a different, detailed subject description and an abstract; and a citation index might contribute a list of other works cited in it and another list of works that cite it. Combining these descriptions could improve bibliographic access substantially.
3. For a more complete search, one may want to extend a search to two or more other systems with a view to use an additional access point. Citations have to be searched in a citation index. The capability to search on other features, such as searching by words within a little or within an abstract, or by the language or date of the document, varies significantly between systems.
4. Following the complexity and vagueness of language, one may prefer using the system that has the best network of cross-references, the best "vocabulary control" to guide the searcher from the searcher's terms (e.g. "coastal pollution") to the system's terms.
5. It may be worthwhile to extend a search to another system as it has special searching abilities, like identifying pairs of words that occur close to each other, or to extend the search by downloading results into a personal computer for more comprehensive analysis ("post-processing").

There are other probabilities. For example, the extent to which texts are subdivided into fields can affect retrieval performance [6].

We can observe that information retrieval theory remains importantly incomplete, even for unitary retrieval systems, until the effects of changes in any one or more of these variables on retrieval results are properly understood.

Conclusion

Automating a catalogue, placing a bibliography online, or providing access to any other electronic resource online is an appropriate technological development. But to think only of an individual online catalogue, of an individual online bibliography, or of any other individual resource-even being aware that there are several different online catalogues, numerous individual bibliographies available online, and different other resources online – is to think in terms of the card catalogues, published paper bibliographies, and the unitary retrieval systems of the past. Instead of thinking of individual retrieval systems, we should now depend our thinking on the awareness that there are large and growing populations of electronic resources and of retrieval mechanisms, increasingly linked by telecommunications networks, and containing data sets that can, in principle, be linked, combined, and rearranged. What could be possible if, instead of thinking of information retrieval in traditional, unitary terms, as when using a bibliography online, we were to adopt the logic of electronic technology one step further and think instead of a collectivity of bibliographies online? We require to think in terms of using a whole electronic reference library, even various libraries, online.

Extended retrieval provides much wider opportunities, but it also creates the difficulties in selecting what is required from so large and complex a universe.

References

1. Belkin, N.J., and W.B. Croft (1987). *"Retrieval Technique." Annual Review of Information Science and Technology* 22:109-145.

2. Buckland, M.K., A. Hindle, and P.M.Walker (1975). "Methodological Problems in Assessing the Overlap between Bibliographic Files and Library Holdings." *Information Processing and Management* 11:89-105.

3. Buckland, M.K., and A. Lynch (1987). "The Linked Systems Protocol and the Future of Bibliogrpahic Networks and Systems." *Information Technology and Libraries,* 6:83-88.

4. Buckland, M.K. and C.A. Lynch (1988). "National and International Implications of the Linked Systems Protocol for Online Bibliographic Systems." *Cataloguing and Classfication Quarterly* 8:15-33.

5. Buckland. M.K., B.A. Norgard, and C. Piaunt (1992). "Design for an Adaptive Library Catalog." In: Networks, Telecommunications, and the Networked Revolution: Proceedings of the ASIS 1992 Mid-Year Meeting May 27-30, 1992. Silver Springs, Md: American Society for Information Science, pp. 165-171.

6. Lynch, A. (1992) "Online Searching on the Internet: The Challenge of Information Semantics for Networked Information." In: Proceedings of the National Online Meeting, New York, May 5-7, 1992. Medford, NJ: Learned Information. Forthcoming.

7. Lynch, A., and C.M. Preston (1990). "Internet Access to Information Resources." *Annual Review of Information Science and Technology* 25: 263-312.

8. Stonebraker, M., and J. Dozier (1991). Large Capacity Object Servers to Support Global Change Research. SEQUOIA 2000 Report 91/1. Berkeley, Calif: University of California, Electronic Research Laboratory.

7

Retrieval of Information and Theory, Experiment and Operational Systems

The process of scientific communications emanating from Users' expressed requirements for information and the formal mechanisms for the storage and retrieval of information in particular in response to queries or requests is examined by the paper.

Introduction

The paper examines the process of scientific communication resulting from users' expressed needs for information and in particular the formal mechanisms for the storage and retrieval of information in response to queries or requests. Formal indexing or coding schemes, Boolean systems, facet analysis, and associative methods, as well as probabilistic models, are reviewed and information-seeking behaviour is discussed.

Scientific Communication and Retrieval of Information

It is a commonplace that science relies on communication. Science is a social activity; scientists' ideas, models, and results have to be scrutinized by their peers, analysed and tested with the feasibility of validation or refutation as well as the construction of further science. With a view to investigate the role of information retrieval and the impact of developing technologies on scientific communication, we may initiate from a simplified view of the process of scientific communication.

Such a diagram is deceptive both in its simplicity and in its circularity. As a publishing scientist, I am explicitly not communicating with myself! My potential audience will not be merely other scientists (who may in fact feed new publications into the process), but also other users of scientific information, e.g. those who apply the knowledge. The diagram also suggests a system with just one communication channel, and furthermore appears to imply a system that always works! Neither is in general the case.

We in the information world tend to work with systems (fragments or sub-systems of this larger process) that are supposed to help to the whole by providing particular linking mechanisms. By and large we work with relatively formal mechanisms (publication, libraries, databases, etc.); we like to think that they are vital to the whole. However, we also know that scientists depend largely on less formal mechanisms (personal contacts, meetings, etc.). Furthermore, from the scientist' s-eye view, there are many sources/ channels of information that may be selected or rejected at different times, for all kinds of reasons. One of our concerns in developing a science of information must be the scientist's experience of the information environment, and the selection and use made of sources, channels, and modes of both getting information and communicating ideas.

The concern in the present paper is mainly with formal mechanisms for the storage and retrieval of information, in answer to queries or requests. But the wider aspects of the communication process will be kept in view. I start with a perspective on the situation that gives rise to the request. Finally, I will return to some features of human information-seeking behaviour.

Anomalous States of Knowledge

We must first of all ask the question, why does a user (scientist) approach an information retrieval system? The simple answer must be following a requirement or wish or imagined need for information. However, the user's perception of this information requirement deserves some exploration.

In Taylor's classic paper, "Question-Negotiation and Information Seeking in Libraries" [14], four stages are identified:

(1) the visceral requirement (i.e. the user's gut feeling of a need for information);
(2) the verbalized need (the user's first effort to put the information requirement into words);

(3) the formalized requirement (the user's expression of the requirement in terms acceptable to the system);

(4) the compromised requirement (the user's revised expression of the requirement after negotiation with the system).

Relevance

One of the most important concepts for an understanding of our present ideas of information retrieval is that of relevance. Relevance is an extremely difficult idea to pin down and has been the subject of much work over several years [12]. It originates from well before the ASK hypothesis, and one way to think of it might be in connection with correctness. An item might be regarded as appropriate to a request if it is in some sense a "correct" response to that request. There are indeed IR theorists who take a modern version of that view: an item is appropriate to a request if the request can be inferred from the item, rather in the fashion of theorem proving, but with an appropriate logic [15].

However, perhaps the dominant view of relevance (and one that is rather more in sympathy with the ASK hypothesis) is a much more subjective one. An extreme version of the subjective approach would be to say simply that an item is relevant to a user's information requirement or ASK if the user says it is, or in other words if the user would like the system to retrieve this item.

Even without agreement as to what exactly relevance is, the idea of relevance is of central significance to theory and experiment in IR, and it is becoming important to IR practice as well. From the experimental stand print, where the concept originated, we need it in order to evaluate different approaches and methods in IR. From there it has fed into theory; recent theories in IR depend upon it. Finally, some methods of IR ask the user to make relevance judgements online and use that information internally as one type of clue to support formulate a new search.

The major assumption is that users can make relevance judgements or recognize appropriate items, even if not necessarily with absolute confidence.

Early Experiment in IR

The approach of the experimental evaluation of IR systems is central to both theory and operational system development. Probably

surprisingly, this idea is only about 35 years old. (Admittedly, 35 years is a long time in the history of computer-based IR systems; but some kind of IR system, such as library classification schemes, predate computers by at least two-and-a-half millennia!)

The early experiments told us a little about the design of IR systems, but they also focused attention in particular areas, and it may be argued that their lasting impact lies in this focusing process. One area is the one already mentioned, that of relevance: the necessity to devise an operational definition of a "correct" response was a major stimulus to the reconsideration of the notion of relevance. A second kind of focus was on the particular aspects of IR system design that seemed important. Many of such aspects that had been endlessly debated in the 1940s and 1950s now appeared to be of relatively minor importance; by contrast, some aspects that had received feeble consideration now became central. One of the later results of this process, as we shall see, has been the concern with highly interactive systems.

Language

Received wisdom in the 1950s was that IR required some kind of formal indexing or coding scheme. (Exactly what kind of scheme was one of the topics of endless debate). Thus, items needed indexing/coding in terms of the scheme, which probably in turn needed a human indexer (though a machine might be taught to do it).

A similar process was needed at the search stage, in connection with the query or need, though an end-user might possibly learn enough about the formal scheme to conduct a satisfactory search. The outcomes of the early experiments, together with the developing technology and changing perceptions of how it might be used, caused a backlash against this received wisdom. It became possible to throw into the computer larger and larger quantities of text, and retrieve on the ground of words in text rather than assigned keywords or codes. At first sight, the necessity for any sort of indexing scheme, at either end of the process, appears to disappear; the user can use "natural" language to search a "natural" language database, without any interference from librarians.

It is explicit that natural language searching is a powerful device that can often produce good results economically. However, it places a large burden on the searcher, and besides, kinds of queries are not well

served. In recognition of these points, many modern databases contain both formal indexing and searchable natural language text.

Formal artificial languages (in which category I comprise library classification schemes) represent particular views of the structure and organization of knowledge.

A number of modern indexing languages, while not necessarily following the rules of faceted classification, reflect an essentially facet-based approach to the organization of knowledge. But the approach also has value at the searching stage, whether or not the database being searched is indexed by such a language. This theme is taken up again below.

Boolean Logic, Search Strategy, and Intermediaries

Long before either natural language searching or faceted division, and certainly long before the modern computer, it became apparent that certain kinds of information retrieval would give advantage from the ability to search on combinations of characteristics, in a way that we would now normally represent by the Boolean operator AND. Indeed, much effort went into devising mechanisms to permit such searching. Prime examples were Hollerith's mechanically sorted punched cards of the 1890s and a scheme of optical coincidence cards first invented in 1915 [13]. Most currently available computer-based systems allow searching using Boolean logical search statements, together with a few extensions to Boolean logic relevant to searching text; for example, an operator to indicate that two words should not only occur in the same record, but also that they should be next to each other. In this respect, they seem to differ little from the punched-card systems of the 1930s.

Feedback in Boolean systems is of a very limited rule (this point will be taken up again below). Furthermore, the use of Boolean logic appears to suggest an analogy with traditional database management systems, where feedback is not normally an issue. However, the use of even a crude form of feedback is a recognition of the cognitive problems mentioned earlier and a departure from the simple input-output model of information retrieval.

The impact of experimental work on the study of search strategy has not been very great. However, there was one experimental result from the 1960s that encapsulated, in a surprising way, the problems latter addressed by the ASK hypothesis and that was seminal in our understanding of the search strategy problem. It is therefore worth describing this outcome.

The requests that were gathered for the experiment could be divided into those where the user talked face-to-face with an expert and those where the user wrote a letter requesting a search. The expectation was that the face-to-face communication would be advantageous to the search by enabling the development of a better search formulation. However, in the event, the reverse was the case: on average, the letter-based requests performed slightly better than the face-to-face ones.

The experimenters' explanation of this result, after studying the data, was to suggest that users often came to face-to-face meetings without clearly verbalized requests, and that intermediaries vowed to suggest formulations that were easy in system terms. The letter writers, on the other hand, were forced to articulate their requirements more systematically before encountering the constraints of the system.

This result made a clear connection between the Taylor/Belkin view of information retrieval and the practical problems of searching and had a big impact on the training of search intermediaries.

The relation between Boolean searching and facet analysis is a simple one: an analysis of the search topic from a facet stand point fits naturally with a canonical form of search statement, as follows:

$$(A_1 \text{ or } A_2 \text{ or}\ldots\ldots) \text{ and } (B_1 \text{ or } B_2 \text{ or}\ldots\ldots\ldots) \text{ and } \ldots\ldots\ldots$$

Here the different facets (or component concepts of the topic) are A, B, ..., and each search term A_1 is one of the ways of representing concept A. Many of "intelligent" front-end systems for supporting users to construct searches assume this canonical form. It is, however, an extremely limited form if interpreted literally: for instance, it fails to appear that one of the A_1 is might itself be a phrase or a combination of concepts.

Associative Methods

Experimenters and theorists in IR have been working for many years with alternatives to Boolean statements. In special, they have been using what might be described as "associative" methods, where the retrieved documents may not match exactly the search statement but may be allowed to match approximately. For instance, the search statement may consist of a list of desirable characteristics, but the system may present as feasibly useful items that lack some of the characteristics. Then the output of the system may be a ranked list, where the items at the top of the list are those that match best in some sense, but the list would contain items that match less well.

The associative approach with the most substantial history of development is the vector space model of Salton and others [11]. In this model, the documents and queries are seen as points in a vector space: retrieval includes finding the nearest document points to the query point. This model leads clustering, relevance feedback, etc. It has been the basis of a many of experimental systems from the early 1960s on, and many different ideas have been incorporated at separate times and subjected to experimental test. Mostly these tests have been along the lines described in section 4 above, with the system treated in input-output fashion.

Tradition, although it turns out to fit very naturally with more recent approaches of highly interactive systems. The probabilistic approach is discussed in more detail in the next section.

It is not strictly important to regard these thee approaches as incompatible. It is feasible to devise methods that make use of approaches based on more than one approach. However, they do suggest very various conceptions of the nature of degree of match between documents and queries.

Probabilistic Models

Once it is assumed that the function of an IR system is to retrieve items that the user would judge relevant to his/her information need or ASK, then it becomes conspicuous that this is essentially a prediction process. These judgements of relevance have not yet happened. Or rather, if any items have been seen and judged for relevance, then those items are no longer of interest from the retrieval point of view because the user already knows about them. The system must in some fashion predict the likely result of the process in connection with any particular item should it present that item to the user. On the assumption that relevance is a binary property (the user would like to be informed of the existence of this item, or not), the prediction becomes a process of estimating the possibility of relevance of each item and of ranking the items in order of this probability [9].

Information-seeking Behaviour

A current experiment investigated various aspects of searching of information-seeking behaviour, including the behaviour of repeated users of the system [18]. The system was accessible over the network in an academic environment and was available to several users through terminals on their desks or very close by. There was no direct cost to using the system, and since it is not tough to use (being designed so that someone walking in off the street could be expected to be able to use it), there was no obstacle of any kind to its repeated and frequent use. Individual users were logged.

Intelligence

It may be noted that I have not yet mentioned any of the work in the artificial intelligence (AI), expert system or knowledge-based system (KBS) areas. There have indeed been several attempts to apply such ideas to information retrieval, though there is in my view less proof for their effect or effectiveness in the perspective of operational systems. The possible role(s) for knowledge bases in IR is the subject of much debate. One approach is to treat the expert intermediary's skill in a system [16]. However, a major component of the intermediary's expertise, at least as represented in such systems, appears to be the manipulation of Boolean search statements. If we can get by without such statements, then much of the point of these systems seems to be lost.

The other sort of knowledge that, in principle, should be of use would be that embodied in a thesaurus, division scheme, or other formalized indexing language. But such knowledge does not seem to fit very easily with established KBS ideas.

8

Computerized Front-ends and Implications for Developing Countries

Introduction

The chapter covers the definition of front-ends, taxonomy of front-ends, examples of and an evaluation of existing front-ends, directions for future research and development, and the implications for developing countries.

The Information Environment

While information technology offers "the prospect of new ways of finding, understanding, storing, and communicating information" [24], there are a lot of barriers to realizing that potential. The number, diversity, and scatter of information sources and systems now available in electronic form challenge the ability of individual researchers to make proper use of these resources. This paper finds out the role of computerized front-ends in retrieval systems as helps to individual researchers seeking to locate information.

The complication of the electronic information environment is well known. Databases now may contain bibliographic records, full texts, numeric data, images, or combinations of these kinds. The retrieval systems on which they are mounted are diverse, with differing interfaces and means of query formulation. The interconnectivity of telecommunications networks internationally gives the potential for interactive access to retrieval systems throughout the world.

While most of the early front-ends were developed as assistance to accessing a small number of commercial systems and the databases mounted on such systems, these resources now represent only a fraction of the resources of potential value to the researcher. Various universities and government agencies now provide public access to online catalogues, campus-wide information systems, and other electronic data repositories that supplement the resources provided by commercial vendors. While access to commercial systems is billed and not allowed for those who are recognized users, many of the other resources on the network do not currently have such access restrictions.

Within the scope of this paper it is not feasible to review in detail the many front-ends already developed. The reader is referred to two recent reviews by Drenth, Morris, and Tseng [10] and by Efthimiadis [12] for extensive lists of references to prior work. This paper gives a framework for understanding the potential roles of front-ends in retrieval systems by exploring: definition of front-ends, taxonomy of front-ends, instances of front-ends, evaluation of front-ends, directions for research and development, and implications for developing countries.

Definition of Front-ends in Retrieval Systems

Front-end system. Synonymous with Intermediary system.

Intermediary system. In online information retrieval, a kind of expert system used to help end users searching online databases. Such systems offer help with query definition, database selection, search strategy formulation and search revision.

While these definitions attempt to explicitly distinguish between software providing help with communications (gateway software) and software providing expert assistance in query processing (front-end systems, intermediary systems, intelligent intermediary systems), in practice the terms have not been used consistently, and a single system may perform diverse functions. For the purposes of this paper, the term "front-end" will be used to encompass all kinds of assistance "which in some way, and to some degree, make the difference or difficulty of database use transparent to the user" [40]. This assistance can range from the purely clerical like automatic dial-up, to fully intellectual, such as selecting the best way to change an unsuccessful search query. The front-end controls what the user can request and how, a well as what the user is given from the external system and the way it is presented.

Taxonomy of Front-ends

With a view to characterize what has been accomplished in the development of front-ends to date as well as to suggest new directions for research and development, it will be helpful to give a taxonomy by which front-ends can be classified. A number of dimensions are useful in distinguishing among the endeavours to provide computer-based assistance to users of retrieval systems.

Resources Accessible via the Front-end

The front-end is the user's "window" on the world of information available on-line. The frontend may be highly specialized, wished tohelp the user in answering a specific type of question. In this case, it may connect to a single database on a single system and focus on only a part of its contents (e.g., locating literature on special cancer therapies in a database like Medline, which covers many other aspects of clinical medicine as well).

Location of the Front-end

"Front-end" means that the software is located somewhere between the user and the system being accessed, but there are multiple feasible locations. Front-ends may reside on the user's workstation, on another computer on the network, or on the host system itself. Meadow [22] has given detailed analysis of the tradeoff in the location of a front-0end. Front-ends on the user's workstation have the benefits of reducing costs by permitting local editing of queries, supporting graphic displays [25], and performing functions like data analysis that may not be available in the host system.

Types of Assistance Provided by the Front-end

The definition of "intermediary system" given above denotes that front-ends could offer assistance in query definition (concept identification), database selection recognition of databases to be searched and the systems where they reside), search strategy formulation (selection of subject terms, selection of other types of terms, selection of logical operators), and search revision (broadening, narrowing, or other changes). Practically, not all of these kinds of assistance may be provided by a single front-end, which may instead focus on a certain step in the process, such as database selection. Going beyond information retrieval, a front-end may also support post-processing functions, ranging from formatting records for easier reading to performing statistical analysis on the content of records.

The Nature of Assistance Provided by the Front-end

When examining the user assistance provided by front-ends, it is helpful to distinguish between two feasible roles for the computer, i.e., computer-assisted vs. computer-delegated [7]. In computer-assisted mode, the system provides suggestions to the user in making decisions. In computer-delegated mode, the system makes decisions automatically, given some initial input from the user. Thus database selection could be handled by advising some alternatives to the user or by automatically making the selection of which database(s) to search, given some initial information about the question to be answered.

User Modeling Capabilities

Front-ends are designed to make easy access to electronic information resources by masking some of the complexity. A further level of assistance could be provided by user modeling capabilities, such that responses would be tailored to special users. As Allen [1] notes, while the term "user model" emphasizes the information about the person, situational, task, or environmental information may also be encoded in the model. In front-ends, user models could be utilized to adapt explanations to the user's level of expertise and to adapt to user preferences. They may affect database selection, query formulation, and the natural language interaction with the user.

Examples of Front-ends

Several front-ends and related knowledge bases are briefly explained to illustrate the state of the art, with special attention to support for accessing scientific, technical, and medical information.

Medicine: Grateful Med and Loansome Doc

To permit physicians and other health care professionals to search a kind of medical databases, like Medline available on the National Library of Medicine's (NLM) MEDLARS system, staff at the National Library of Medicine have developed Grateful Med for the PC [30], with Version 6.0 scheduled for release in June 1992 [23]. It helps with menu-driven offline entry of strategies. Once on-line, it automatically reformats the terms entered into MEDLARS commands, executes the search, saves the outcomes logs off the system, reformats and displays the citations. The Grateful Med software creates suggested controlled vocabulary terms (Medical Subject Headings) based on retrieved Medline citations, When a strategy results in zero retrieval, a help screen is available that provides suggestions for modifying search strategies. COACH, an expert searcher program to help Grateful Med users improve their retrieval, is currently under development.

Medidine: Unified Medical Language System

The goal of the National Library of Medicine's Unified Medical Language System (UMLS) project is to give easy access to machine-readable information from different sources, including the scientific literature, patient records, factual data banks, and knowledge-based expert system [17]. The barriers to integrated access to information in these sources comprised: the variety of ways the same concepts are expressed in the different machine-readable sources (and by users themselves), and the difficulty of recognizing which of many existing databases have information relevant to certain questions. The UMLS approach to overcoming these barriers is to develop "knowledge sources" that can be used by a wide variety of application programs to compensate for differences in the way concepts are expressed, to recognize the information sources most appropriate to a user query, and to carry out the tele-communications and search procedures necessary to retrieve information from these information sources.

Environment: ANSWER

ANSWER is a standalone microcomputer-based workstation designed for use by health professionals and related personnel in US state and federal agencies responding to dangerous chemical situations. It was developed by the Toxicology Information Program of the National Library of Medicine for the Agency for Toxic Substances and Disease Registry. ANSWER illustrates the fusibilities of using local data access and front-end capabilities in support of problem solving in emergency situations. ANSWER includes a CD-ROM database with information on the medical and hazard management of exposure to over 1,000 dangerous substances; a database of information on previous chemical emergencies;

a gateway to the National Weather Service's online information (automatic dial-up, log-on, and data capture for state, regional, and local weather information); an air dispersion modeling package for conditioning plume path and dispersion; a front-end for access to chemical, toxicological, and hazardous waste files locate in various governmental and private sector on-line systems; and a report generation capacity for editing, sorting, merging, and transforming retrieved data files.

Environment: Eco-Link

Eco-Link was evolved as an electronic research system to take benefit of electronic sources of information on the environment and to coordinate their acquisition, storage, and presentation [39]. It integrates a large variety of data from electronic sources relating to the environment. The heart of the system includes download-filter-manage software routines that automate access to electronic databases and process the acquired information so as to merge data from a broad range of various sources in a common set of locally constructed databases.

Chemistry: Graphics Front-ends

Chemical structure searching presents a requirement for customized front-ends, allowing the scientist touse two-dimensional chemical structure diagrams. Graphics front-ends help the offline building of chemical structure graphics and subsequent uploading to a host computer, as well as the capture (downloading) of retrieved records. Warr and Wilkins [37] have reviewed the basic features of a number of these graphics front-ends, such as STN Express, the front-end software that helps access to STN international databases. STN Express enables one to prepare off-line the strategy formulation (including structural query formulation) and then upload the search strategy line by line after logging on. Offline chemical structure building is menu-driven.

Engineering: Ei Reference Desk

Engineering Information Inc. (Ei) has been developing an integrated software package that is designed to bring together both the searching and retrieval of documents [4, 28]. Users will have a discretion of browsing through electronic tables of contents for engineering journals, searching COMPENDEX PLUS on CD-ROM, accessing other databases through a telecommunications link, and marking documents for automatic ordering and delivery from Ei's document delivery service. Each work of the Reference Desk has been introduced as a separate application but integrated within the Windows graphical interface. A planned enhancement is an electronic mail function.

The Livermore Intelligent Gateway

The Livermore Intelligent Gateway develops a framework that links distributed, heterogeneous computer resources and provides a single user interface such that a "virtual information system" can be tailored to any user's needs [8]. Besides extensive data access capabilities, the Gateway system provides powerful analysis and processing tools to complete the creation of an integrated information environment.

TOME SEARCHER and IMIS

TOME SEARCHER is microcomputer software that intends to provide the inexperienced online user with a series of facilities [34]: choice of database(s) related to the subject of a search; guidance in formulating the scope of the search; natural language input of the search topic; guidance in clarifying and/or amplifying the topic; automatic conversion of the topic into a Boolean search statement; automatic insertion of synonyms and spelling variants in the search statement; estimate of likely yield of a search statement; and guidance in narrowing or broadening the statement if the estimated yield does not match the output specified by the user.

Easy Net

Perhaps the best-known front-end is Easy Net, which offers access to Multiple databases on 13 hosts, comprising many science and technology databases [32]. It gives searchers the option of selecting a database themselves or allowing Easy Net to do so based on answers to a series of questions concerned to the subject and type of material required. Searching can be accomplished using menus to help in constructing a search strategy or with commands based on the Common Command Language.

Wide Area Information Servers

The Wide Area Information Server (WAIS) project seeks to determine whether current technologies can be used to create end-user full-text information systems [19]. The WAIS system is composed of three different parts: clients, servers, and the protocol (Z39.50) that connects them. The client is the user interface, the server does the indexing and retrieval of documents, and the protocol is used to send the queries and responses. Questions are formulated as English-language queries, which are then translated into the WAIS protocol and sent to a server that translates the encoded query into its own query language and then searches for documents satisfying the query.

Evaluation of Front-ends

Front-ends are designed as tools for users. To assess their performance and to identify areas in requirement of improvement, it is necessary to evaluate them. As noted above, front-ends may work in computer-assisted or computer-delegated mode. For those decisions that are computer-assisted, one must condition if the advice is helpful. For those decisions that are computer-delegated, one must condition if the computer's decisions are appropriate. Where assistance is not offered, one must condition if the targeted user group has the necessary expertise to function unassisted. Because the front-end controls what the user can request, one must condition whether it is "habitable" [38], where a habitable language is one in which its users can express themselves without straying over the language's boundaries into un-allowed questions. Furthermore, one must consider whether the output options meet the users' requirements. In addition, there is a requirement to analyse what effort is required to use the front-end. Van Brakel [33] suggests using the activities of a human intermediary as a framework for evaluating the capabilities of a front-end.

Directions for Research and Development

While the instances given in this paper hint that there are already a number of front-ends available to scientists and others who wish to do their own searching, additional research and development are required to create more useful front-ends. Besides completing evaluations as described in the previous section, a number of other issues require to be investigated as outlined below. It should also be noted that development of front-ends may be aided by new computing tools such as user-interface management systems (UIMS) [15].

From Directories to Resource Selection Aids

There is currently a great deal of activity in developing databases of databases or directories. Instances include the Directory of Biotechnology Information Resources maintained by the National Library of Medicine and the Listing of Molecular Biology Databases maintained by Los Alamos National Laboratory. Other instances are guides to library catalogues and the Internet Resource Guide. Work with WAIS and UMLS is finding out ways to use directories for resource selection. This is a potent area for further research, since sophisticated help with search strategy formulation is of little value if an inappropriate resource has been selected.

Coping with Null Sets and Large Sets

Studies of end-user searching frequently disclose that such users often formulate strategies that retrieve nothing or that retrieve very large sets. Prabha [27] reviews a number of strategies for reducing large sets. Front-ends must be designed to help users modify strategies to avoid both situations.

Front-ends for Non-bibliographic Databases

Much of the effort to date has focused on creating front-ends to handle query formulation for different bibliographic databases. As Jarvelin [18] points out, there is also a requirement for assisting with access to various numeric and other types of non-bibliographic databases. While some of the front-end functions would correspond to forms of assistance required for accessing bibliographic databases, others, such as data conversion between varying data representations, must be dealt with in accessing numeric databases.

Multilingual Facilities

As Vickery and Vickery [35] remark, a required further enhancement of front-ends would be provision of multilingual facilities. They suggest that such a front-end could have these features: (1) screen displays would be available in all the languages covered by the system; (2) the interface would accept input of a user query in each of these languages and would refine the question by interacting with the user in the language of input; (3) the terms of the refined question would be translated into the language of the selected database(s); and (4) retrieved records would be translated into the language of the user. As one instance of such multilingual support, Halpern and Sargeant [13] mention a front-end for bilingual searching of Medline that has been developed by INSERM (Institut National de la Sante et de la) Recherche Medicale) and the host Telesystemes-Questel. It supports bi-lingual access at both the command and question level. At the command level, menus and help screens are presented in French only. At the question level, subject searching can be done in French or English, taking advantage of a French translation of the controlled vocabulary Medical Subject Headings.

Knowledge Acquisition

One of the problems involved in the design of more sophisticated front-ends is the dearth of extensive knowledge collected from experts about how they search. As human intermediary expertise is better understood, the problem of knowledge acquisition by the front-end remains. If performance of front-ends is to improve over time, then some provision for modification or learning must be introduced.

User-Friendly Systems

Vickery [36] has remarked that a front-end "accesses existing online systems, with all their constraints and deficiencies, so it can only be as successful as the online search system permits it to be. An interface does not address the difficulty of restructuring the database or the search system to make retrieval more intelligent." Harman [14] argues that attempts to develop more user-friendly front-ends are inherently confined by the design of the under-lying retrieval systems. WAIS is a current instance of efforts to create both a more user-friendly front-ends and a system that is easier to use in searching., based on statistical methods, allowing natural language input, and returning lists of records in order of likely relevance. Research is required to evaluate and further develop these optional approaches to retrieval so that future front-ends are not so constrained. Knowbots [9] – knowledge robots transporting the user's request out into the universe of digitized information where outlaying knowbots will search for responses—may well be part of that future, but there still must be provision for human oversight of the information retrieval process.

Conclusion: Implications for Developing Countries

Keren and Harmon [20] suggest that nearly all publications that deal with information work in the developing nations cite one or more of the following problem areas: "lack of appreciation by national decision makers for the role of STI in development; the absence of an substantial infrastructure for information storage and processing; the absence of infrastructure for information use and absorption by users; and economic, administrative, technological, cultural, educational, and structural impediments to substantial information flow." Given this context, it is necessary to ask what role computerized front-ends might play in overcoming barriers to information access and use in developing countries.

A key lesson that there is the feasibility with front-ends of accommodating some differences (e.g. language spoken) among users of information systems and of providing some guidance in the use of information systems tailored to the requirements of particular user groups. As the telecommunications infrastructure gradually develops, making possible access to remote information resources, it will be important to investigate how best to design front-ends to meet the requirements of particular user groups in specific countries or regions. Moreover, as indigenous information sources are developed, front-ends have a role to play in integrating access to indigenous and external information sources where both are suitable to the users' needs.

9

Human-Centred Approach to Designing Information Systems

Introduction

In relation to viability, validity and acceptability of the information support provided, the design of information systems could be considered. Information is an inevitable ingredient in much that we do. We spend much time gathering, refining, and interpreting information. This process of digesting information has become increasingly complicated as the store of information has become larger and more diverse. The size of the information store makes it problematic to consume all relevant information.

The increasing diversity of information sources, forms, and languages makes it difficult to recognize and interpret all proper information. Often indigestion and sometimes "information poisoning" result.

Information technology seems to provide the means whereby these problems can be overcome. Hypermedia, multimedia, natural language processing, expert systems, and CD-ROM are notable instances. A number of commentators over the past 40 years projected that technologies such as these would soon support us to deal with the information explosion. Each of these communications has, at best, been a bit too optimistic.

One could argue that the proclamations of success were premature because the cost and/or power of computer technology, and related technologies, did not evolve as quickly as anticipated. While this may be true, I believe that more subtle problems have disturbed progress. Put simply, enabling technologies like those noted above may be necessary but they are not sufficient for success. To help this assertion, consider the following two instances. In the late 1970s and early 1980s, we undertook an attempt to put hard-copy procedural information online.

It appeared intuitively obvious that problems associated with the growing size and number of technical manuals could be lessened, or perhaps eliminated, by moving to computer-based information systems.

Two studies were performed in the context of aircraft operations manuals [5, 6]. Of special interest here is the first study, where one condition involved putting on the computer display the exact same information, in the same format, as in the hard-copy manuals.

Experimental consequences for this condition indicated the computer-based system was substantially inferior to the hard-copy presentation. The problems seemed to be due to the inherently limited screen size and the distinct feasibility of getting lost in the display hierarchy. Fortunately, means were devised for alleviating these problems and a derivative of the display system discussed by Rouse, Rouse, and Hammer [6] is being used in the Boeing 777 aircraft. Nevertheless, the "lesson learned" is explicit—simply putting information on a computer does not necessarily make it more useful than presenting it in more traditional ways.

The second instance concerns an effort in the mid-1980s to develop intelligent bibliographic information retrieval systems, primarily for use by engineers and scientists. Five studies were undertaken to understand how different computer aiding schemes affected users' abilities to retrieve information of value. The outcomes of this series of studies are reviewed by Morehead and Rouse [3].

Three of the studies considered the impact of providing connections among articles based on reference lists. As we expected, such links helped considerably. This led us to add further connections based on citations of articles. In this way, an article was linked to both its ancestors and its descendants.

Much to our surprise, the citation connections substantially degraded users' performance. Users tended to wander down citation paths long after they ceased to be productive. We changed the system to display the productivity metric of articles selected divided by articles viewed. In this way, the decrease in productivity of citation paths became evident to users and they abandoned citation paths much sooner. The "lesson learned" here is also clear—providing more connections among information elements is not necessarily advantageous and may be detrimental. Thus, the intuitively obvious advantages of enabling information technologies are not always realized. The straightforward cause is that intuition is not always right, as numerous lottery customers will attest. Rather than betting on technologies, users would be much better served if we first focused on the advantages sought, and then considered alternative means of providing these benefits.

Human-centred Design

The kinds of problems noted earlier can be avoided, and the capabilities of enabling information technologies can be percepted, by adopting a human-centred approach to designing information systems. Human-centred design is a process of assuring that the concerns, values, and realizations of all stakeholders in a design effort are considered and balanced [8]. Stakeholders include users, customers, maintainers, investors, and so on. Further, the designers of information systems are stakeholders in these systems.

While this paper importantly focuses on users, were we to discuss the design, development, implementation, and servicing of an actual information system, we would consider all of the stakeholders. Four of these issues (i.e, evaluation, demonstration, verification, and testing) are well known to designers of information systems and are usually addressed in a proper manner. These four issues are not discussed within the confines of this paper. Interested readers will find a detail treatment of these issues in Rouse [8].

The main three issues in the figure (i.e. viability, acceptability, and validity) are sometimes addressed with sufficient rigour by designers of information systems. Human-centred design includes pursuing all of the issues in Figure 1, starting at the top.

Thus, the first question asked is "What matters? While the last question asked is "Does it run?" Rouse [8] discusses a four-phase methodology, and associated methods and tools, for pursuing the seven issues in Figure 1. In this paper, discussion focuses on elaborating the nature of viability, acceptability, and validity. The use of these constructs is latter illustrated in the context of a few applications.

Viability is concerned with benefits and costs. Contrary to the apparent beliefs of several designers of information systems, the primary benefits to users seldom involve having the opportunity to use an information system.

Users typically use an information system to make better-informed decisions, solve problems, order products and services, save time, and so on. Costs may contain access charges, however, such costs are often paid by third parties. For most users, costs comprise the difficulty and time involved in learning to use and in using the system, and the difficulty and time associated with using the outputs of the system. Thus, for instance, one of the costs of using conventional computer-based information retrieval systems is the difficulty and time of wading through the hundreds or thousands of abstracts obtained, and locating and obtaining source documents.

Acceptability concerns the extent to which a way of doing things fits in with individual and organizational preferences and constraints. For example, the hardware and software of an information system should be compatible with other hardware and software employed by users and their organizations.

Applications

In this section, three instance applications are discussed: (1) maintenance information systems; (2) sales transaction systems; and (3) design information systems. The objective of these illustrations is to show how human-centred design influences the nature of the products and systems that outcome.

Maintenance Information Systems

The application concerned the difficulty of transforming large, blueprint size hard copy, often called C size, to small, computer-display-size images [2]. The context of interest was helicopter maintenance. A very potent element of human-centred design is initial stress on defining the true nature of the problem to be solved.

From the standpoint of the humans involved in this context, the problem of interest was helicopter maintenance, not reading blueprints. Thus, relation to validity the primary concern was providing information to support maintenance activities rather than finding a way to aces blueprints on a mall display.

This perception led us to focus on the tasks to be done rather than on the nature of blueprints. It became clear that information is used in various ways depending on the nature of the task, i.e., problem solving vs. procedure execution. This conclusion led us to adopt Rasmussen's abstraction-aggregation hierarchy [4] as source of organizing maintenance information.

Sales Transaction Support

Computer-mediated sales are an increasingly prevalent approach to selling is retail stores, banks, airlines, and several other domains. Probably not surprisingly, there has been considerable interest in improving the user-system interface of such systems. Of particular concern, following the high turn-over among people performing such jobs, has been decreasing or possibly eliminating the requirements for any extensive training in the use of these systems. We undertook two endeavours in this area, one in the domain of retail sales and the other in passenger reservation systems.

In all the cases, we were asked to improve the usability of these systems by focusing on the user-system interface. We employed the human-centred design methodology to pursue these endeavours.

In both cases, we focused initially on viability, acceptability, and validity for a period of 4-6 weeks. We discovered that usability problems, while important, were by no means the predominant concern. The advantage sought in both cases was increased sales and the cost was the time needed to make sales.

For both endeavours, the initial focus on viability, acceptability, and validity led to stress on sales support rather than solely on improved operability of computer terminals. While usability and the user-system interface still got much attention, it was given in the context of supporting the tasks that really mattered. The consequence was system designs that were substantially different from those originally envisioned.

Design Information Systems

The application under design information systems focused on access to and utilization of science and technology information in the perspective of designing aerospace systems.

The motivation for this endeavour included a long-term interest in the value of information [7, 11], as well as a practical perspective requirement to develop design information systems. In keeping with the human-centred ideas to design we began by fousing on viability, acceptability, and validity. These issues were pursued using questionnaires, interviews, and observational techniques including a large number of designers [9]. We found that very little science and technology information is accessed by formal means.

Why don't designers take benefit of science and technology information? One answer is that they perceive little advantage and great cost in accessing this type of information. They attach no advantage to using the information system per se.

They are related to making informed design decisions. They become informed by asking other people in their organization, a conclusion also reached by Allen [1]. Why do they depend on subjective opinions rather than the "hard" objective information provided by science and technology?

A primary cause is that they find published research results to be applicable in general but not to their certain problems in particular. They want contextually based answers to their questions rather than generic simplifications. In other words, they question the recognition of available science and technology information. There are also acceptability problems. Almost all science and technology information is created, written, and published for consumption by scientists and technologies. Designers sometimes have the specialized expertise, or the patience, to penetrate this information. They find the context and format of presentation full unacceptable.

The crux of the designer's dilemma is depicted in Figure 2. Each transformation in this diagram requires time and attempt. Both time and effort increase as one moves to the right in this diagram. It is easy to see why a designer would not want 1,000 abstracts of research articles on human memory to answer a question relating to usability of radar modes. The cost of answering questions in this way far outweighs the advantages.

The above conclusions concerning designers' realizations of viability, acceptability, and validity caused us to focus on designers' tasks and information requirements rather than on the nature of science and technology information. Thus, rather than focusing on how to get designers to access and utilize science and technology information, we looked at the information requirements to help design decision-making.

Figure 2
Alernative Transformations in Answering Questions

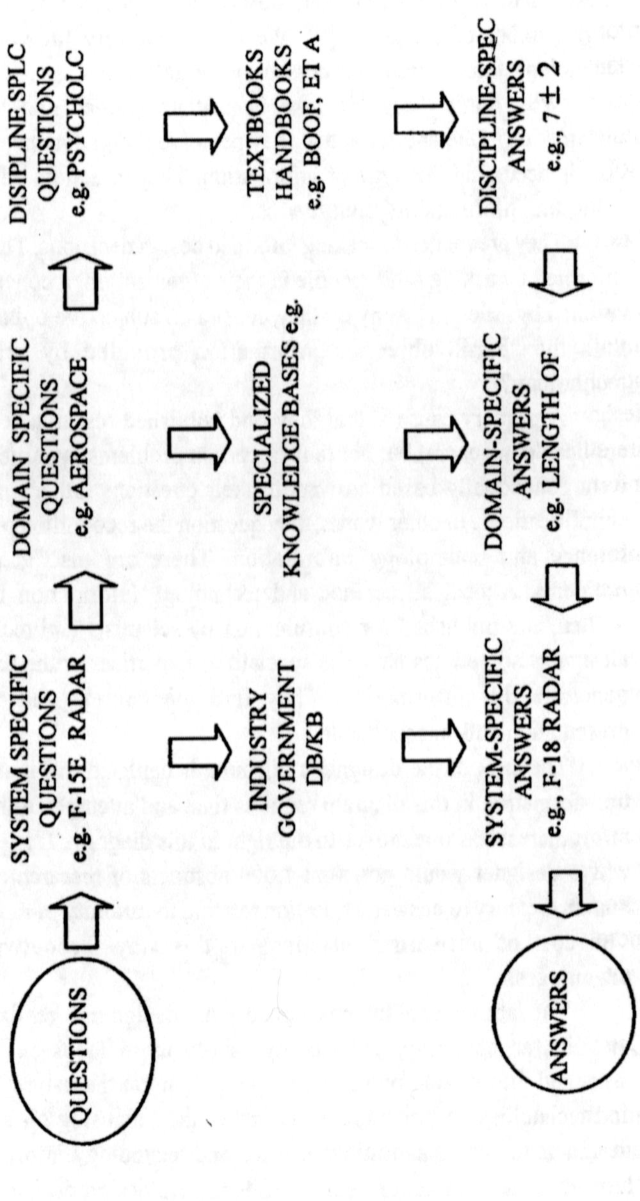

Such requirements should drive the way in which science and technology information is created, organized, formatted, and accessed if this information is intended to support design.

After considering option representations, we concluded that information seeking in design could be represented as a process of asking questions and pursuing answers in the perspective of a "design space" involving a set of archetypal tasks focused on attributes of the design artifact and characterized in relation to abstraction and aggregation [10].

Lessons Learned

The human-centred design issues of viability, acceptability, and validity have been discussed in the perspective of several examples, involving systems for bibliographic information retrieval, aircraft operations, maintenance information, sales transaction support, and design information. In this section, the lessons learned from these efforts are summarized. First and foremost, it is inevitable to recognize that information access and utilization are seldom ends in themselves.

The advantage sought is successful task performance, not information seeking. Thus, primary tasks of interest do not include operating an information system.

Regarding primary tasks, the information requirements associated with these tasks would dictate information system design. The existing organization and format of information should not, to the extent feasible, constrain the nature of an information system. It should also be noted that the means in which information needs are satisfied are likely to vary with tasks despite the fact that the same information content may be needed for two or more tasks.

Finally, by focussing on the issues of viability, acceptability, and recognition within the human-centred design framework, one is much more likely to resolve the right problem and solve it in an acceptable way. The outcome is information systems that are both usable and useful.

Conclusions

The information explosion continues unabated. The promise of information technology has long been started as a means of containing, and probably counteracting, this explosion. This paper has argued and illustrated with several instances that the problem is not amenable to technology panaceas. Instead, success is much more likely if the concepts, principles, methods, and tools of human centred design are used to condition contextually relevant information requirements, as well as synthesize support systems that satisfy these needs.

10

Designing Interactive Systems and Theories of Human Mind Process Information

Introduction

Today, a question generally stands before us how best to produce and provide the information being needed by all sorts of users. Hypertext and hypermedia have been introduced as solution to this question. The new generation of information systems must be user-oriented and task-driven, and their design should depend on knowledge about the manner in which the human mind processes information. Extensive reference is made to the cooperative hypermedia authoring environment SEPIA.

I start from the assumption that the world of today—and, particularly, that of tomorrow—depends more and more on the availability of the right information at the right time and in an adequate quantity and quality. Not judging in this context whether this development is good or bad, a question remains on how to produce this information and how to give it to clients, students, teachers, engineers, readers, and users in general. My first claim is that hypermedia systems will provide a solution to this problem. They represent the starting of the development of a new generation of information and publication systems. It is my second claim that the development of these information systems has to adopt the approach of user-oriented and task-driven system design. It is my third claim that the application of this approach has to depend largely on knowledge about human information processing, i.e. cognitive theories. In summary, I claim the inherent capabilities of hypermedia systems will meet the needs of cognitively adequate human-computer interfaces and the demands for task-driven provision of functionality required to support a variety of work activities.

The aim of this contribution is to show for selected areas what is required in order to live up to the expectations raised by the concept of hypertext and hypermedia. The paper is structured as follows: First, I introduce the concepts of hypertext and hypermedia. Second, I present five basic needs for user-oriented and task-driven system design. Third, I describe the proposed research and development strategy in the context of the cooperative hypermedia authoring environment strategy in the context of the cooperative hypermedia authoring environment SEPIA. SEPIA is an instance of how the design of an interactive system is largely based on theories of human information processing, in this case on cognitive models of authoring hyperdocuments. SEPIA is part of the recent research activities at the Integrated Publication and Information Systems Institute (IPSI) of the Gesellschaft fur Mathematic und Datenverarbeitung (GMD) in Darmstadt, Germany.

Hypermedia Systems

Basic Concepts

First, we require to distinguish between hypertext and hypermedia. In my usage, hypertext uses the structural aspects. This concept is based on the idea of a non-linear organization of pieces of information ("nodes") that can be referenced and concerned to each other by "links" in an associative manner and constitute a network structure (directed graph including cycles). An important feature of hypertext is the capability of having machine-supported connections within and between documents. On the other hand, I use the term hypermedia if the nodes consist of multimedia contents, e.g. sound, complex graphics, pictures, video, or animation.

I claim that hypermedia systems will provide qualitatively new means for producing, communicating, and comprehending knowledge and will quickly change the conditions of the information society [26,27]. Additional information will be given as we go along. Since the expectations about the potential of hypermedia systems are very high, the role of hypermedia in a comprehensive information environment has to be clarified. In my view, expectations will not be met by depending solely on the concept of hypertext and hypermedia. Rather, these are the crystallization nucleus for the development of a new generation. They must be complemented by considering and integrating existing outcomes and future achievements in the following spheres:

- ergonomic design of human-computer interaction
- database management systems
- information retrieval
- knowledge-based components
- publication and high-quality layout systems
- telecommunication and computer networks

Current hypermedia systems are merely a first demonstration of the elementary principles that raise our interest in what is still to come in the future.

Authoring versus Retrieval

Discussions about the results of computer technology for the information society seem to address primarily problems of how to supply information (presentation, retrieval, filtering, etc.). While these are valid issues, at least an equally important aspect is largely neglected: a prerequisite for information retrieval and presentation – not merely in hypermedia systems—is that this information must have been produced. Therefore, we have to give tools for authoring and production. The quality of the next generation of hypermedia systems will rely on the extent and quality of support in authoring environments. Most of the hyperdocuments recently produced rely on the method of "turning (existing linear) text into hypertext." There may be value in turning existing paper or linear electronic documents into electronic hyperdocuments. But the results rarely show what an innovative hyperdocument could actually be like.

User-oriented and Task-driven System Design

I propose that the design of interactive systems in general should adhere to the following five requirements:

(1) *User-oriented design.* One should take into account the limits and the capabilities of the human information-processing system when designing features and mechanisms of human-computer interaction. This concerns mainly the design of the user interface. It is important to have potential users partaking in the design process.

(2) *Task-driven design.* Even a very user-friendly system is worthless if it does not give the extent and quality of performance necessary to solve the problems that are part of accomplishing the overall task. A detailed analysis of the task and the corresponding activities is needed with a view to decide on the kind of support required by the user and then provided by the computer system.

(3) *Theory-model guided design.* To realise usability and utility, it is important to have an adequate model of the different processes and knowledge structures included in the problem-solving activity of the user. I propose that they models be based on cognitive theories of human behaviour.

(4) *Empirical-based design.* The use of models and theories means the use of empirical investigations to test and validate the theoretical assumptions and their applicability. This means rapid preparation of prototypes for testing the ideas with users and engaging in a step-by-step design process.

(5) *Technology-knowledgeable design.* One has to keep in mind the role of available technology can serve as a means of inspiration for new applications in different domains. Beyond this, it has been argued [24] that it should be an end to progress conceptually one step ahead of prevailing technology and provide requirements to be met by future interactive systems on the ground of cognitive and social theories of human behaviour.

SEPIA: A Cooperative Hypermedia Authoring Environment

In this section, I will describe how my ideas that the design and development of interactive systems can and should be relied on theoretical considerations and empirical outcomes in the field of cognitive science were reflected in the search and development plan for SEPIA (Structured Elicitation and Processing of Ideas for Authoring). SEPIA and its chief design principles were first mentioned in Streitz et al. [28] but did not comprise the cooperative aspects.

The R&D Strategy for SEPIA

Our R&D strategy that addresses the cognitive processes, the product, and the social aspects of the authoring activity is characterized in Figure 1, exhibiting the relationship of the activity under investigation, the theoretical ground, and the resulting components of SEPIA. Paying attention to the process aspect needs developing and refining a model of the cognitive processes of writing and transforming these results into needs as in our activity space concept.

The Authoring Activity

While publishing is communicating knowledge, authoring, and in special writing, is knowledge production and transformation. From our writing is a complex problem-solving and design activity with various constraints. The final product—in terms of a hyperdocument—can be viewed as an externalized representation of internal knowledge structures that have been developed by the author. Thus, authoring tools that are particularly geared to hyperdoucments offer much better facilities for conveying the message and intention of authors: authors can externalize knowledge in a format that is nearer to their knowledge structures than was feasible with traditional linear documents. Making additional properties of the author's knowledge structure (as part of hyperdocument) available to the reader facilitates integration rather than delinearization and thus more detail processing on the recipient's side. Documents produced with these instruments keep authors' knowledge structures alive by preserving, e.g., their argumentation and theoretical structures, which can be utilized for subsequent processing.

The Role of Cognitive Theories for the Design of Authoring Systems

Based on an analysis of the cognitive processes of writing [1, 11, 10], authoring can be characterized as a "journey of discovery". On this journey, ideas are not only translated into text ("knowledge telling"); they are also generated and refined, because the production of words and phrases triggers new associations ("knowledge transformation"). The widely mentioned model of Hayes and Flower [11] stresses the problem-solving aspect of writing. Based on the analysis of thinking aloud protocols, it recognises three main sub-processes (planning, translating, and reviewing). A model that reflects basic differences between novice and experience writers has been proposed by Bereiter and Scardamalia [1]. Knowledge transformation is conceived as an interaction between two problem spaces: the "content space" and the "rhetorical space".

Supporting the Authoring Process via Activity Spaces

On the ground of research writing, we distinguish three closely related sub-problems that an author must solve to present a document: (1) the content problem, (2) the rhetorical problem, and (3) the planning problem.

Applying the principle of "cognitive compatibility" [24], we can use this decomposition into sub-spaces as a basis for dedicated requirements of components of the authoring environment. We need that these (cognitive) problem spaces be "matched" in SEPIA by corresponding activity spaces (see figure 3). Each activity space gives specific objects and operations to facilitate the author's activities when working on these sub-problems. Since argumentation is a decisive cognitive activity that plays an important role in writing for a large number of document types, these three spaces are supplemented by a fourth called "argumentation space".

Objects and operations of the content space facilitate the development of a domain model. This can also include access to background material from either internal (e.g. previous documents) or external sources (e.g. querying a database). Therefore, SEPIA uses the structuring facility of hypertext to support collecting ideas in textual and graphical nodes, their grouping in topic-related clusters by composite nodes, and connecting them via typed links.

In the rhetorical space, the author creates the reader-oriented, final document. To a large degree but not exclusively, it is produced on the ground of transformations of the material in the content space.

In the planning space, the author is able to externalize his writing plans regarding goals, construct issues to be related to in the document and establish an agenda of the authoring activity. Consequently, this space serves as a meta-space for coordinating the activities in the other three and controlling the progress of the design process. The formulation of issues may cause

- the identification of important topics that are elaborated in the content space;
- the creations of positions and claims that have to be supported in the argumentation space; and
- the structuring of the document in the rhetorical space.

For the development of an issue structure, the author can depend on a set of dedicated nodes and links.

The argumentation space supports the development of an argumentative structure by providing proper design objects and operations based on an extension of the well-known argumentation schema developed by Toulmin [30]. Using the argumentation space, the author can elaborate an argumentation by creating support or objections on varied levels, by formulating contradictions, and by constructing argumentative chains (for details, see Streitz et al. [28]). When "travelling through activity spaces," the author does not require to follow a predetermined route.

Beyond the structural aspects, hyperdocuments are very much characterized by the kind of media that is used. In general, all atomic (content) nodes carry multimedia information, comprising text, graphics, pictures, and sound. At present, we are working on the integration of video as the content of a node. This means of using multimedia capabilities, i.e., as part of nodes and in combination with other media, has to be distinguished from using them for communication purposes as, e.g., in audio and video conferencing systems.

Supporting the Social Process: From One Author to a Group of Authors

Considering that especially large and complicated documents are prepared by a group of authors, our system should be able to support the social processes involved in team work. For this reason, we had to develop social cooperation models and extend SEPIA from a single-author to a multiple author environment by providing corresponding cooperation modes.

First of all, authors have to be able to access and intend to work on the same part, they have to be prevented from destroying each other's work. In most of the cases, the overall task is classified into sub-tasks that are assigned to specific authors or subgroups of authors. The authoring environment should help this division of labour. This is facilitated by the modular structure of hyperdocument networks and accomplished by introducing the notion of "composites," which permit a set of nodes that belong to one sub-task to cluster.

Conclusion

I presented the hypertext and hypermedia as a strong concept for the creation, structuring, and presentation of information. In a second step, I introduced the approach of user-oriented and task-driven system design. Building on this, I mentioned the application of cognitive theories of human information processing for the specification of design requirements for a hypermedia authoring system. And in the last, I mentioned the user interface and the functions of the authoring environment for one author and various authors. Reviewing my three claims from the introduction, I can state that my experience in following this approach has been very positive. I do not think that another concept of information structuring would have been as proper as the hypertext concept. Its inherent opportunities for modularity, flexible decomposition and combination, reuse of prevailing material, guided tours, group-specific views, annotations, clustering of information, graphical presentation, and navigation of document structures are what is required for the complex task of authoring large documents in teams. There is still one aspect missing. We completed building the prototype system only currently. The task ahead is to give the system to a group of real users outside the laboratory and have them use it. Their feedback will be considerable for the evaluation of our design decision and their implementation. Based on this information and our own utilization and thinking, we will review our decisions, redesign this prototype, and produce a new version.

11

Multimedia Interface Design

Introduction

The sound graphics, text etc. are the different presentation media. The term multimedia has also been used by the paper in this sense. The possible benefits of a multimedia approach are discussed and some examples are given of how different media affect knowledge comprehension in human beings. An indication is given of what multimedia facilities are recently available. The PROMISE multimedia interface project is described, and in main a feasible approach to the formulation of a multimedia design methodology is proposed. Some initial guidelines on multimedia interface design are provided. Although some of the ideas expressed here come from work in process control, they are likely to be generalizable to wider domains.

The term "multimedia" has two feasible meanings. Firstly, the "media" can refer to storage media such as WORMs, CD-ROM, and disks. Secondly, it can refer to the presentation of information using various media such as sound, graphics, text, etc. [10]. In this paper the second meaning applies throughout. The idea of using multiple media to develop communication between humans and computers is not new. A paper of 1945, "How We may Think" [7], suggested a multiple media view that was later reasessed [8].

Some well-known early experiments with multimedia were carried out at the MIT "Media Lab" in 1977 [6], and Maekawa and Sakamura [14] also described an early multimedia machine that was being implemented at the University of Tokyo. The system had an optical disc,

100 Mbyte disc, a high speed resolution graphics display, a TV camera, and sound input/output. These collections of multimedia devices were very expensive and it is only currently that a lot of multimedia tool kits have come to the marketplace at a relatively low cost.

But why should we be interested in multimedia interfaces? Well, even a cursory study of human beings communicating information between each other will show the significance of the use of multiple media in the communications process. Human beings generally use at least two sensory channels (visual and auditory) but frequently use a third—touch—as well, and within these communication channels, a rich variety of media are employed. When one artificially insertion the richness of the set of communication media being used (for example by taking a tape-recording of a meeting), the subsidization in communication power is explicit.

Since human beings do seem to be able to communicate more effectively between each other than with computers, the idea of employing additional media in human-computer interaction seems a sensible one, whose insertion is likely to improve the communication process. The early stumbling blocks that prohibited the implementation of multimedia facilities on computers were lack of power and storage. Now, these problems have largely been overcome and multimedia tool sets are thus becoming available on both personal computers and high-performance work-stations. The technical difficulties of providing a variety of media with acceptable performance and at a reasonable cost are not the only stumbling blocks that may prevent the exploitation of multimedia facilities. Another key problem is that of devising a methodology to help multimedia interface design. Being able to give multimedia interfaces is not enough. One must also be able to know when to use which media and in what combination to solve a particular interface problem.

What are Communication Media and How Do They Differ?

Although we generally think initially about the physical aspects of communication media (screens, colour, sounds, etc.), the chief attribute of a medium is that it gives a language for communication. This language will mix up a syntax, semantics, and pragmatics, with the physical aspects of the medium providing constraints on the syntactic feasibilities. Traditional computer media have generally been restricted to one sensory channel (e.g. text [visual], graphics [visual], sound [auditory]), but even within one sensory channel, a rich kind of media can be supported. The visual channel, for instance, can help graphics, tables, diagrams, pictures, maps, graphical animation, and 3-D graphics, all of which communicate information in various ways. The auditory channel can helpspeech, verbal gestures, realistic sounds, artificial sounds, and music. The sensory channel can include vibration and sensory input that might result from, for example, a data glove. Some information already exists to guide us on the relative claims for different media for effective information transfer. Auditory media, such as radio, make dialogue salient. For example, children given a story in audio only or with a visual + audio combination (same soundtrack) recall discussion better when it is given as audio only.

Television presentation seems to be better for action information, which has developed recall when presented via television [5]. Whilst audio information seems to stimulate imagination, spatial visualization is better handled visually, as might be anticipated. Other studies have indicated that diagrams are better at conveying ideas, whereas text is better for detail [22]. However, the visual channel does not often dominate. Walker and Scott [24] found that human beings judge light as being of a shorter duration than a similar tone, and when these are presented together, the auditory channel dominates. Pezdek [21] carried out experiments to condition if the visual channel dominated over the auditory channel in the comprehension of information on television. Whilst there was proof of visual domination, the presence of the auditory channel actually improved comprehension and vice versa.

Text is generally better for communicating complex information to experts, whilst pictures are better for exploratory learning. In specific, visual representations are excellent for synthesis. These ideas are shown in Figure 1, where the usability of varied channels (visual and auditory) is contrasted with the previous knowledge and experience in the knowledge area. For some tasks, text can be a very effective medium of commination. Each varied medium of commination, therefore, has properties that will increase or restrict its capability for sending particular types of knowledge.

Multimedia technology can deliver information like a fire hose delivers water. Just as drinking from a fire hose is not an sufficient way to quench one's thirst, high powered multimedia presentations can overload the senses and not successful to communicate information effectively. Multimedia bases on the important truth in the Chinese proverb that tells us a picture "is worth more than a thousand words." Unfortunately some pictures do not support to control the flow of information, and actually make it worse.

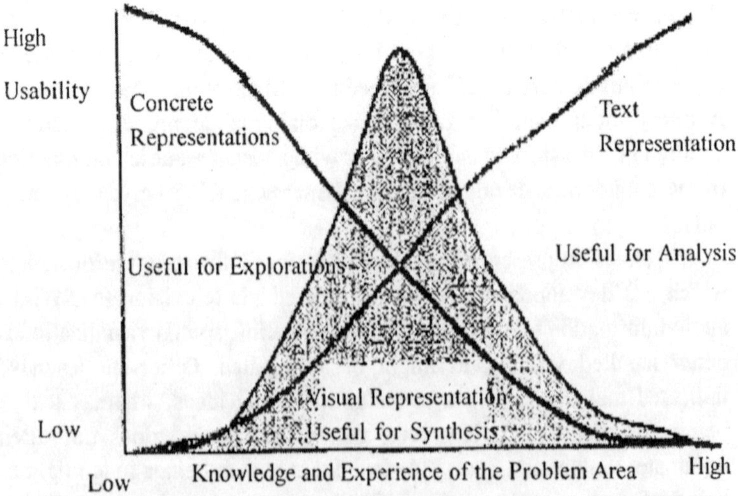

Are Human Beings Aware of the Capabilities of Different Media?

Human beings in general, and computer interface designers in special, are not really aware of the capabilities and limitations of various media. Early computer output was restrained to text. This is a medium that most people deem, since it has been used for hundreds of years. Therefore we have an intuitive understanding of how to communicate with text, at least at a fairly basic level. When graphics became feasible on computers, the situation did not materially transform because graphics had also been used by human beings to communicate (often in conjunction with text) for many years. When colour became available, however, the situation deteriorated colour was used in a completely indiscriminate manner in early interface design. It was not surprising that the quality of interfaces deteriorated. Most people cannot opt their own wall-paper or clothes with a real colour sense. It was much later that designers realized that the spare use of colour was the basic to good interface design. It is rather interesting to reflect on why human beings (in the Western world in particular) do not have good colour sense. Many White [25] makes the interesting point that "imagery" (which in her definition encompasses paintings, sculpture, and television as well as computer graphics and video) has been utilized as a primary learning tool for centuries.

The invention of the printing press transformed all that, and the chief mechanism for learning became the printed word. Ironically, towards the end of the twentieth century we have moved back to a world where imagery is important again, and it has transferred the word as a major political communication medium. There is, however, little research on imagery and its effects.

What can the Technology do Now?

The technology has moved quickly in the past some years. The enabling technologies needed to support a multimedia workstation go far beyond provision of the media themselves. A typical list [15] would comprise:

- Bit-mapped displays
- Audio and video support
- Device independent graphic rendering
- Control and synchronization
- Data compression
- Networking support
- High CPU/disk performance
- Authoring tools

To illustrate how far recent workstations have come in being able to deliver such a collection of enabling technologies, Malleo-Roach cites the SUN SPARC station as an instance and provides the figures given in the table.

To give an idea of the costs related multimedia support, he suggests three feasible configurations: "minimal", "enhanced", and "operational", with costs at about US $10,000 and US $35,000 for the first two (the third not yet being available). He expects an "operational" version to be available in 1995 for about US $10,000.

Bit mapped display:	1152x900 bit-mapped display, most models giving 8-bit pseudo-colour.
Device independent	All SPARC station support Open Windows 2.0 with XII
Graphics:	NeWs Imaging
Audiovisual:	Every SPARC station has built-in audio capabilities (8 KHz single channel. Videopix (a

	video frame grabber) is also available).
Data compression:	JPEG compression support for Video Pix. Uniflix-video compression/decompression tool kit for full-motion video.
Control synchronization:	No total and comprehensive solution, but a several mechanisms are offered such as share money, interprocess communication, times, semaphores and threads.
Networking:	Client-server support. Multimedia as natural extension of the client-server model.
Authoring:	A number of tools are available comprising Hyper News, Cats Meow, and Mediawrite.
High CPU/disk:	Sufficient Performance

Multimedia capabilities have also already arrived on most of the personal computers. There are multimedia extensions to Windows, and Apple now offers "Quick Time" on the Macintosh. Quick Time offers three new components: the Movie Toolbox, the Image Compression Manager, and the Component Manager. The Movie Toolbox gives facilities for generating, editing, and playing back moving images. The Component Manager enables new devices (such as VCRs, camcorders, etc.) to be appended as well as third vendor software modules. The Image Compression Manager uses one of three compression techniques for animation, video, and photos.

The JPEG (Joint Photographic Experts Group) algorithm is utilized to compress photographs. It removes data that is redundant to the human eye. Compression ratios of between 500:1 and 5:1 can be realized with a full screen colour image taking about 10 seconds to compress. The video compressor can achieve ratios of between 25:1 and 5:1 giving about 15 seconds of compressed video per megabyte. Boards are available for capturing video directly from cameras.

User Centred or Design Centred?

Articles on multimedia tend to stress the technological side rather than utility aspects. There are several who appear to view multimedia techniques as a technology looking for an application. This technological push view of multimedia is summed up in the introduction to an extended set of articles on multimedia in a current edition of Open Look [19]:

For while multimedia has the potential to transform computing, several of the components that develop it are already available—it's just that users haven't brought them together yet......Admittedly, the one thing that multimedia's been waiting for is applications. But they....are now coming on stream. In other words, we have the technology, why don't you users want it? Following the availability of the CD-I ROM and the richness of the media, educational technology has been a big target area for multimedia development. A number of people extol the virtues of multimedia education, however, one does tend to get the impression that the designers start with a multimedia tool kit and then try to find an application. As a result, a lot of people are rather sceptical about recent developments and the progress really made. Tools for the construction and manipulation of collections of multimedia material are becoming largely available on successively cheaper hardware platforms. In terms of the educational use of these systems, however, it is unclear that any development has been made.

The endeavour in developing the technology has not been matched by a similar concern with the pedagogy........At present it is an article of good faith that multimedia is a good thing for education and training. There is no proof that multimedia enhances learning, or makes it more cost effective. [12]

Thus, the significance of multimedia applications lies not in what it can do but in what user goals it can solve more effectively.

The PROMISE Multimedia Interface Project

The overall purposes of the PROMISE project (Process Operators Multimedia Intelligent Support Environment) are two fold:

(1) the design, construction, and evaluation of a multimedia tool set for improving user interfaces to advisory and diagnostic expert systems applied by single operators in process control environments;
(2) the development of a methodology to help designers using the tool set.

The Media Supported

The PROMISE system is multimedia, as it supports many ways of communicating information, and multimodal, as several styles of interaction are supported. The system supports a lot of multimedia options [2], comprising:

- text, graphics, and sound output
- full colour

- live and still video output
- text and Mouse input
- two-dimensional animation
- unmediated video
- natural language output (speech)

The Environments

The multimedia approach in PROMISE is being applied in two different types of environment that will support us in evaluation—a real-time application and a simulated one. The real environment puts serious constraints on the evaluation environment, as the clock cannot be stopped and unanticipated events can occur. Such an environment also poses other difficulties from an evaluation standpoint. Errors cannot be deliberately introduced or reproduced, and controlled experiments are not easy. Therefore a simulated environment where we can control the nature of the upsets and monitor operator performance will also be utilized. The two application areas opted are control of a chemical plant (DOW Benelux) and the application of power station simulators (Scottish Power).

The Unique Features of Multimedia Usage in Process Control

Most multimedia ideas grew out of work in computer education. The educational multimedia approach includes the use of video computers, interactive television, and electronic books to give a richer educational environment. It is envisaged that a user will be able "to browse through vast libraries of text, audio and visual information [4]. These libraries will be highly inter-linked utilizing a technique known as "Hypermedia", a concept developed from Hypertext that was first defined in the 1960s and led to the Xanadu system [18]. Most of the recent literature about multimedia approaches derives from the educational sector. These educational applications tend to be activated by the learner alone where the user of the multimedia system is in full control.

In opposite, the process control environment places extremely demanding requirements on the architectural of a multimedia presentation system.

- the operator may be engaged in different distinct tasks simultaneously, for example monitoring, tracking alarms, etc.
- New tasks and hence interactions may be provocated at any time

by either system or operator.

- The process state may be really dynamic, so information may need to be presented quickly and in a form that is readily understood by the operator.

The Architecture

The overall architecture is shown in Figure 3.

The actual realization of an objet is derived from:

- designer options: the designers specify alternative renderings of an objet and give measures of their preferences for such rendering;
- resource limits: the availability of the physical rendering resources;
- multimedia options: given a choice, what would be the choosen rendering?
- Operator preferences: are there special operator needs (i.e. colour blindness)?

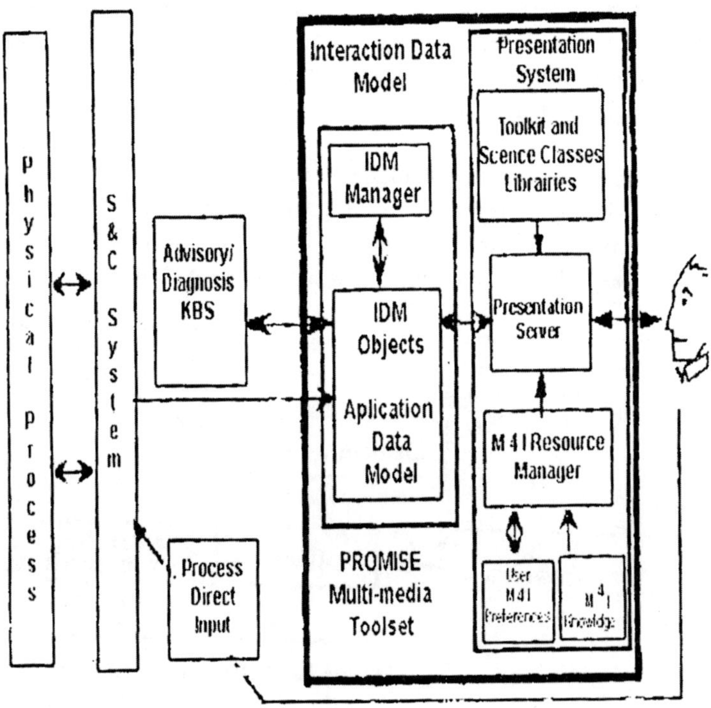

Figure-2

At the far right are the dynamic system to be controlled system to be controlled and the "supervisory and control system" that controls it. The PROMISE system is an advisory system so that the operator can fully ignore it if required and can control the process separately. In fact, no direct control of the system is feasible through the PROMISE terminal. An "advisory/diagnostic knowledge based system" is shown in the figure, though such a system is not a real part of PROMISE. At the heart of the tool set is the "interactive data model." This module models the appropriate portions of the plant and all objets rendered to the operator. It is therefore a basic player in consistency maintenance. The "presentation server" actually renders the images, sounds, etc., under control of the "resource manager" which decides what media will be employed keeping in view the designers' preferences, the current resource usage, the user preferences, and general rules about rendering (the M4I Knowledge in the diagram).

Recently, this tool set is being established in the chemical plant and in a nuclear power station simulator so that experiments can be carried out on the effectiveness of multimedia interfaces. In parallel, a series of experiments are being undertaken in the behaviour laboratory at Loughborough University.

How does One Design a Multimedia Interface?

Although the project is ongoing, we can already give some guidelines as to how to design a multimedia interface. Our approach is one of experimentation combined with pragmatism (Figure 3).

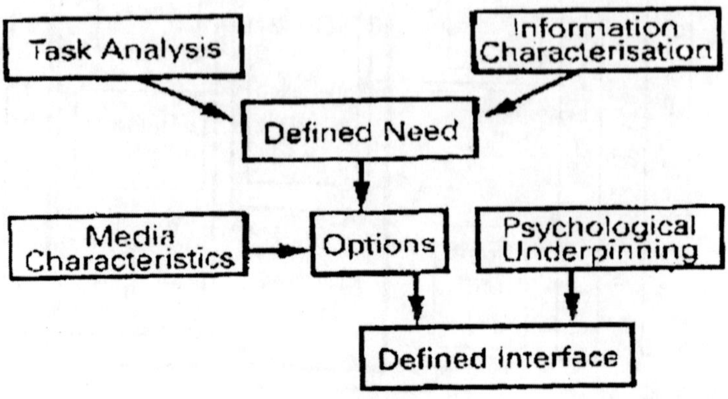

Figure-3

A task analysis [20] will be carried out on the operator task to establish the information needs. These needs then must be characterized in terms of a defined information processing requirement using a knowledge characterization scheme. The options that the different media provide are then matched to the needs to obtain a set of multimedia feasibilities. Finally, an envelope of defined interfaces can be derived by checking the possible interfaces against our knowledge of the human cognition system.

The knowledge characterization scheme recognises a lot of important information communication features that describe the knowledge to be communicated to the operator, for example. More details are given in Alty and Bergan [3].

- the number of dimensions needed;
- Ordering or sequence;
- Relationships:
- Dynamic;
- Static;
- Persistence;
- Instance;
- Information content;
- Urgency;
- Context change;

There are, of course, a number of. We then map these information requirements onto appropriate media using another list of media properties, for example:

- ICON is 0-D has no ordering, limited relationships, static, is persistent, and has limited information content.
- PICTURE is 2-D, strict ordering, probably strongly associated with real world static, persistent, and has high information content.
- VOICE OUTPUT is 1-D, strict ordering, strongly associated with real world, dynamic, non-persistent, and has medium information content.

Some Initial Guidelines

Multimedia interface design has only one objective-that of achieving some goal in a "better" manner. It is therefore important to clearly establish the goals to be achieved and what is meant by "better".

In the PROMISE application, we decided early on that the basic problem in process control was information overload with too little time for cognitive processing. Thus our major objective is to use multimedia in such a way as to buy time for the operator by rendering the information in such a manner as to enable it to be assimilated more rapidly. Other goals comprise error reduction and better job satisfaction. Multimedia design is therefore critically bound up with the tasks being undertaken and the skills of the operators at the interface. Even so, we can make some general observations:

Real World Sensing

Multimedia interfaces permit us to reconnect the operator/user with the real sense world. The history of process control ha been the gradual separation of the operators from the system they are controlling. In former times, operators were able to see, hear, and feel the plant. We have developed a media-poor world that the multimedia approach can recreate. When operators close a valve they should see and hear it close. In PROMISE, we expect to have a microphone icon that can be moved round the process diagram. The operator can then hear information from chosen parts of the plant.

Maintaining Information Source Integrity.

Human beings generally do not know how they use information. From a set of sensory inputs they "know' what decision to take. It is therefore necessary to preserve the integrity of information sources, particularly if we are not absolutely sure what is important. In the PROMISE project, for example, our studies disclosed that converting a particular test to a number lost a great deal of important visual information. Now we preserve a video still of the test so that the operators can still make a complete judgement.

Exploiting Human Cognition

There are particular aspects of human cognition that lend themselves to a multimedia approach. Overloading of one sense can often be avoided by using a second sense in parallel. In specific the audio + visual approach can be particularly powerful.

Changing Context

This aspect does seem to be best dealt with applying the audio channel. Auditory warnings are most effective and allow the operator to concentrate on other aspects of the task.

Simulation

The visual approach is, of course, specially well suited to simulation. A useful combination is that of real video and overlaid graphics.

Use of Non-verbal Sounds

Very short sounds are fruitful for alarms or status identifiers. Continuous sounds are more difficult to use effectively. They are best used when identifiable changes really matter. Their use for absolute measurement should, of course, be avoided. The critical issue is whether the important changes can be recognized by the human observer. Continuous sounds can also be very irritating.

Conclusions

I hope that this paper has shown that the key issue facing multimedia technology implementers is not primarily a technical one (although technical performance is important) but a design one. We need to know where and when particular media combinations will enable us to achieve our goals more effectively. Because the advantages (or disadvantages) or multimedia usage depend upon the tasks being performed, it is difficult to set up precise laboratory studies and apply the results directly to real life situations. The answer here is probably more longitudinal studies in real situations. However, we are now reasonably confident that our list of guidelines will eventually extend into a methodology.

There are issues that have not been addressed in this paper. For example, dynamic allocation of multimedia resources raises major issues about interface consistency. We believe that, provided the representations change only occasionally and only in critical resource situations, this nee not be a serious problem. However, this is a matter for debate.

12

System of Machine Translation

Introduction

Having made a speedy review of the history of machine translation, machine translation process is sketched by the paper. The capacities of recently available systems are indicated. The establishment and use of these systems are mentioned, as are the factors to be considered in their evaluation. The Japanese endeavour and experience, as well as international experience and prospects, are outlined.

History of Machine Translation in a Nutshell

Weaver was the first to make an attempt to use computer for translation purpose around 1945 at the very beginning of digital computer development. During the 1950s, there were a number of research efforts were made on machine translation. A famous system is the Georgetown University-IBM joint project of machine translation from Russian into English. The Government of USA invested a substantial amount of research money in this area in the late 1950s and early 1960s, particularly to develop the Russian-English system. Around 1960, 20-30 widely scattered research groups in the United States were involved with machine translation and natural language processing. However, many years of research effort did not produce really usable translation results, and therefore the US Government stopped investing machine translation research and development in 1966. After that, the boom of machine translation there faded quickly, and US researchers turned to the more basic field of computational linguistics. Europe, Japan, and the Soviet

Union started machine translation research in the middle of the1950s. In 1959 the Electro-technical Laboratory in Tsukuba, Japan, demonstrated English-Japanese machine translation. Kyushu University prepared a machine translation computer that translated Japanese to English or German and the reverse. I started research on machine translation and natural language processing in 1961 when I completed my M.Sc. degree and entered research life at Kyoto University.

At that time, we had several difficulties in natural language processing by computer because we could not handle Chinese characters. We had to struggle for more than 10 years to solve these difficulties. By around 1975, we had arranged for comparatively easy Chinese character input and output. But really satisfactory input/output was finally reached with the widespread usage of Japanese word processors at the beginning of the 1980s.

Although we encountered various difficulties, we competed a comparatively good machine translation system called TITRAN in 1978. This translated the titles of research papers from English into Japanese. First time it was use on a trial basis by the researchers at Tsukuba Science City to quickly scan recent research information. The success of this system encouraged the development of Japanese-English and Japanese-French title translation systems, which were completed in 1980 and 1981, respectively. The Japanese Government, attracted by the success of this title translation and decided to launch a national project of machine translation that aimed at the translation of abstracts of scientific and technical papers between Japanese and English. The project was started in 1982 and lasted four years. I was the project leaders, and four organizations, namely Kyoto University, Electrotechnical Laboratory, Tsukuba Information and Computing Center, and Japan Information Centre of Science and Technology (JICST), cooperated with each other. We prepared two prototype systems, one from Japanese to English and the other from English to Japanese.

After the completion of project, the Japanese to English system was further improved at JICST, and the dictionary was enlarged from 70,000 words to 540,000 words and is now in regular operation at JICST. An abstract that is compose of about 300 Japanese characters on the average is translated in 25 seconds. Some pre-editing and post-editing are done by outside companies, which take about three weeks for 1,000 abstracts. This translation speed is more than two-time that of human translation. The approximate of translation by machine is about 60 per cent that of human translation. JICST is now translating about 91,000 abstracts of Japanese scientific and technical documents into English in a year. These translated abstracts are in the JICST database and can be accessed from the United States and Europe as well as from inside Japan.

This national project had a great impact on Japanese industry. Several computer companies and other information-related companies started the development of machine translation systems in the early 1980s. Todays there are around 10 commercial machine translation systems, some from Japanese to English and others from English to Japanese. Furthermore, several other companies are developing machine translation systems for commercialization.

text submission — preprocessing — segmentation and tagging — parsing

semantic interpretation — text generation — solution extraction and postediting — result presentation

Figure-1
The Machine Translation Process

System Configurations

The machine translation process is shown in Figure 1. Morphological analysis conditions the word form, including infections, tense, number, part of speech, and so on. Syntactic analysis conditions which word is the subject which the object, and so on. Semantic and contextual analysis conditions the correct interpretation of a sentence from the multiple outcomes produced by the syntactic analysis. Syntactic and semantic analyses are very often combined and executed simultaneously. The outcome is the internal representation of a sentence. Then the internal representation in the target language is often the same as that of the source language, but sometimes a change in the internal representation is required. The generation phrase is just the opposite to the analysis process.

Present-day machine translation systems are still rather imperfect, and we must be skilled to use such imperfect systems. However, if they are used with care we can get advantage from machine translation in both translation speed and translation cost. The technology will make rapid progress, experience will be acquired, and grammars and dictionaries will be improved step by step. Therefore, we should not undermine the usefulness and the cost-effectiveness of machine translation in the near future.

A machine translation system consists of components, as shown in Figure 1. For the analysis of a source language sentence, a set of grammar rules and the dictionary of the source language are important. The same applies for the target-language generation.

The transfer dictionary contains information on the correspondence between the source language word (phrase) and the target language word (phrase). The rules of grammar for a language generally range from a few hundred to more than one thousand, and dictionaries consist of 50,000 or more ordinary words and many special terms for a subject field.

One of the problems in machine translation systems is text input. If electronic media such as floppy disks are the usual way of text input, there is no obstacle. But if printed pages are to be input, either human typing or optical character reading (OCR) has to be used. In the first case, the speed and the expense of typists are the problem. In the other, the problem is the expense of an OCR and the proofreading and error correction by humans. Japanese text input is very problematic for European or American organizations. They can use Japanese OCR, but they have to employ Japanese persons for error correction tasks.

Machine translation is automatic, but the output of translation is poor in quality. Errors are included in translation and sometimes no translation comes out at all. The machine gives up on the translation when an input sentence is too complicated. Therefore, post-editing is a necessary task for current machine translation systems. For human translation, two-stage translation is generally adopted; namely raw translation and brushing-up. Post-editing in machine translation may similar to the brushing up process. Some brushing up is required even for human translation, and this is, of course, much heavier in machine translation. Post-editing is done either on printout paper or on a computer screen. The latter is more advantageous and economical because no printout is required during error correction. Editing, such as the insertion of figures an tables, is also very easy on computer screens today. Page formatting can be done very conveniently on the computer, and only the final results need be printed out.

Pre-editing is sometimes required. The segmentation of a long sentence into two or more shorter sentences is very often performed in particular. Pre-editing and post-editing have a particular correlation. When a heavy or elaborate pre-editing is performed, very simple post-editing is sufficient, and vice versa. However, two persons have to be employed in this case, one for pre-editing who knows the source language, and the other for post-editing who is a native speaker of the target language. In any case, the post-editing is not avoidable, and the overall cost of pre-editing and post-editing is often much more than that for elaborate post-editing alone. Therefore, many machine translation users do only post-editing.

The organizations that practise machine translation systems must not imagine a situation in which "verybody who needs copy comes to a copying mahine, puts in documents, presses a button, and receives copies." Today machine translation systemsare not that simple. Organizations must employ professionals to operate a system with pre-editing, dictionary maintenance, and so on. An organization must sometimes change the flow of its documents to get the maximum from a machine translation system. Such changes comprising the training of people in document-writing sections to write in a clear, unambiguous style. This is finally profitable to both human readers and the translation machine.

Ability of Current Machine Translation Systems

Today, machine translation systems are not perfect, so that we have to be very careful about the use of these systems. Otherwise we cannot the anticipated productivity. One of the important factors in the use of machine translation systems is the text categories for machine translation. Headlines of new articles the titles of papers can be translated quite easily if the subject areas of these texts are particularly restricted to a narrow domain. Technical information and news articles are appropriate for machine translation without post-editing if the readers do not care about the sentence structure of translated materials and just want a general idea of what is happening (information-gathering reading). The most widely used text category for machine translation is the operation and maintenance manuals of industrial products, such as computers, automobiles, nuclear plants, and so on. The texts themselves are quite simple, but the volume is enormous. Therefore machine translation is inevitable.

Evaluation Factors of Machine Translation Systems

There is a growing interest in machine translation. Some people have proper understanding of the capability of present-day machine translation systems, but several others have the idea that machine translation can perform perfectly, that it will deprive translators of jobs, or at the opposite extreme, that the machine cannot do anything significant, and that a machine translation system is useless.

For the proper use of existing systems, there is need for a kind of common standard for the evaluation of machine translation a well as detailed knowledge of how machines translate sentences. Serious discussions have just been started about setting up such a standard, but it will take a long time for wide agreement, because there are several factors to consider. Evaluation factors will differ according to the purposes of usage. This further complicates establishment of a standard. The following are factors that must be considered in the evaluation:

(1) The cost of purchase, operation, and maintenance; training, text input, dictionary enhancement for ordinary words and for particular terminology; post-editing, final text preparation, and the relation between translation quality and cost.

(2) The speed of text input, pre-processing (including the handling of tables, figures, and so on), machine translation, post-editing final text format arrangement (including tables, figures, and so on), and the relation between pre-editing and post-editing time.

(3) The quality in respect of fidelity, intelligibility, and naturalness of style.

(4) The capacity of the system for improvement in respect of dictionary change, enhancement of the system's main dictionary and user dictionary, grammar improvement, specially for sub-language expressions in a specific domain, and the extent to which users are allowed to improve the dictionaries and the grammars, and to chalk the method after improvement.

(5) The capacity for system extension from one text field to another and from one pair of languages to another.

(6) The extent of endeavour required of users in terms of the number of operating staff required, including the pre-editor, post-editor, and dictionary maintenance person; the period of time required for testing and tuning, for adapting the organization's documentation system structure to machine translation, and for controlling source language expressions when authors prepare original texts.

(7) The capacities and limitations of the system for dealing with grammar, semantics, discourse—comprising anaphora and ellipsis—dictionary information, software speed, learning capability, interactive translation or post-editing, vagueness resolution, and for producing only the best possible translation output or all the possible outputs for a sentence.

Japanese Machine Translation Systems

The Japan Information Center of Science and Technology (JICST) is translating abstracts of scientific and technical papers from Japanese to English by the improved version of the Mu machine translation system that we developed in 1985. Sentences in abstracts are comparatively long, and sentence structures tend to be very complicate. Therefore, a particular degree of pre-editing is performed on the original Japanese abstracts. Post-editing is also done for the translated English abstracts. There is a complementary relation between the pre-editing and post-editing. That is why when a heavy pre-editing is done, the post-editing is light, and vice versa. JICST is now measuring what degrees of pre-editing and post-editing are best from the view point of overall cost.

Many private companies are engaged in machine translation. Although they do not yet make a profit, they invest a host because they consider that natural language processing will be a key technology in he future information society. The systems given below are typical ones in Japan. Some other companies are developing small systems on personal computers. Those marked with an asterisk are R&D systems.

ALT J/E: Information Processing Laboratories, NTT*

ARGO: CSK (JE)

AS-TRANSAC: Toshiba Corp.

ATLAS-I: Fujitsu, Ltd.

ATLAS-II: Fujitsu, Ltd.
CONTRAST: ETL*
DUET-E/J: Sharp Corp.
HANTRAN: CBU
HICATS E/J: Hitachi, Ltd.
HICATS J/E: Hitachi, Ltd.
KAN-TRAN III: Carozelia Japan*
LAMP: Canon Inc.*
MELTRAN-J/E: Mitsubishi Electric Corp.
MU: Kyoto University*
MU2: JICST
PAROLE: Matsushita Electric Co., Ltd.
PENSEE, PENSEE II: Oki Industrial Co. Ltd.
PIVOT: NEC Corp.
RMT E/J: Ricoh Co., Ltd.
SHALT: IBM Japan, Ltd.
SHALT/JETS: IBM Japan, Ltd.
STAR: CATENA Resource (on Unix)
SYSTRAN: Systran
THE TRANSLATOR: CATENA Resource (on Machintosh)
Translation Word Processor SWP-7800: Sanyo Electric Co., Ltd.
Transer/EJ: Nova
UNNAMED: Nippon-Data General Corp.*
XJE: SPIRIT*

Two or three nationwide online machine translation services via computer network are commercially used.

Japanese Governmental Efforts

The Japanese Government, the Ministry of International Trade and Industry (MITI), the Science and Technology Agency (STA), and recently the Ministry of Post and Telecommunications (MPT), in particular has shown interest in machine translation. The STA in cooperation with MITI supported the national project of machine translation (Mu project) during 1982-1986. MITI was the Chief promoter of the First Machine Translation Summit Meeting in Hakone in 1987, which was succeeded by the second in Munich in 1989 and the third in Washington, D.C. in 1991. MITI realized the importance of dictionary construction for machine translation, development of which needs a long time and a heavy investment. Individual companies independently construct their own MT dictionaries. This is a waste of money. MITI established in 1986 a neutral organization for MT dictionary construction named Japan Electronic Dictionary Research Institute (EDR). 70 per cent of the financial support comes from the Government and the other 30 per cent is provided by eight major electronic companies. It constructs a kind of neutral dictionary based on concepts that are matched to lexical items and phrases of individual language. Within the project length of nine years, the EDR will set up a dictionary of 200,000 concepts and its corresponding English and Japanese dictionaries for machine use. The project is now in the improvement stage and its quality is being tested by a limited number of users. When the dictionaries got completed, they will be available to any organization in the world at a proper price.

MITI supports another project conducted by the CICC (Centre for International Cooperation for Computerization). The project consists of the development of a multilingual machine translation system between the Japanese, Chinese, Malaysian, Thai, and Indonesian languages. The project began in 1987 and is continuing. They successfully demonstrated a first prototype system in 1990.

Dictionary

Dictionaries are drawing increasing attention from more and more types of people. This is true not only of language dictionaries but also of terminological dictionaries in every field, and also of encyclopaedias. People are mainly interested in learning the meaning of terms that appear in newspapers, books, TV programmes, and so on. In particular, they want not only the definition of a term they encounter but also that of related terms. People want on the one hand to get the knowledge of the specific details of a problem and, on the other, to grasp the total picture or to have a general understanding. This is one of the chief reasons for consulting dictionaries. In the language area, thee appeaed a few new good language dictionaries. In the language area, there appeaed a few new good language dictionaries, such as the Longman dictionaries of contemporary English and the COBUILD English Language dictionary. These dictionaries triggered discussion about what constitutes a good dictionary. Dictionaries are increasingly becoming more and more important in the computer processing of natural language. Not only machine translation but also man-machine dialogue systems, information retrieval systems, and so on require good dictionaries for their own objectives.

Here we have to clarify what kind of information must be included in a dictionary. Dictionary construction requires much time as well as a big investment. It is rather difficult to change and reconstruct one. Therefore, there must be a careful design at the outset.

It is not easy to construct a bilingual dictionary because a word of a source language has varieties of meanings or concepts, and for each meaning there exist many similar words and expressions in a target language. Very often there are cases where concepts in a language similar to several concepts in another language, and it is not easy to fix minimum "gains" for concepts that have one-to-one correspondence to linguistic expressions in both languages. When we consider the multilingual dictionary, we have first to identify minimum "grains" of concepts in each language and culture, and then to determine those that are common to the concepts set for all the languages concerned. In this way, a neutral multilingual dictionary depends on the language set.

Bilingual dictionaries are problematic to construct, and so multilingual dictionaries of several languages are even more difficult to construct, particularly when these languages have very different cultrual backgrounds. It is very hard to identify pivot concepts through which words and phrases can be exchanged between every language pair. It would be feasible to establish pivot concepts for major conceptual words, but it will be very difficult for many other concepts in ordinary life. These concepts, specially those strongly related to human life, must be explained in terms of the cultural background where the language is used. Therefore, for very detailed machine translation dictionaries of ordinary words, it is essential to construct bilingual dictionaries. It is difficult to construct multilingual dictionaries covering several languages that reflect fully different cultural backgrounds.

Multilingual dictionaries will be feasible, however, for concepts in natural science and technology, which are less dependent on different cultures. Also, if high quality translation is not essential, we may be able to construct multilingual dictionaries among particular sets of languages.

Another question that requires to be discussed is how to use dictionary information. Dictionaries are useful not only in machine translation but also in natural language processing systems such as dialogue systems and information retrieval systems. Internal organization of a big dictionary is important from the view points of speed and flexible reference to the concerned information. Hypertext structure will help people use complex electronic dictionaries. We have to develop more powerful ways for using electronic dictionaries.

State of the Art in Europe and the United States

There were many basic research projects in Europe in the 1960s, but the first system that aimed at practical use of the Systran Russian-English machine translation system at CEC Euratom, Ispra, in the late 1960s. Systran English-French was introduced to the EC Commission in Luxembourg in 1976. After long trial use and improvement of the system, it started semi-operational use at the beginning of the 1980s. Now Systran English-French is very satisfactorily used by several translators in the EC computer net-work communication. For instance, the translation speed is 40 pages (pages averaging 250 words) per minute, or minute, or 500,000 words per hour. On the average, minor corrections are important at about 10 spots on a page.

The EC Commission has many other Systran Systems for language pairs, such as French-English, English-German, English-Italian, French-German, etc. The translation quality of these systems is less good in comparison to the English-French system.

The EC has to deal with nine languages in the Community. This might have meant that 72 systems of machine translation from one language to another had to be constructed. To avoid this problem, it deemed necessary to develop a multilingual machine translation system that could translate one language to all the others at the same time. The EC began preliminary investigation for this multilingual machine translation system in 1978 under the EUROTRA project. The official EUROTRA project was launched in the early 1980s for the seven languages then used in the EC (extended to nine languages afterwards), and several researchers from every EC country participated in it. However, the R&D of multilingual machine translation systems was very difficult, and the project was stopped at the beginning of the 1990s. The EC has shifted its research from machine translation to dictionary construction and language industries.

Germany has launched a speech translation projected called VERBMOBILE.

The United States had leading research groups in machine translation at its beginnings, but unfortunately the US Government stopped R&D in machine translation and stopped governmental research funds in 1966.

In the US private sector, there are few commercial machine translation systems, such as Systran, Logos, Weidner, and soon Glovalink.

Canada is a bilingual country using English and French. The Canadian Government was interested in machine translation long ago, and supported several R&D projects. It has no pre-editing nor post-editing. It is fully automatic. When a complex sentence comes in that the system cannot handle, it is displayed on the operator's screen and is translated and typed in immediately. The Canadian Government has a large translation bureau under the Secretary of State, and does daily translation manually. The bureau is now using the Logos English-French system on a trial basis as well as translators' workstations developed internally.

The International Association for Machine Translation

As mentioned before, Japan took the initiative for organizing the first Machine Translation Summit Meeting, and already three summit meetings have been organized, in Hakone (Japan), Munich (Germany), and Washington, D.C. (USA). We also organized the International Forum for Translation. The objectives and activities of the Association are outlined:

(i) Purposes

1.1 The International Association for Machine Translation (IAMT) brings together users, developers, researchers, sponsors, and other individuals or institutional or corporate entities interested in machine translation (MT) for the purpose of promoting and fostering, by every available means, the development and active use of MT systems. The IAMT offers opportunities and occasions to exchange information, study MT technologies and applications, and discuss and establish reference criteria or standards in areas of common interest to its members.

1.2 The specific concerns of the IAMT may include:

1.2.1 Collection and compilation of information.

The IAMT may serve as a repository for historical and current documentation on MT, converting the texts to machine-readable form when and as feasible.

1.2.2 Exchange of information

The IAMT may serve as a clearing-house for current information of interest to MT users and developers, including:

- For users: translation market trends, available MT systems, types of MT applications, introduction of MT systems, approaches to text file input, pre-and post-editing strategies, evaluation of MT, etc.
- For developers: theories of MT, MT technologies, improvement of MT, approaches to dictionary-building, databases and other files available for exchange etc.

1.2.3 Dissemination of information

The IAMT may publish information of general interest in the sphere of machine translation, such as :

- A regular newsletter on MT
- An MT handbook, including agreed definitions of terminology
- Bibliographies

1.2.4 Standardization

The IAMT may develop and propose reference criteria and standards in such areas as:

- Common document format for MT input
- Exchange format for dictionaries
- Design of controlled language
- Evaluation of MT output and MT systems

(ii) Activities

2.1 The IAMT shall convene the biennial General Assembly of its membership. The Assembly shall preferably be held in conjunction with the MT Summit, a technical forum that is open to the general public and that shall also be convened by the Association.

The IAMT may also undertaken the following activities:

2.2 Sponsorship and support of workshops, symposia, and conferences on MT and related technologies and applications.

2.3 Organization of tutorials and training courses on MT applications and skills involved in the use of MT.

2.4 Organization of tutorials and workshops on MT technologies.

2.5 Establishment of technical committees, special interest groups, and study teams.

(iii) Membership

Membership in the IAMT shall be open to active or potential MT users, developers, and researchers, and to any other individuals or institutional or corporate entities with interest in the purposes of the Association. There shall be three categories of membership: (1) individual, (2) corporate, and (3) institutional. All of these must belong to a regional association, except where there is no suitable association in the region where a person interested IAMT lives.

(iv) Organization

4.1 The IAMT is the federation of Regional Associations for machine translation (one each in Europe, the Americas, and Asia).

4.2 The organs of the IAMT shall be the General Assembly, which is the supreme governing body of the Association, and the Council, which executes the decisions of the General Assembly and carries out the business of the Association.

4.3 The IAMT shall have a permanent Secretariat. The location of the Secretariat shall be decided by the General Assembly.

The Japan Association for Machine Translation (JAMT) is trying to extend its membership and to become the Asian Association for Machine Translation. The CICC is considering the linkage of Asian countries for the exchange of technology on machine translation. For example, we can imagine the establishment of a machine translation centre in each country, where R&D and services of machine translation will be performed, and these centers working together for the progress and wider usage of machine translation. The IAMT will play an important role in such activities in the future.

13

The Sub-Language Concept

Introduction

Sub-language concept is a form of communication that is concerned to natural language but is domain specific. Following a brief discussion of obstacles to the introduction of a "telephone computer era" (based on the use of a combination of the telephone, personal computer, workstation, and television set), the "sub-language" concept is presented, this being a form of communication that is related to natural language but is domain specific.

Prologue

We are witnessing one of history's major technological events: the advance of the telephone-computer era. In a several years, we have devoted our research toward the solution to the problems of this coming age. The consequences of this research are presented here. However, it is not enough to put down some concepts from which a solution may be utilised. The solution therefore is also in the form of a completely implemented system that now exists as a commercial prototype ready for product development—the New World of Computing system.

Obstacles to the Development of the Telephone-Computer

The next decade will see the telephone, personal computer, workstation, and television set integrated into a single, ubiquitous instrument - the telephone-computer. The telephone-computer will cause a rapid, widespread acceleration in the use of information processing and telecommunications.

As a consequence to this major development, the market for both computer hardware and software will rapidly expand in both quantity and quality. This market will soon far exceed the recent market for personal computers, workstations, and large transaction processors. Current hardware capabilities are already sufficient for this development: 30 MIP processing chips, voice digitizing, image processing and communication chips, 8 megabyte main memories, and 100+ megabyte peripheral memories are quite sufficient for the bulk of processing to be done. 144 K bits per second, error free, and soon 1,500 K bits per second, telecommunications, with packet switching, are now becoming available; capabilities can be expected to stay well ahead of foreseeable needs. New technologies, like flat screens, and parallel processing chips will all increase this radical change in the human-computer interface.

What will the era of the telephone-computer be like? This question has been the focus of our research over several years. One thing is clear: in the confluence of computer technology and telecommunications technology, we are witnessing one of history's important advances in human communication. Industry is ill-prepared for this rapdi increase of the information technologies. There are dislocations in the current software industry that work against the full development of the telephone-computer.

One important symptom of these dislocations is the high cost of software development. Industry is really aware of these symptoms, as evidenced by their relation with "open systems" and "software engineering" approaches. However, the roots of these problems lie elsewhere. In this paper we will recongise these roots and an approach that substantially corrects them.

Sub-language: A New Paradigm

We put here a simple, basic concept, that of a "sub-language." A sub-language is a form of human communication that is domain particular, appropriate to that domain, and, consequently, highly efficient. Using this concept, we put forward a new example for human information processing and communication. We then utilize this paradigm to lay our the new world of computing that will characterize the telephone-computer era.

We have learned to impose structure on the jumble of our moment-to-moment experiences so as to originate order and provide perspective. In the words of William James:

What is this "natural language" that we use? The nature of natural language has played a useful role in linguists' development of a general concept of human communication, in the codification and maintenance of purity of national languages, and the training of language teachers. Language, in the sense used by linguists, might more appropriately be thought of as combined family of linguistic mechanisms, often expressible as grammar rules. The phenomenon of information processing and communications although exhibiting in a given cultural community the relation to such syntactic forms, also has features better characterized, we believe, by the notion of "sub-language."

Consider the sentences in Figure entered by the trust officer of a bank in his ongoing discussion with his computer. Does this look like English? It is not. Certainly it is a sub-language of English, one that has been geared to the concerns of the trust officer. In such a defined context, the phrasing is no longer ambiguous or indecipherable. The concerns of a human individual engaged in a particular task environment can be characterized by that person's immediate sub-language. The inevitable characteristic of a well functioning team is their common sub-language.

The stability of a given sub-language is got in the stability of the task we perform. When we return again and again to a task, and to that group in which we interact in doing that task, it is the sub-language that codifies and externalizes our ongoing considerations. And it is the ongoing, ubiquitous changes in that sub-language that track our decision-making process.

As an illustration, consider a specific work environment, say that of a person working as secretary for an industrial manager. One aspect of that person's environment is their typewriter. The technology of the typewriter keyboard has not changed in several years, even though a more efficient layout of the keys is known. The causes for this stability are not hard to envision the keyboard does not change following the strong social inertia resulting from so many people having been trained on the existing one. There are several other aspects of the typing, filing, and sending letters, reports, etc. where there are both physical and social inertia that mitigate against change in several aspects of the secretary's concern. The moment to moment sub-language of such a person is incessantly shifting as a required address must be found, a letter retrieved from a file, a phone call answered. But a part of all of these sub-languages remains inevitably constant-that part related to the mechanics of typing, phoning, filing, where the physical and social inertia are high. This part can itself be characterized as a formal language. It is briefly these highly stable sub-languages that can economically be constructed into computer systems. Word processors are in ideal instance of how the inertia of a remarkable part of the secretarial world can be exploited.

Figure-1

There is one sphere where the computerization of sub-languages is already highly evolved and sophisticated, namely programming languages. The stability of the Von Neumann architecture has resulted in an evolutionary development of sub-languages that exploit this stability. We will say that the computer "understands" a sub-language to mean briefly the same as when we say a computer understands a programming language. Namely, it carries out instructions in the way they were aimed at be carried out, whether in the sub-language of a programmer or the sub-language of a professional when referring to work-related matters. Stable, domain-specific sub-languages, from simple word processors to the cryptic, icon-oriented yet absolutely sophisticated sub-language of a NASA space flight control room, can be handled by a computer as easily as any traditional programming language. Computers can be programmed to know the highly idiosyncratic, often cryptic sub-languages of individuals and teams from different walks of life. The academic disciplines of linguistics, foundations of mathematics, and computer science provide firm theoretical underpinnings for the study and computer implementation of sub-languages.

A precise overview of these underpinnings discloses in sharp focus the full sub-language paradigm. The concept of "sub-language" is abstractly equal to the concepts of "recursive function" and "Turing machine". Thus our "sub-language" paradigm is equal to Church's thesis that human information processing can be characterized by these formalisms.

The sub-language paradigm can also be considered as the combination of two other well-established paradigms of computer science, namely object-oriented programming and compositional semantics. In this form, sub-language is abstractly equal to "computer" that is, the set of all "sub-languages" coincides with the set of all machine languages of computers.

A computer can "understand" a given task-specific sub-language far beyond its use as a simple query language to a database. Consider a middle-level manager in a large engineering setup (see Figure 1). He transforms the estimated time of completion of one of the tasks for which he is responsible by typing instructions to his computer; the computer answers by carrying out the indicated actions. The sub-language of engineering management is that "understood" by the computer, just as the manager would expect a staff assistant to have replied in a pre-computer era.

The Implementation of Sub-languages

How are sub-languages implemented in the computer? Members of one class of sub-languages are already implemented in computers, namely programming languages. How are they recently implemented? A compiler is written that embodies both the syntax of the language and the semantics. The compiler accepts a sentence of the language and returns a single, machine language program. When used in interactive mode, this program is then implemented. This is, the abstract computer that understands the programming language comprises a hardware computer with its own machine language and the compiler, which translates the programming language into machine language. To transfer the programming language, one rewrites the compiler. There are compelling causes why this is a bad technology for implementing sub-languages, comprising programming languages. Before discussing these causes, we present here a radically various technology.

Let the computer be a Universal Language Processor (a hardware computer with a universal language processor replacing the compiler of a certain language, if you like). It operates in two modes:

(1) It accepts, one at a time, the rules of grammar and their related semantic procedures that define the sub-language, building them into its internal grammar table.

(2) It accepts an input sentence, parses is in accordance with the grammar, uses the resulting parsing graph to compose the associated semantic procedures, evaluates them, outputs the result, and cycles.

Thus it is a simple, straightforward implementation of compositional semantics.

A new object class can be easily implemented as a new subclass of the "noun" object class; when an instance of the new object class is created, first its record as an example of "noun" is developed, and then a link from this record to an example of the data structure of the new class is added. As an example, suppose one were building a new sub-language to be utilized by the structural engineers in an aerospace company. Suppose the company already had made a major investment in files of stress data and, say, FORTRAN procedures that processed these files. The new object class, a sub-object class of "noun" would be developed whose associated data structure was that of the stress data files. Syntax rules for noun phrases that engineers commonly used in referring to the stress data would be added, their corresponding semantic procedures consisting largely of calls to the appropriate FORTRAN routines. Such queries as: "Plot the stress against wing tip loading for both Model A12 and Model 14 wing aileron designs" would be soon available.

The manager enters:

"Task G will be delayed 10 days."

The computer :

1. changes properly the data base entry for the duration of task G;
2. recomputes a Pert chart for the entire project;
3. for those tasks that will experience a remarkable delay, generates e-mail to the affected managers, identifying the reason and potential consequences of the delay;
4. sends any changes in critical path tasks to the Project Manager.

Figure-2

In today's highly visual world, sub-languages are seldom limited to written text. But how can this total integration of media be implemented? Certainly the identification of the object class with its encapsulation of structure and process is a major step. Another step concerns the extended "alphabet" available to all sub-languages. All letters and characters of the usual alphabet as well as the whole extended ASCII character set; all graphic "events", such as clicks of the mouse and movements of the cursor; and all "interrupts" from internal and external sources (properly screened and identified) can be utilised in the input string that is fed to the language processor. (The computer, like human beings, has "fingers" for pointing and "intonation" and "gestures" it can use.) In this regard, all sub-languages have the same terminal vocabulary, namely this extended alphabet. Once this is established, grammar rules can supply the recursive, flexible link between the input string and the internal object classes. For instance, one can at any time introduce a new icon, placing under it any sentence or phrase of the sub-language that is then evaluated in line whenever the icon is clicked during input of a query. In figure 4, an airline mechanic is seen working on the radar nose-cone of a Boeing 747 aircraft. He turns to his computer for detailed technical support. He has already entered information recognising the particular aircraft he is working on and has called for a display of the nose-cone area.

The computer-generated photo image of the relevant area (plus an invisible back-plane drawing outlining all significant parts) provides a highly efficient medium for communication. For instance, he may type "leak" and click his mouse on the image of the place he suspects is leaking oil. The computer may respond with the spoken word: "tighten" and blink the bolt it recognised in its diagnosis as the probable cause of the leak. In response to a sparsely stated but technically involved question, the mechanic receives an immediately useful response that reflects a high degree of built-in understanding.

A maintenance professional is entering instructions into his personal, fully mobile, telephone-computer. It eliminates any need for the usual truck-full of manuals. The professional's efficiency is greatly increased, since the computer tailors its responses to the specific installation. Astute use of hypermedia links from one data display to another rapidly provides pathways to the details the professional really requires. References constructions (e.g., "What about the other connector?) play potent roles in effective dialogue. Note that pointing to and blinking remarkable areas in pictures and drawings constitutes visual "pronouns" (e.g. "voltage there?" or "tighten 'that'," "[show schematic icon] of 'that' ").

The Creation and Basing of Sub-languages

The typical industrial manager will have several sub-languages, for example:

- schedules and deliverables
- budgets and fiscal control
- personnel assignments and administration
- correspondence

Underlying each of these, and a part of every sub-language, are the general dialect of the manager's natural language, a total graphics package, text editor, electronic mail, voice messaging, etc. Once he has chosen to use, any one of his sub-languages, all of these services will be soon available; the manager will not be aware of which service a phrase of his question may have invoked as he proceeds in his normal way: "Send this draft budget to my section managers with the following message: . . .(voice)..... "; "Fix a meeting with them sometime on Wednesday afternoon."

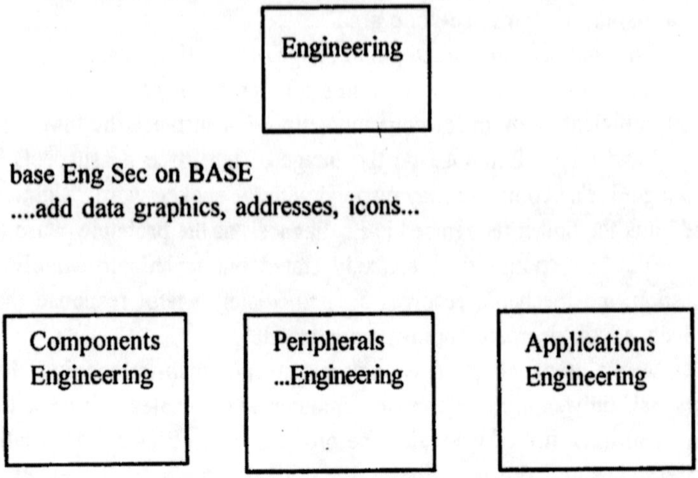

Figure-3

How are sub-languages created? In the beginning, there is one sub-language, BASE. It comprises a limited dialect of English that is sufficient to handle expressions concerning typical relational, or entity-attribute databases with inheritance. It also comprises a graphics package, text editor, electronic mail, etc., as mentioned above. To develop a new sub-language, say "Finances," one "bases" it on BASE: base Finances on BASE, or, for that matter, on any pre-existing sub-language that may be available. Then, selecting this new sub-language: enter Finances, one has all the capabilities of the based upon sub-language: enter Finances, one has all the capabilities of the based upon sub-language soon available. One can then extend this new sub-language in various ways (these will be discussed below).

In Figure 3, engineering manager E.D. Moore creates a sub-language to share with his three subordinate managers. Now any of the four of them can use, modify, and extend this common sub-language "EngSec." Thus they combinedly maintain a common, up-to-date view of their joint activities (e.g., preliminary designs, personal schedules). This is the importance of being able to "enter."

There is a strong asymmetric relationship between a sub-language and all of the sub-languages on which it is based, either directly or indirectly. Suppose one sub-language, "Accounting," is

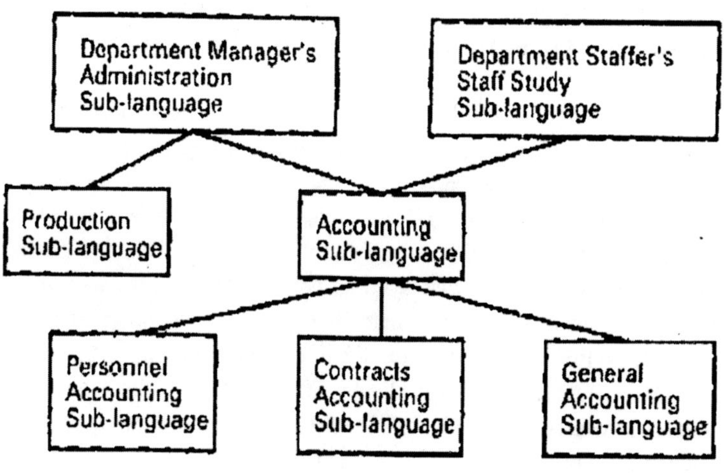

Figure-4

based on another, "Personnel Accounting": base Accounting on Personnel Accounting. Any changes in Personnel Accounting are soon reflected in Accounting; however, Accounting can be transformed in any way without affecting Personnel Accounting. This asymmetric relationship is characteristic of basing.

In Figure 4, showing the accounting sub-languages, the people in the Personnel Accounting Section are the only ones who have the right to enter the Personnel Accounting sub-language; therefore, they are the only ones who can change it; the similar holds for the Contracts Accounting and general Accounting sub-languages. Accounting is based on each of these three. No one has the right to enter Accounting; therefore no one can make any changes in it. Of course, it is automatically always up to date with the latest data from Personnel Accounting, Contracts Accounting, and General Accounting.

Networking in the Telephone-Computer Era

Local area networks (LANs) are a very transient aspect of our computer environment. Once Integrated Service Digital Network (ISDN), Broad-band ISDN (BISDN), and packet switching are completely implemented and installed, file transfers will be sufficiently fast to current LAN services between any two telephone-computers.

At that time, obviously, telephone-computers will have telephone numbers, indeed will be the terminal equipment represented by one's telephone number. Simpler forms of telephone communication, such as voice, e-mail, fax, and electronic messaging, will be subsumed within a much broader spectrum of telecommunication services mediated by the telephone-computer. When one telephone-computer calls another, pairs of windows are created; one window of each pair appears on the monitor of each computer. Each participant controls one pair of windows.

The participant controlling a given pair of windows can enter any of his sub-languages; then any of the wide-ranging data and graphics thereby available can be displayed on both windows of the pair. If both participants have the right to enter the given sub-language, then both can address this sub-language jointly. For instance, in Figure 5, a banker calls Bob Moore, one of this clients. The banker exhibits Moore a bar graph of the changes in Moore's DetEd stock over the last quarter, and the banker soon instructs the computer to bring this information forward. The banker shows Moore the implications of the changes he is advocating, and Moore's questions are quickly answered with the supporting data displayed by the computer. A change is made, and its effect is just seen by both parties. Once a transaction is decided upon, it is immediately implemented by means of a transaction transfer to the appropriate stock exchange.

We have already shown how a manager can create a sub-language and then give the right to his subordinates to be able to enter it, thus creating a common sub-language. A sub-language on one telephone-computer can be entered from a separate telephone-computer, provided the requesting person has been authorized. The combination of basing with the single, worldwide telephone network relates to a powerful set of capabilities. To see the importance of basing, consider the matter of virtual address space.

Figure-5

There is just one common virtual address space, down to the byte level, for all telephone-computers, for all these resources in the telephone-computer age. This address space is blocked into pages, which are also the packets that move over the telephone lines. International agreements long ago, have developed a universal address standard, namely the telephone number. When one starts a new telephone and is assigned a new telephone number, one is thereby automatically assigned one's own slice of "virtual memory," one's own corner of the world's address space.

Companies that maintain large data and powerful processing resources have the whole world as their market because they are uniquely identified and reachable through their telephone number. It remains to provide the means of establishing the addressability to these resources. That is the role of basing. Basing one sub-language on another establishes addressability among the data and process pages that found the physical expression of these sub-languages.

Here once again, in Figure 6, is the maintenane professional working on the nose-cone radar of a Boeing 747 aircraft, his computer by his side. Consider the networking aspects of this maintenance situation. In the strong sense of sharing address space, the computer is networked, with the Boeing maintenance shops in Seattle, Washington. That is, a sub-language in this computer is based on the Boeing Maintenance sub-language in the Seattle shops. None of the maintenance material is in the computer being used by the maintenance person. First, the recognition of the aircraft being serviced is established. In answer to a call for a full-colour, annotated image of the radar nose-cone area, the pixel data sets come, via ISDN, from a single source the high transaction rate server in Seattle. As some processing is being done locally, all maintenance data and diagnostic analysis are being done in Seattle. The bane of having out-of-date maintenance manuals will be a matter of the past. The addressable page is both the unit of storage and the packet of telecommunication. If the maintenance professional is still vexed, clicking the mouse on a special icon will make an immediate conversation with a maintenance specialist at Boeing in Seattle. Both monitors will exhibit the same material, both people can utilise their mouse to point, and both an have a voice discussion of the problem at the hand.

Figure 11 speaks of the point that all of the database records, semantic procedures, utility routines, pixel data sets, etc., are stored as pages, and that only the important pages are brought into main memory.

Figure-6

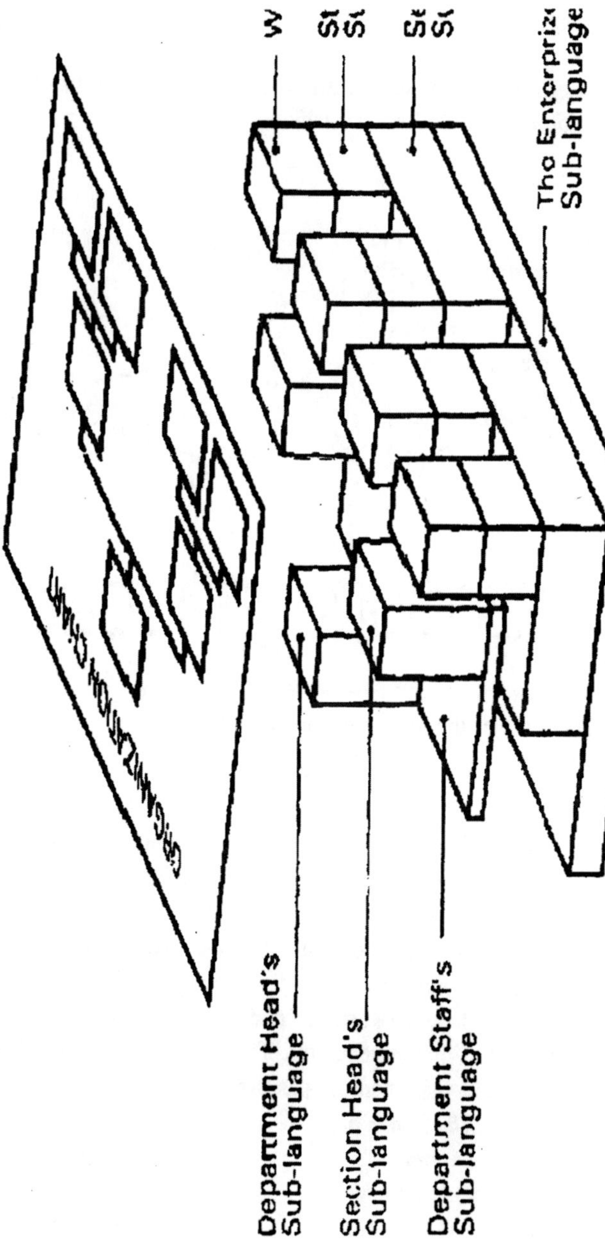
Department Head's
Sub-language
Section Head's
Sub-language
Department Staff's
Sub-language
Tho Enterpriz
Sub-language

We see that by using basing and networking, several if not most of these pages will be drawn from distant stations at the time they are needed.

Each individual item of information in a network of sub-languages has its ubiquitous address by which it is reognised.

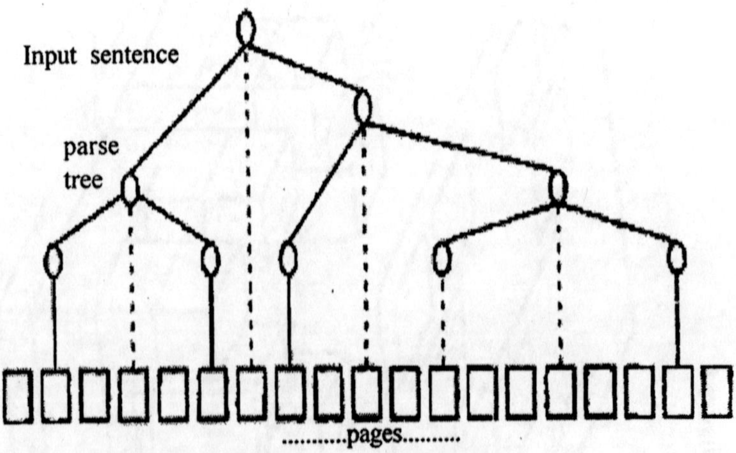

vertical links of the form------ are to procedures
vertical links of the form —— are to data

Figure-7

In recent database technologie, the database comprises largely links from one node of the database to another. The "links" in our semantic net database comprise page addresses. Thus for a network of more than one telephone-computer, the links within a database may refer to pages that remain anywhere in the net anywhere in the world. A database in such a network is "distributed" in an intrinsic way; the basing procedure implements this. The size of a page is 2,024 bytes.

The 64-bit page address has the following structure:

Byte offset on a page	2^{11} bytes
Page number	2^{21} bytes
Telephone number	2^{32} bytes

Thus, around four billion telephone-computers can be accommodated. Each telephone computer may hold two million pages,

Figure-8

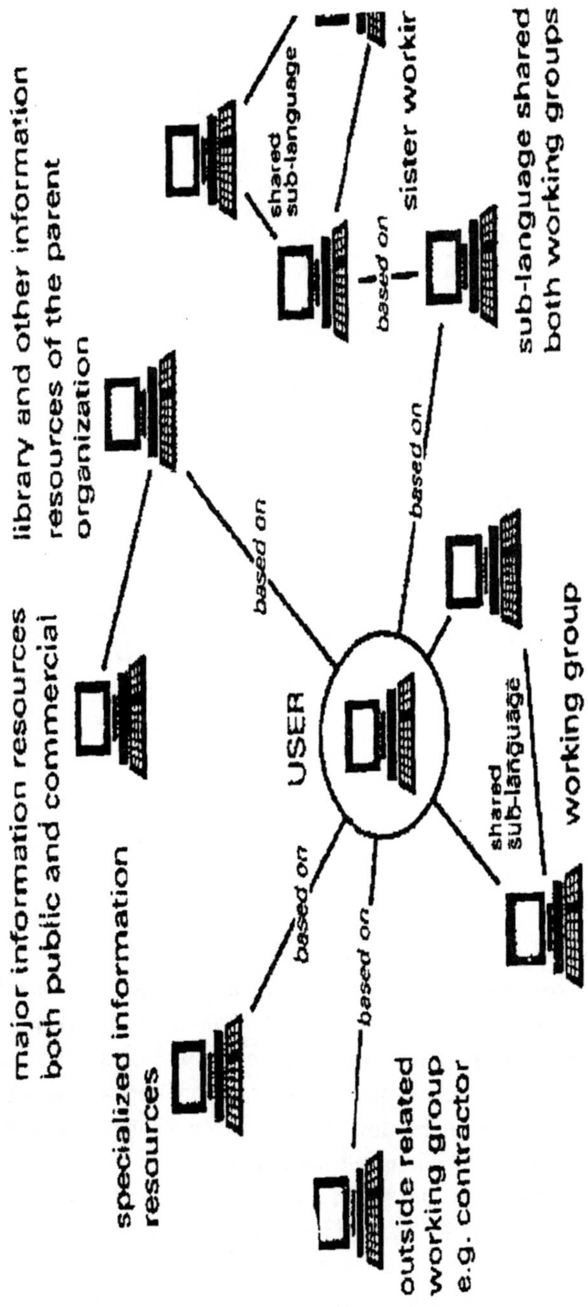
major information resources
both public and commercial
library and other information
resources of the parent
organization
specialized information
resources
USER
based on
based on
based on
based on
based on
based on
shared
sub-language
shared
sub-language
sister workir
sub-language shared
both working groups
working group
outside related
working group
e.g. contractor

that is four billion bytes of information. Thus the bound on directly addressable data and processes, the size of the single virtual memory, is 10 19 bytes.

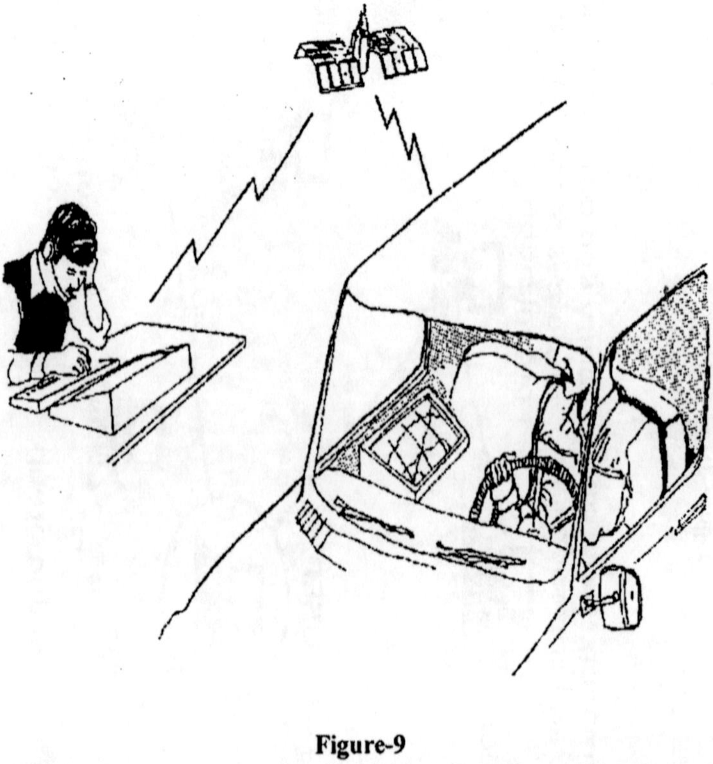

Figure-9

Figure 13 Displays a maintenance professional working for a loal service company. The professional's mobile station is working in at least two networks: the first, previously illustrated, is with the home maintenance station whose server keeps all records for the field locations served and all the maintenance information. The second is the dispatcher network. The central dispather can see on the map displayed before him the location of all maintenance trucks as they move about the city. When the dispatcher gets a call requesting maintenance service, he can type in the address of the caller and just see its loation on the map, spot the nearest maintenance unit, click it with his mouse, and talk with the maintenance person directly to relate the new service.

All of the World's Information

What needs to be addressed? The obvious answer is anything that may at some time be an object of attention in some sub-language. Each object class will have its own grain and often its own particular means for the identification of its relevant elements. It is interesting to note that several, if not the majority of, objects referred to by sub-languages do not have "names" in the lexicon. Consider the marriage of Edward D. Moore and Patricia Jones Moore. Friends of the Moores often refer to their marriage; for instance, "her daughter by her second marriage," but it does not have a name.

Texas Instruments FB74 transistor may name a class of its instances as they exist in a great kind of circuits, or alternatively, of its example in circuit drawings (as sub-drawings). In either case, they will inherit the properties (such as impedance) of the FB74 transistor class. In the latter case, one can recognise the particular transistor either by "the FB74 transistor used in the monopole section of the shift register" or by pointing at the transistor and clicking the mouse while viewing the circuit diagram.

How is the addressability difficulty for all of the world's information solved? We recognise the notion of the Archival Station. You call up a station that supplies information you wish to be accessible to one of your sub-languages. A form appears on your monitor and you are asked to fill it out. After doing so, you put your charge card in the card-reader slot in your telephone-computer. You are then free to base your sub-language on any to the Archival Station provides it with all its requirements for billing, notification, etc. The act of basing automatically recognises authorization information necessary for security. The Archival Station only infrequently starts a call to you. Your computer calls it, requesting a page. Since the request is sent as one of your own pages, it carries not only the requested page address but also the return address as well. Thus it carries all the information the Archival Station requires to identify you and your account and provide you with the information you need.

All telephone computer users in each of their sub-languages have complete freedom to choose and base on whatever information resources they desire, paying for accesses to only those pages needed in the course of their pendent displays (as, for instance, in the French Minitel System).

The New World of Computing Applications Development Environment

The most serious difficulty facing the computer industry today is the prohibitive cost of software development. Without a big improvement in this sphere, the telephone-computer will remain underutilized.

So what is the software development environment for application programming in the era of the telephone-computer? Each sub-language expresses the way a person views an area of interest; a meta-sublanguage has as its focus the associated sub-language itself. This meta-sublanguage is the appropriate software development environment of the applications programmer. In this environment, he can extend the vocabulary and grammar rules of his user's sub-language to encompass the idiosyncratic expressions of the user's domain, construct here the utilities required for efficiently building and maintaining the semantics of these expressions, and develop the new object classes, their data structures and processes, that bring the important efficiency to the computer's support of user needs. The result is a programming environment that is domain specific and highly developed.

The same language processor that handles are "English" sentences for the client also handles the "Pascal" or "C" statements for the applications programmer. So it is straightforward matter provide the meta-sublanguage access to the lexicon and grammar is added, the name of the semantic procedure is put into the meta-sublanguage's lexicon, linking to both the source code file and the paged object code.

The applications programmer maintains and extends the client's sub-language by dealing directly with the syntax rules and associated semantic procedures of the sub-language. To add a new ability for the client, the programmer first enters the client's sub-language, types "metalanguage" to enter the meta-sublanguage, and then types "RULE". The meta-sublanguage answers with the prompt "SYNTAX" and the programmer adds the syntax for the new grammar rule. If this comprises a new part of speech not identified by the sub-language, it is automatically added to the proper table. The meta-sublanguage then prompts for the semantic procedure, which is then programmed directly on-line. When the procedure has been completed, the system:

(1) compiles the procedure;

(2) links the result to the resident code;

(3) puts the result on a page;

(4) puts the syntax into the grammar table linked to this page.

	Sub-language	*Meta-sublanguage*
language:	"English" "French"	"Pascal" "C"
Subject matter	domain of user's interest	User's sub-language

user: "What is the cargo and destination of the British start?" application programmer: "dump record for British Start'

Figure-10

Note that linking is done only with the comparatively small resident code. The programmer types "return" and is back in the client's sub-language, with all the client's data, grammar, and prior added extensions and can try out the new rule in this actual client environment. Again, entering the meta-sublanguage, the programmer can edit the procedure and literate.

In Figure 11, the Trust Officer of a bank has called the applications programmer to request a new analysis procedure, "the ABC value," to be applied to different equities. One new rule of grammar with semantic procedure defining the notion of the ABC value is all that the programmer need add. It can then soon be used by the banker in far-ranging queries.

Just as any given sub-language can be extended by adding new syntax rules and their concerned semantic procedures, its meta-sublanguge can be extended by adding syntax and semantics proper to the context of applications programmer.

We see in Figure 12 that the BASE sub-language has been extended to an Accounting Sub-language. The Accounting Sub-language contains all the terms and syntax that are generally used in the accounting world. For example, it may consist of an object class of procedures and data structures for double-entry bookkeeping. Meta-accounting comprises an extensive family of accounting utilities and a convenient syntax for using them. Thus, a metasublanguage becomes highly domain knowledgeable. When attentively crafted, it can have the look and feel of a specification language, yet after macro expansion and compilation, creates efficient object code.

Such a sub-language/meta-sub-language may be marketed by a software firm specializing in accounting. The source code for the semantic procedures will not, of course, be shipped with the package. The ABC Co. buys this package, and their small group of application programmers tailor the ABC Co.

Figure-11

Accounting sub-language to the special practices and jargon of their own accountants. They lose nothing of their company's pre-existing capabilities; they simply add rules that embed their own existing files and particular procedures in the "accounting English" that the package provides. Now the whole panorama of the sub-language hierarchy starts to come into focus. Each office of the enterprise has its own sub-languages, which may be associated to each other through basing. Several of these sub-languages will also be based on other information resources, comprising archival stations. Several will have been extended to include domain-specific application packages. But this is only half

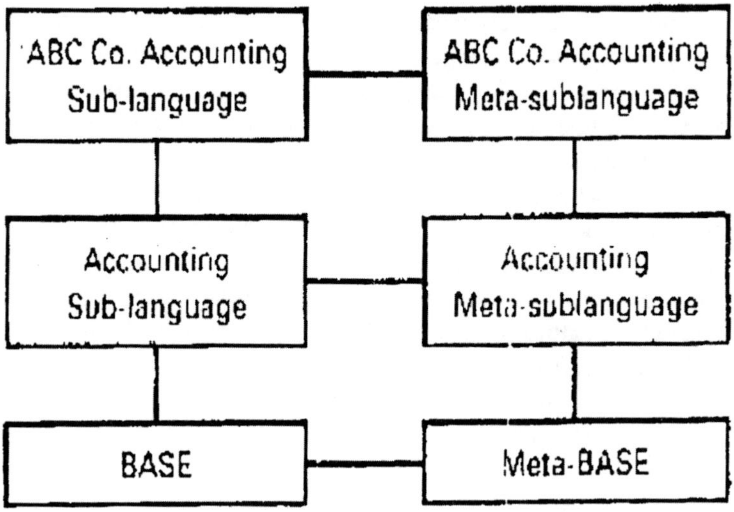

Figure-12

Toward an Efficient Organization of the Software and Data Provider Industry

A sub-language does not have to be a complete, self-contained "language". It may, for instance, consist of only those syntax rules and associated semantic procedures that are the tangible implementation of a new object class. By recognising the object class by a new, otherwise unused, part of speech, the encapsulation of the processes and data of the object classes is achieved. As this new object class is automatically made a subclass of "noun" and thereby link to other properly related object classes in a natural way. To realise this other half of the picture, consider how easy it is to change a significant part of a sub-language, in opposite to the difficulties this would entail in current systems. One rather narrow facility that almost all sub-languages will want to comprise is a graphics package. A graphics package exists now, consisting of syntax rules, semantic procedures, and utility procedures, and these in turn call proper Postscript operators. The package only supports two-dimensional drawings. Suppose some software house that often works close to the UNIX or DOS level produces a considerably improved graphics package that supports three-dimensional drawings. The applications programmer in any applied software shop, say one specializing in spreadsheet packages, can go into the meta-sublanguage of any appropriate sub-language and type: "delete from file": followed by the name of the file comprising the recent graphics sub-language syntax, then after having mounted the new graphics system in the floppy disk drive, type: "extend from disk." The result is the replacement of one graphics package by the new, updated one. Everything else remains the same; no data are disturbed, no relinking of the whole large system is needed. And when the new spreadsheet package is purchased, the client will be able to analyse and change their pre-existing database along any three selected attributes in a beautiful three-dimensional display.

The door is now open for a proliferation of software development at all levels, a layering of development levels, different branching hierarchy of specialization. It is just like a hierarchy that characterizes the textile industry,automotive maintenance industry and, infact, today's computer hardware business. The monolithic, application-independent "tools" niche in the lower levels within this far broader context.

Near the top of this hierarchy, software houses that realise themselves as specialists in their client's domain rather than in computer software can succeed in small, specialized markets because their development environment is already highly specific to their requirements. The outcome is the considerable reduction of software development costs. This opening of the competitive market to the innovative specialist will produce sub-languages that can be fully understood by the telephone-computer and imbue it with a really penetrating understanding of the subject domain.

Let us suppose that some software house that specializes in the graphic aspects of merchandising has developed a package, including television camera, for building catalogues. A women's apparel shop has purchased this package, preparing a Spring Sales catalogue. How is the catalogue material to be related to the rest of the apparel shop's information system? The software house assumed rightly that video sequences and other catalogue material would be directly concerned to items of merchandise given by their clients, and that the names of these items would already be in the client's lexicon as noun phrases. This was enough; what other connections from these items-inventory levels, prices, etc.-are maintained by the stores is immaterial to the catalogue-building package. So when the store personnel are in the midst of preparing a catalogue, and the catlogue package asks for the description of the merchandise item to be related to a particular graphic, the store personnel reply using their store's item number. The catalogue package procedure then connects the graphics to this item record in the database; it is, therefore, indirectly connected to all non-catalogue aspects of store management.

Well layered software development:

ABC Co Sub-language		XYZ Co. Accounting
catelogue maker		Accounting
persenting manager	word processor	spread sheet
	NEW WORLD OF COMPUTING SYSTEM	
UNIX/OPEN WINDOWS	or	DOS/WINDOWS
networking		graphics chip
windows		graphics
assembler		signal processing

Figure-13

When a customer, perusing the catalogue over the telephone-computer, clicks the mouse on a graphic and types: "Send me one of those in size 14, colour blue," the following occurs:

(1) The pronoun "me" is assumed to be the peson on the phone to the store's telephone-computer, who is therefore recognizable from the page address of the page sent to the store containing the request; from this the store, utilizing a standard utility procedure, goes to the customer's telephone-computer for the number of the customer's credit card (entered by the customer in the computer slot as a part of logging in), which recognizes the customer's account, credit rating, nd other information.

(2) The syntax of the catalogue package, through a graphics package the software house had based on, comprises the RULE: <click>. The semantics of this rule retrieves the item number added by the catalogue package with this graphic.

(3) The store's order-processing package, purchased from a different software house, comprises the verb "send" with the associated semantic procedure that carries out the appropriate processing of the whole transaction.

(4) The underlying English comprises all of the other rules important to complete the parsing, and therefore the processing of the request. The customer's telephone-computer exhibits the text: "Mrs. Smith, we are pleased to send you a Calvin Klein dress, catalogue item 08249, size 14, colour blue. Your account will be billed for $124.99 plus $7.50 shipping and tax, for a total of $124.99 plus $7.50 shipping and tax, for a total of $132.49. You can expect delivery in 3 to 5 days. Thank you for your order."

As another instance, a furniture store ha purchased a software plus equipment package that supports customers visualize potential purchases. In Figure 14, the sales person has put the floor plan of the customer's room on the scanner (seen in the background). As the customer selects furniture items, their recognizing numbers are typed in and the mouse is clicked at the appropriate site on the floor plan. The package then exhibits (perhaps on a giant, room-scaled screen), from any viewpoint, how the room will look. Colours, fabrics, furniture orientation, etc., can be changed and the just effect seen.

The scanner package which recognises the inputs to the ultimate graphic process, would be very easy to implement using the standard graphics package of the BASE sub-language. The output graphics pose considerably more difficult problem. How can the cost of development of such sophisticated software be amortized? Inputs would perhaps be pictures of each item taken from a prescribed set of angles. The output would likely use ray tracing to receive the shadows and textures just right. This package, however, would consist no other aspects, whether it be furniture, automobiles, microsopic pictures of tissue, a "blow-up" schematic of the nose-cone of air-plane, or whatever. The specialists building such packages would not require to know anything about accounting or linguistic. Their deliverable product would likely be a chip, together with grmmar rules and procedures for extending meta-sub-language rather than a sub-language. Providing the outcome as meta-sublanguage syntax provides the applications programmers that use it a great deal of flexibility. Thus, the resulting packge can be easily tied in with other packages (such as the scanner package in the

Figure-14

Figure-15

application cited here, a catalogue-building package, a medical lab package, or one used in evolving the graphics for the Boeing maintenance package used by the airplane mechanic who was shown working on the nose-cone.). This means that the high development cost of such a package could be disseminated over a wide market consisted of software houses closer to applications, and labs with their own strong programming groups each having its own distinct clientele (like the furniture store).

Several exciting capabilities are being displayed in academic and industrial laboratories. However, in today's software development environments, the cost is prohibitively high; and it will be a long time before these capabilities will find their avenue into any but military and space applications. The software development environment presented here radically reverses that trend by supplying a simple, linguistic linking at the meta-sublanguage level.

The Vision and the Realization

So here is our paradigm: It is the incessant re-evaluation and adjustment of the relevant view that characterizes human information processing. A succinct expression of this approach is a sub-language that is describable as a formal syntax and denotation semantics. When the basic conceptual structure of a task environment is changing only slowly, a sub-language, providing a natural computer adjunct in accomplishing that task. Programming languages are the proper sub-languages of system programmers and their very restrained application is the implementation of operating systems and language processors. Probably it is only dearth of a clear and relevant paradigm that ha delayed even applications programmers from having an appropriate way to communicate with the computer. It is now time for the rest of us to be provided with the sub-languages proper to our concerns sub-languages that are natural and efficient for our communications with the computer and for our communications with each other through the computer. Then the computer will find its proper niche as a medium of communication tying people, information resources and processing power together into the efficient focus of our appropriate sub-language. This is our vision. However vision alone will not give the better answer.

How do we realize our vision? How do we solve the many technological difficulties that lie in the path of such a development?

The problems now faced by the software industry are explicit and indeed are identified by that industry; the first of these is by far the most stringent.

(1) The high cost of software development

(2) The combination of multiple media, of data and of geographically dispersed people and resources into a coherent user interface.

(3) The computer's current inability to comprehend references to internal contents of files-to know what we are pointing at in a picture to be able to respond the questions using a table of data from a journal article, or to know to inform others of a change in an item of data.

(4) The problem in getting any single relevant item from all the world's information without being blocked by the numerous barriers of ambiguity, and non-focused indexing.

In the quest of a solution to these problems, we have first put forward a clear paradigm: The sub-language is the proper focus of software development. From the vantage point of this paradigm, follow three quick changes in software system architecture:

(1) A single, grammar-driven language processor that comprises language extension utilities.

(2) Segmentation at the language-processing level using a page-address structure compatible with networking.

(3) Hierarchical sub-languages sharing a common, worldwide address space to solve the distributed data and distributed processing problems.

In presenting our vision here, it has been necessary for us that our ideas really work, and that our words are supported by a solid, working system. The New World of Computing System exists. We have embodied the quick changes into a complete, rounded system. We have gone farther by extending this system to include capabilities that elucidate and amplify the fundamental concepts. The several technical designs, both indicated in the above presentation and implied by the illustrations, have been completely implemented in this single, integrated system. We have successfully tested and demonstrated every technological capability needed to achieve every aspect of our vision. Thus, the foundation has now been laid, a technical solution has been achieved for that new world of computing the era of the telephone-computer.

14

MITI's New Programme: Real World Computing

Introduction

In 1992, MITI (Ministry of International Trade and Industry) started a new R&D programme called "Real-World Computing" (previously called "New Information Processing Technology") as a 10-year Japanese national project to follow the Fifth Generation Computers project that officially ended in June of that year. The purpose of the new programme is to lay the theoretical foundation and to pursue the technological realization of human-like flexible information processing as a new example of information processing toward the highly advanced information society of the twenty-first century. The paradigm seems essential for the qualitative advancement of current information technology and for providing computers and users with flexible information access and collaboration in the real-world environment.

The programme covers a wide range of information technology: fundamental theory and novel functions for application to percept flexible information processing, and computational bases for massively parallel and distributed processing, comprising neural computing and optical computing/interconnection. Though the programme, which is open to the world, it is also aimed at that Japan make a greater international contribution to basic science and generic technology, which should be the common property of mankind.

The existing paper, after reviewing the background, outlines the content of the Real-World Computing programme and gives details on research and growth in the programme.

Background

Social Background

Supported by the growth of computer and communication technologies, information technology is generating innovative change in society. This innovative change is not only affecting industrial activities like new wealth and services and rationalized production and distribution systems but is also enhancing national living standards, regional progress, and educational and cultural development.

The information network is developing from an intra-organizational network to an inter-enterprise network and, further, to one bringing together homes and individuals, and, likewise, information processing is developing beyond enterprises to comprise homes and individuals.

As a result, information to be processed will largely increase not only in quantity but also in quality and variety, and a new technological ground that enables everyone to easily and efficiently take advantage of the various information resources of the network will be required for such an information network society.

Given the social background and the technological needs for various application fields of information processing, computers should become more humanized and possess the ability to assist and collaborate with humans in the real-world environment.

Technological Background

Computers have developed dramatically with the aid of technological progress.

In the first stage, as is shown in Figure 1, computers evolved along the line of conventional von Neumann architectures in the spheres of numerical computation, document processing and management of database storage and retrieval, since those application spheres have clear algorithms and are appropriate for processing by conventional computers. The second stage of development was directed toward the manipulation of symbols and logic, casting light on the intelligent thought processes of humans such as logical (deductive) inference.

Today, computers have come to provide very computing power and far surpass human ability in solving well-defined problems, where the algorithms for solution exist and can be conspicuously stated in programming languages.

Nevertheless, computers are still not very flexible when compared to human flexibility in information processing in the real world, where several problems are ill-defined and not easy to describe in algorithmic terms. It might be called the "algorithm crises" compared to the so-called software crisis.

Real-world Computing Paradigm

In order to cope with real-world problems and to open a new horizon in information-processing technology, it is inevitable to pursue research on the basic ways of human-like flexible information processing, and to embody the consequences as new information-processing technologies for use with the developing hardware technologies.

In recent yeas, fundamental knowledge about the information-processing capability of humans has been a rapidly accumulating, and hardware technologies for massively parallel computing systems are expected to reach our hands by the beginning of the twenty-first century.

Given these circumstances, the concept of "Real-world Computing" is proposed as a new example of information processing that intends to furnishing the "real-worldness" (or "flexibility") of human information processing to information systems.

With a view to make the twenty-first century a globally prosperous information network society where humans and information systems collaborate more closely and flexibly, the Real-World Computing programme, which intends to developing novel fundamental generic technologies in the spheres of information processing, is a topic of vital concern.

The Concept of Real-World Computing

In the changing environment of our daily life in the real world, we humans evaluate various kinds of information, comprising ambiguity or uncertainty, and receive the important information for making predictions, plans or decisions in a flexible way. Such an information-processing function is characterized by the term "flexible information processing" or "real-world computing," in opposite to the conventional rigid information processing performed by computers that assumes complete information in a pre-assumed world or problem domain.

Information processing in general is a function that has been received by humans and creatures in the process of evolution in surviving and adapting to the changing real-world environment. Although it is a versatile function, it can be classified into the following two categories: (1) logical information processing and (2) intuitive information processing.

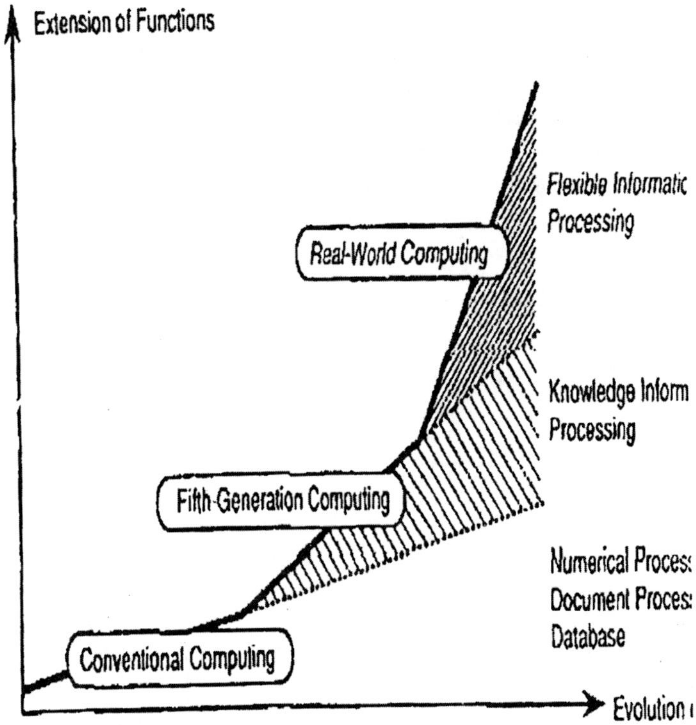

Figure-1
Extension of the Functions of Computing Systems

Logical information processing, is characterized by the worlds conscious, analytical, deductive, serial, intensive, digital, and symbolic. Contrarily, intuitive information processing is characterized by the worlds unconscious, synthetic, inductive, parallel, distributed, analogue, and sub-symbolic.

Basically, information-processing technology is intended to complement or alternate for our information processing function through mechanization of both of the two aspects divided above. Historically, however, machines that were theoretically and technologically appropriate for logical information processing developed into conventional digital computers. They progressed very quickly, assisted by the tremendous growth of hardware technologies, and serial and sequential information processing have been set up as today's ruling paradigm (see Figure 2).

On the other hand, intuitive information processing has been studied in the research fields of pattern recognition and learning. The original model was Perception currently neural network computing has been the case. However, intuitive information processing is still not mature in current information technology. Conventional computers are far behind humans in this aspect, and their lack of flexibility is following the unbalanced development of those two aspects.

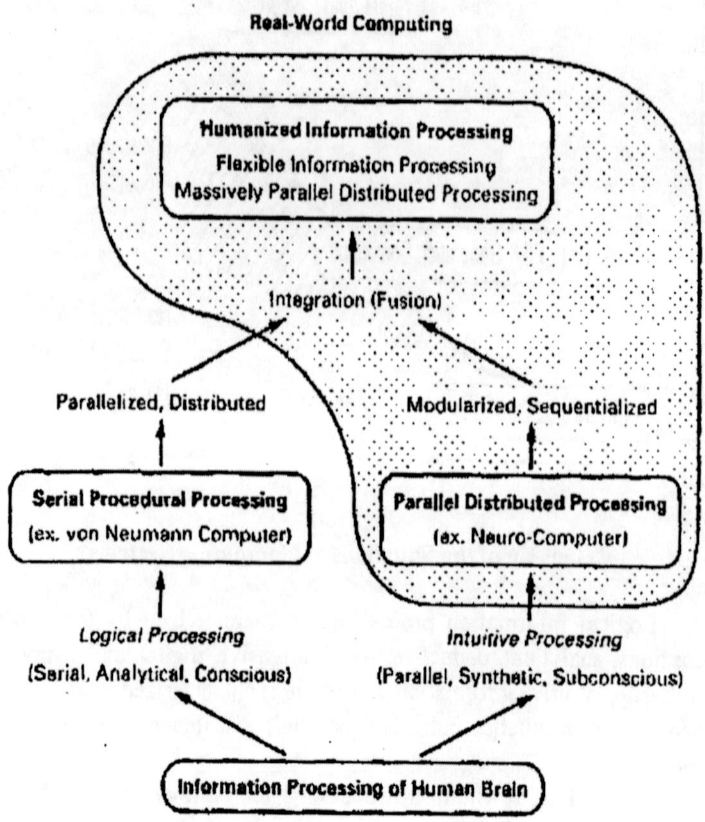

Figure-2
Separation and Unification of the two Aspects of Information Processing

Outline of RWC Programme

Purpose of Research and Development

Information systems of the twenty-first century will be based on not a single but different key technologies, like those for massively parallel computing, optical computing, neural computing, and logic-based computing. These technologies require to be flexibly integrated into information systems in order to meet with real-world problems.

The main objective of the RWC programme is to lay the technological foundation for the advanced information society of the twenty-first century. This programme is intended to establishing the ground for flexible and advanced information technologies that are closely allied to humans and are capable of processing a variety of information in the real world. Such technologies seem necessary for creating a cooperative relationship between humans and computers and for generating innovative and generic technologies toward the advanced information society of the twenty-first century. The primary goal of this programme is not to develop a single computer but to contribute toward the realization of these significant but not yet established technologies.

Herein, we will attempt to establish the theoretical foundation for these technologies, to explore their potentials, and to create some particular style of their integration. Some potent real-world problems will be tackled for confirming the feasibility and usefulness of the new technologies. By disclosing these experiences to the public, it is also intended that Japan will help to the development of the common knowledge and wealth of humankind.

In order to accomplish these fundamental and ambitious goals, it is very important and imperative to develop international and interdisciplinary cooperation in the research spheres and to support collaboration among industries, national institutes, and universities.

Subjects of Research and Development

The research and developments in the RWC programme are classified into the following mutually concerned subjects:

- theoretical foundation
- novel functions for application,
- computational bases.

A three-storied structure as shown in Figure 3 is the fundamental framework for the organization of research and development in this programme.

Theoretical Foundation

The research end is to setup a new theoretical foundation for flexible information processing. For this purpose, it is important to expand and generalize the conventional framework of information processing and to clarify the principle, or "soft logic" commonly underlying changing information processing.

The research topics are:

- Evaluation of information and processing models
- Flexible representation of information
- Flexible storage and recall of information
- Learning and self-organization
- Integration of information and of processing modules
- Optimization methods

In special, integration of multi-modal information (and of heterarchical processing modules) and learning and self-organization (optimization and adaptation) are the most basic issues, and how to implement these in a framework of massively parallel and distributed information processing will be a key point.

Novel Functions for Application

Research and development on novel functions for application should be directed toward investigating elemental novel functions, which are on the whole important for percepting flexible information systems to solve a wide range of real-world problems.

Research topics are divided into the following categories:

- Flexible recognition and understanding multi-modal information
- Flexible inference and problem solving based on flexible information base
- Flexible interactive environment for man-machine communication
- Flexible and autonomous control

Some typical application problems will be handled for exploring the integration of these elemental technologies and for demonstrating their effectiveness.

These novel functions will be implemented on the following computational bases.

Computational Bases

RWC involves processing large volums of spatio-temporally distributed information at a high speed, while keeping in view their mutual interactions. As a new computational basis to support it, computing systems that can exploit parallel and distributed processing at many processing levels should be developed. For this objective, research and development from the following perspectives is important; how to integrate these technologies will also be investigated.

- General objective massively parallel computing systems
- Neural systems as a kind of special-purpose system
- Optical computing systems

In the below section, more detailed contents for each research subject will be explained.

The objective of research is to lay the theoretical basis for the technological realization of human-like flexible information processing as a new era of information processing.

With a view to provide a theoretical foundation for flexible information processing, it is important not only to continue in-depth study in these research spheres but also to clarify the theoretical framework of "soft logic" commonly underlying these fields and to intend to constructing a new unified theoretical base for dynamic RWC. Here, probabilistic and statistical formulation of problems and non-linear dynamics in conjunction with learning and self-organization will be a key approach.

It will be important to expand and generalize the conventional framework of information processing in all aspects of information representation, processing, and evaluation, and to systematize fundamental theories and elementary novel functions for application on the flexible framework.

The followings are conceived of as the most basic issues of common concern :

- integration of multi-modal information (and of heterarchical processing modules);
- learning and self organization (optimization and adaptation).

Figure-3
Organisation of Research and Development

Real-World Computing Programme

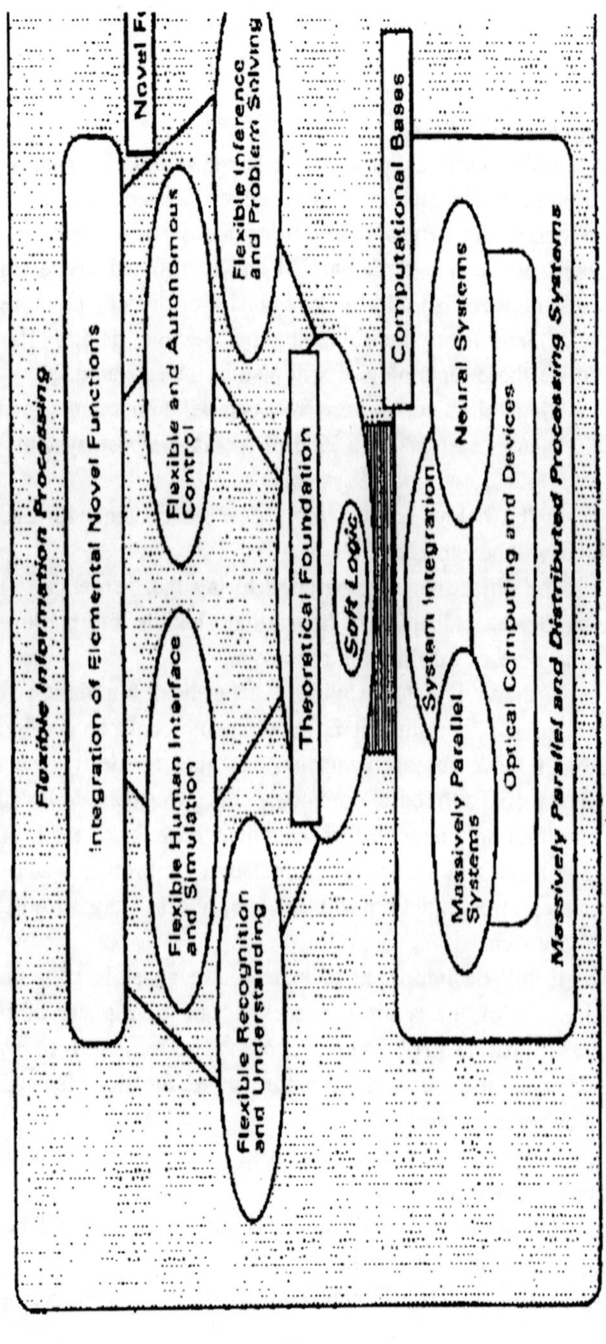

Flexible Representation of Information

With a view to treat various kinds of information in the real world (such as images, speech sounds, and languages) and to construct heterarchical flexible systems, it is first of all important to establish a flexible framework for information representation. The framework should be flexible enough not only to represent different kinds of information in unified manner but also to represent certainty of information. It should also be appropriate and efficient for implementing associative memory and learning/self-organization procedures.

Evaluation of Information and Processing Models

For actively interacting with the real world and learning of self-organizing from experience, RWC systems should have a flexible and systematic framework (criterion) for evaluating the importance of various kinds of input information, the output information that is a consequence of processing, and the processing models themselves.

Flexible Storage and Recall of Information

The highly sophisticated work of the human brain's memory is a key to the flexible information processing of humans. RWC systems should have such flexible memory functions to store and associatively recall different kinds of information. Thus the research should intend to establishing the theoretical analysis of associative memory and developing new efficient mechanisms for flexible associative memory.

Integration of information and of Processing Modules

Information processing such as inference, prediction, and planning can be considered as an integration process of different kinds of information and knowledge. It is necessary to carry out the theoretical research to analyse these information-integration processes and develop a new flexible way of controlling the processes. Multi-variant data analysis methods will give the methods of information integration, although most of those are confined to the linear transformations. Non-linear extension of those methods will be important.

Neural network models are considered as giving a type of non-linear extension. Regularization theory will give a method for incorporating various kinds of constraints.

Cooperative processing by a large number of processing modules is also an important issue of information integration. Research on the integration. Research on the integration of processing modules will be important. Investigating the information-integration process of human cognitive systems will also be important as means of inspiration.

Learning and Self-organization

Apart from information integration, learning or self-organization is one of the most important topics of flexible information processing. It will play a considerable role in constructing adaptive autonomous systems, complicated heterarchical systems or flexible databases. Thus, it is important to construct computational theory of learning/self-organization for exploring the "learnability" of different concepts or structures and to develop novel, efficient algorithms.

Optimization Methods

Information-integration processes can be formalized as optimization processes. Learning and self-organization can also be considered as optimization procedure. Solving thee optimization problems usually postulates a large amount of computation. With a view to surmount this difficulty, developing approximately correct optimization methods that can be executed effectively on massively parallel systems will be a potent area of research.

Novel Functions for Applicant

The purpose of research and development is to investigate elemental novel functions in the various application fields, closely cooperating with the theoretical foundations, and to embody those in respective application fields or integrate them to demonstrate new flexible information systems.

RWC systems support should approximate various human activities by acquiring and processing different types of information in the real world such as images, speech sounds, tactile sensations, and so on, which are huge and modal and moreover subjected to incompleteness and uncertainty by nature. Thus, the RWC systems require novel functions with flexibility of different types. Terms such as robustness, openness, and real-time reflect different attributes of flexibility. Therefore, the basic issue for novel functions is how to percept such flexibility.

The novelty of the functions should originate from new concepts of theory or algorithm suitable to RWC. The bottlenecks of conventional information processing should be alleviated through new types of flexible functions such as integration of symbol and pattern and learning/self-organization. Merely, combining conventional technologies or making ad-hoc systems for specified tasks is not what is desired.

Since flexible information processing intends to expand the abilities of information processing beyond the limitations of the conventional one, the range of expected application fields is quite wide. These spheres can be classified into the following categories:

- Flexible recognition and understanding of various kinds of information, such as pattern information-images, speech sounds, and symbolic information like natural languages;
- Flexible inference and problem solving based on flexible information bases that accept direct treatment of information and have capabilities of learning and self-organization;
- Flexible human interface and simulation for percepting mutual interaction between humans and the real world;
- Flexible control and autonomous systems interacting with the real-world environment.

The following are conceived of as necessary directions to pursue for realizing integrated systems of novel functions:

- Real-world, adaptable, autonomous systems.

The former means cooperation with the real world. The latter refers to cooperation with humans.

The basic novel functions should be evaluated from the viewpoint of how they contribute to realizing these two systems and from the view-point of how they make breakthroughs in their own technological fields, related to the attributes of RWC, namely, robustness, openness, and real-time.

In the following, we will investigate research topics that seem important for the perception of both systems.

Flexible Recognition and Understanding

We can easily and flexibly recognize and understand different types of information in the real world, like images and speech sounds. This ability is a typical instance of intuitive information processing and will be indispensable for enabling RWC systems to possess autonomy and to undertake smooth communication with humans. It will also form the ground for inference and problem solving at higher levels.

Several efforts have been made in research to mechanize these functions, but the state of the art is still far behind the level of human ability. The problem of realizing recognition/understanding in the real-world environment lies in the incompleteness, uncertainty, and ambiguity inherent to natural patterns and further in the ill-defined and ill-posed nature of the problems themselves.

Therefore, a new framework for solution is required that admits these difficulties and can integratively include various constraints (knowledge) and also subjective value judgements, for example flexible frameworks such as optimization, constraint satisfaction, Bayesian inference, hidden Markov models, learning/self-organization from instances, or a new paradigm of parallel computation unifying these.

Flexible Inference and Problem Solving

Conventional AI percepts intelligence by reducing human intelligence, such as inference and problem solving, to problems of logical operations and retrieval in knowledge representation by symbols. Such methods are efficient for restricted or rigorously abstracted problem domains, but for the types of problem solving needed in the real world, they face many difficulties, such as the limitation of clandestine representation and manipulation, combinatorial explosion and knowledge acquisition.

In the real world, much information and knowledge contains inconsistency, incompleteness, and uncertainty. There are many cases where the problems to be solved themselves cannot be described completely, and problem formulation is required based on a user's incomplete statements. Apart from real-time problem solving is also a potent factor. Therefore, a new scheme of flexible inference and problem solving is necessary to cope with these problems. This will be achieved by expanding the conventional framework to a more flexible one.

Flexible Information Bases

Flexible information bases to handle various kinds of information and knowledge in the real world are important in the sense that they will support intellectual activities of humans in the forthcoming era of high utilization of information networks and also in the sense that they will form a basis for novel functions such as flexible understanding and recognition, inference, problem solving, and action control.

So far, many kinds of databases have been proposed and developed, such as relational, object-oriented, deductive, and knowledge bases. However, there are still several problems with the conventional databases and knowledge bases, which rely mainly on symbolic and logical representation and retrieval.

Two new technologies should be focused on here. One is the flexible representation and memorization of the kind of real-world information within a unified framework for an inner information model ensuring tractability. The other is the flexible and semantically correct retrieval of the needed items corresponding to the intentions of users.

Flexible Human Interface and Simulation

Novel ways of using RWC systems must be developed in parallel with the development of the individual novel functions mentioned above. This new information processing will give a new environment that enables broad, cooperative relationships between humans and computers and enlarges human intelligence activities.

Users will be able to interact with the computing systems by such natural means as spoken language, gestures, and facial expressions, and will be able to get information by means of real-time 3-D images, etc. This ways that users can concentrate their intelligence efforts on more creative activities, freed from learning the exhausting skills needed for communication with traditional computers through narrow channels. Related research topics to realize such an information processing environment will include broad-band multi-modal interface (linguistic and visual communication, including recognition of human body actions facial expressions etc.) information display system with virtual reality cognitive and behaviour models comprising sensor fusion to understand human intentions.

RWC will also percept novel simulation technologies to solve very complicated and difficult problems. This will assist human thinking, creative activity and decision-making by means of visualizing phenomena that have no inherent visual appearance. Instead of performing costly and time-consuming physical experiments that may not always be precise the computing system will provide users with powerful tools to simulate very large-scale complicated systems and to predict their behaviour in real-time. Prediction of untapped phenomena and future events such as the global environment and weather forecasting will be an important application of RWC.

Flexible and Autonomous Control

Research needs to focus on the development of the technologies required for the perception of flexible autonomous coordinated systems operating in the real world in real time. Robots are typical instances of such systems and applications include aids for the elderly or physically handicapped. Such systems will be composed of different functional modules that interact with each other in realization decision making and action control. On the other hand the real world where the system operates is subject to incompleteness and ambiguity in the available information to dynamic change in the physical environment and limitations on available time and space. Therefore the potent problems to be solved are how to integrate these different functions and how to control the interactions between the functional modules with a view to achieve desired goal states under such real-world constraints.

Computational Bases

Massively Parallel Systems

RWC requires a computation framework that can process various kinds of information and integrate them felxibly. A system that implements an RWC application is likely to consist of many modules that can exploit parallel and distributed processing at several levels both within and between modules. Several parallel computation paradigms have been proposed including concurrent purpose oriented data flow data parallel neural network probability-based information processing, etc. RWC will perhaps be realized by some combination of these examples.

These paradigms re naturally adopted to a massively parallel system and they need a huge amount of computation to solve practical problems within a reasonable span of time. These observations how that a massively parallel system for RWC is important to support the computational power, and it must be purpose to efficiently execute the multi-paradigms flexible itself, adapting itself to application environments for optimal performance while minimizing the workload on the users.

The research and development will comprise the following topics.

Massively Parallel Architectures

The following are fundamental technologies that should be pursued in the development of general-purpose massively parallel system :

1. *Model.* Flexible execution models, which can be bases of general-purpose architectures, should have the capabilities to fill the gaps between the language models and hardware. Flexibility that permits a mapping of a virtual computer onto actual processing elements should also be pursued.
2. *Architecture.* The massively parallel system should be based on a general-purpose architecture that supports different paradigms efficiently. It is also necessary to study hardware architecture that supports different paradigms efficiently. It is also necessary to study hardware architecture in consideration of future device technology and packaging technology for a successful implementation of the massively parallel system.
3. *Interconnection Network.* The interconnection network should give high-speed communication that is comparable to computation speed. It should also give support for dynamic load dissemination, global synchronization, and global priority control. In implementing the high-speed interconnection network system, not only silicon technologies but also optical technologies should be considered.
4. *Robustness/Reliability.* Hardware-oriented robustness that can tolerate expected component unsuccesses in massively parallel systems should be examined. System components should have self-checking and self-repairing features. The total system should have a maintenance architecture or facilities to maintain system reliability.

In the first half of this programme, a prototype system that comprises 10 4 processing elements will be constructed and developed as a platform. The platform system is used for tools of software development and a research platform for novel functions. Fundamental research on massively parallel model and architecture are concurrently undertaken. In the second half, a massively parallel system is expected to have the order of 10 6 processing elements. It will have the capability to execute different types of RWC applications at real-time speed. The architecture will be based on the new massively parallel computing model to be studied in this programme.

Operating System for Massively Parallel Systems

The operating system for a massively parallel system should be designed to support the execution of different processes (parallel programs) concurrently with high throughput and to build a user-friendly software environment that hides hardware details and makes parallel programming easier. The research topics are as follows :

1. Hierarchical Structure. To percept a functionally distributed management system for flexible processor management, the operating system may need a hierarchical structure. Hierarchical structure makes the system scalable. Some substantial mechanisms to control to control activities and its hierarchical structure and the reduction of overhead for controlling parallelism or executing critical sections should be considered.
2. Network Management. Advanced intelligent routing, addressing, synchronization, stalemate prevention, flow control, and failure preclusion should be included into a flexible network management system.
3. Resource Management and Load Distribution. In the massively parallel system, the elimination of synchronization overhead, access contention, and communication overhead will become more serious issues. To overcome these problems, the operating system should be capable to gather management information autonomously and undertake statistical management or adaptive management. Memory management and virtual systems for different resources should also be pursued for efficient scheduling and load distribution.
4. Fault Tolerance. In the massively parallel system, resource management should be done in a manner that permits for expected component failure rates. Therefore, it is important to handle the failure preclusion system as a normal process. Multi-route processing will also be needed for tackling failures.

Languages for Massively Parallel Systems

The language for the massively parallel system must be capable to describe the coordinated operations of a number of processes. The problem is how to find the available parallelism in the problem domain, and to be able to execute it with as much parallelism as the underlying system can provide. Varied compilation techniques and run-time implementation techniques scalable to near about 1 million processors should be studied. The following items should be considered:

1. *Language Model.* Language model is a description model for flexible programming languages of massively parallel systems. The model must be simple and be sufficiently close to the underlying architectures so as not to restrict their computing power, and at the same time provide powerful source of abstraction to develop software programmability, portability, and reusability. In the research for a language model, fundamental research on supporting flexible language, model of describing coordinating and cooperating actions, inheritance, and reflections should be followed.
2. *High-level Languages for Massively Parallel Systems.* The primary goals of high-level languages for massively parallel systems should be ease of programming and the capability to describe computation on the scale of 1 million processors. One viable candidate will be an appropriate amalgamation of concurrent object-oriented, functional, and declarative constraint-based approaches. Currently available purpose-oriented models are aimed at process more than 1 million processes, so the following extensions will be required: introduction of a description system permitting hierarchical decomposition of complexity; diversification of message propagation systems; introduction of reflective functions for adapting and evolving objects; and declarative description of purpose relationships.

Environment for System Development and Programming

1. *Programming Environment.* The requirement to develop a programming environment that can support multi-paradigm programming is expected. Tools for debugging, graphically monitoring and analysing load balance, communication characteristics, etc., will also be needed. Since these functions may require hardware support, the architectural design should take these needs into consideration.
2. *System Development Support Environment.* The needs of an environment supporting the development of the massively parallel

system include two features separate from conventional ones. One is the support for the interconnection network development, where the overall functions such as robustness, dynamic load dissemination and global synchronization mechanisms, and performance of the interconnection network should be evaluated, in advance, by system-level simulation. The other is support for the architecture development of processing elements, where a set of basic functions for processing elements should be conditioned through a functional assessment of the different subsystems, including the interconnection network.

Neural Systems

In recent years, neural networks based on the model of the brain have been receiving attention for their abilities of learning/self-organization and different kinds of flexible information processing. However, these networks are still limited to small-scale applications as the neural models used are very simple and the learning is mostly based on the back-propagation technique and requires a huge amount of computing time. Usually neural networks are simulated on conventional computers, and the simulation speed is very slow, particularly on large networks. Therefore, how to feed high-speed processing on a neural network is an important subject, and it will be desirable to have special hardware.

In the RWC programme, the feasibility for large-scale neural networks will be explored to create flexible information-processing systems that can operate in the real world. The research and development will comprise: research on new models, hardware architectures, and software environment; development of a prototype system on the scale of 10,000 processing (neuron) units to give a platform for research on neural models and applications. Later, a final system is to be evolved, which is expected to be on the scale of 1 million neuron processing units. In the last stage, the neural system will be integrated with the massively parallel system to make flexible information processing a face.

Neural Models

A flexible information system for RWC can be implemented using a large neural network that transformed its own structure adaptively through interaction with the real-world environment. Realizing such a huge neural network will require research on new models:

1. *Neuron Unit Models.* Simple neuron unit models have so far been used with success in particular areas. However, more advanced applications will demand more sophisticated neuron models. To begin with, the feasibility of already proposed models, such as the chaos neuron model, the complicated number neuron model, and the neuron logic model, must be evaluated. At the same time, research must be undertaken on new neutron models.
2. *Modularization and Hierarchization.* In the learning process of a large neural network through interaction with the real world, new knowledge should be gained without destroying existing knowledge, and information should be efficiently retrievable. This means the necessity of modularization and hierarchization of knowledge. Concerned important research topics are: learning mechanisms using centralized or distributed control for the objective of percepting modularization, hierarchical structuralization and functional differentiation of a large-scale neural network, evaluation criteria for this and interaction among modules, etc.
3. *Learning and Self-organization.* Layered or hierarchical neural networks are effective in spatial pattern recognition, while recurrent neural networks are effective in spatial pattern recognition, while recurrent neural networks are effective for recognition and generation of temporal patterns, and also for application to optimization problems. Since they will play a more considerable role in the future, it is important to do research on the methods of learning and self-organization for recurrent neural networks. Another potent research topic is the topology and size of a neural network, which are the most critical parameters for generalization ability of the network in learning by instances. A network should be large enough for learning and small enough for generalization.
4. *Associative Memory.* Association is one of the basic functions created by neural networks. Spatial or temporal patterns are memorized distributively and recalled on the principle of best match. It is important to theoretically clarify the principles of this association function and to work out an engineering mechanism to implement it. Concerned research topics are memory capacity, topological structure of memory, etc.
5. *New Analog Computing Principles.* Information processing by a neural system is based on the analog non-linear dynamics of the

system. New principles of analog computing in neural systems, comprising chaos dynamics, must be clarified from this point of view.

6. *Integration of Different Paradigms.* Research must be done on models for integration of different paradigms. For instance, the integration of a neural network and logical processing and the integration of pattern processing and symbol processing will be needed for implementation of a neural system. The representation of input/output information in a neural network is necessary in that it functions as an interface when different paradigms are integrated, and in that it substantially affects the processing performance of the network. Therefore, theoretical and experimental research on input/output representation will be an important issue.

Neural System Hardware

Real-world application of neural networks might need a large network, on a scale of 1 million neurons. Such a large neural network may be modularized and comprise of sub-neural networks, each of 1,000 neurons that are completely interconnected. The hardware of the neural system must support such a huge network at high speed. The target processing speed is 10 TCUPS (Tera Connections Updates Per Second). In the design of neural system hardware, general-purpose and scalable mechanisms should also be incorporated so as to permit a wide variety of neural network models, as at present it is not clear which model is the best and different other new models are likely to be unveiled in the future.

Hardware for neural systems can be divided into the following three: neuro-accelerators, VLSI neuro-chips, and engineering implementation of neural networks.

A neuro-accelerator consisting of special-purpose parallel processors should be evolved for neural network processing. A large number of architectures for this have been proposed. A typical architecture consists of hundreds of processors and archives 1 GCUPS.

A VLSI neuro-chip is the hardware for implementing neuron unit(s). The domain of neuro-chip architecture is so large that it ranges from digital circuit chip to analog circuit chip. Digital circuit neuro-chips have different benefits such a high noise tolerance, high processing accuracy, and direct applicability of the ordinary computer manufacturing technology. They are suitable for stable operation in a big system. In addition, it is easy to implement other variations using the pulse-density model or the like so as to produce new neuro-chip feasibility. On the other hand, analog circuit neuro-chips make it possible to reduce the hardware volume because it has fewer operation circuits. This is beneficial for developing large-scale networks. In addition to analog circuits have the potential for implementing dynamic and complex neural networks such as the chaos neural network. It is also feasible to consider the use of digital-analog hybrid neuro-chips which add the strengths of both digital and analog circuits.

The engineering implementation of a neural network is the third approach in which the functions of the neural network are implemented through hardware logic without the use of neuron unit hardware.

It is not easy to compare these approaches, since each approach is unique in connection with learning capability, scalability, and so on.

In a neural system, all neuron units exchange their activation values. Therefore, the interconnection network architecture is an important point in design. Methods of time or frequency multiplexing are feasible solutions to this problem. Related important technologies comprise wafer scale integration, three dimensional architecture, and optical interconnection. CAD and silicon compilers are considered to be important design tools.

Neural System Software

Different kinds of neural software systems are needed for the research and development of neural systems:

1. *Simulation System.* A flexible, general-purpose neural simulator for large-sale neural networks would be a powerful tool. The needs for such a simulator are high speed processing, machine independence, for such a simulator are high-speed processing, machine independence, extensibility, convenient user interface, and different types of utility routines. It is also important that such a simulator has mathematical analysis tools to describe and analyse the convergence or cognitive performance of individual networks.
2. *Neural Network Language.* Neural network processing should be described using a high-level language. The construction of such a language stipulates the following research and

development: expression of ambiguous information, analysis of best-match operations, combination with logical programming, and integration with simulators.

3. *Operating System.* When the number of hardware neurons is smaller in comparison to the number of units in a neural network, a virtual mechanism to fill in this gap will be important. Related research topics are: mechanisms for mapping the neural network onto the hardware, scheduling of resources, etc.

Integration with a Massively Parallel System

It is highly probable that a neural system will be one of the processors for such specific purposes a associative memory, pattern recognition, and combinatorial optimization. This implies that the neural system will be combined or integrated with other computing systems. The forms of integration range from close connection to loose connection. An instance of close relation is neural systems combined as associative memories to the processing elements of a massively parallel system, and an example of loose connection is a massively parallel system throwing problems such a optimization to the neural system.

Optical Computing Systems

Light is expected to be a new information medium, following its extended transmission capacity and massively parallel processing capability. Optics will give new device technology and new architectures and algorithms in the RWC programme that aims at flexible information processing using massively parallel distributed processing. Research topics will be divided into the following categories.

Optical Interconnection

Optical interconnection combines the advanced electronics technology represented by VLSI with optical communication technology and thus eliminates information transmission difficulties in electronic systems like propagation delay, line-to-line cross-talk, space fctors of wiring nd mounting, and large power consumption.

By using high-density multiplexing technologies in the area of time, space, and wavelength, optical interconnection device, architecture, and design technology will offer high-speed and large-capacity optical interconnection having such flexible functions as reconfigurability and self-routing. These are also basic technologies for realizing optical neural systems or optical digital systems.

With a view to develop optical interconnection, the following issues re important:

- Ultrafast (sub-picosecond) optical interconnection devices for large-capacity interconnection by using time classification multiplexing (TDM).
- Space-parallel/functional optical interconnection devices for reconfigurable high-speed interconnection by applying space division multiplexing (SDM).
- Wavelength-parallel/functional optical interconnection devices for large-capacity/reconfigurable interconnection by applying wavelength division multiplexing (WDM) and wavelength-selective self-routing technology Passive optical interconnection elements comprising micro-optics and diffractive elements for developing optical components having benefits of both stability and high-density optical interconnections.
- Advanced opto-electronic integrated devices and circuits combining vrious material systems/functions for compact and smart users for the next generation due to the aforementioned devices
- Research on interchip and intra-chip optical interconnection for high-speed and flexible optical interconnection networks between processing elements, between processors and memories, and between memories.
- Modularization of opto-electronic devices and passive optical elements for combination and miniaturization of optical interconnection components.

Optical Neural Systems

Optical neural systems aim at realizing real-time processing of images and other spatially disseminated information or spectral information through learning and associative processing, applying massive and flexible interconnectivity of light.

With a view to develop such systems, the following issues are considerable:

1. *Optical Neural Models*

- Models for direct input and processing of 2-D/3-D image information by neural networks

- Novel-type theoretical models utilizing physical phenomena of light, such as bistability , chose and phase-conjugation, etc.
- Expandable modular models comprising of a number of unit modules
- Models for implementing optical analog devices that are low in accuracy but very appropriate in large-scale configuration at high speed.

2. *Optical Neural Devices*

Large-scale optical array devices that can vary synaptic connection weights identification electric/optical learning signals

3. *Optical Neural Systems*

- Design technology for the dissernation the functions, hierarchization of the system, and perception of accurate processing through system integration with digital computer.
- Learning methods for getting knowledge from training signals, storing them as structured knowledge, and technologies for increasing learning speed.
- Human friendly I/O interface technologies for direct processing of multimedia information and also for image data base permitting direct search of images by key image.

Optical Digital Systems

Optical digital systems aim at realizing massively parallel and accurate processing of images and other spatially applying information or spectral information with logical computation principles disseminate massive and flexible connectivity of light.

To develop such systems, the following components are needed.

1. High-speed binary/ multi-valued optical devices and their two dimensional combination with low power consumption:

- Space-parallel optical logic devices with encoding signals in the form of spatially coded pattern
- Wavelength-parallel optical logic devices with encoding signals in the form of a combination of light with various wavelength
- Passive optical devices for micro-optics, planner optic diffractive optics, and high-precision optics

2. *Optical Logic Circuit*
   - Reconfigurable optical interconnection between optical logic devices
   - Functional modularization of optical logic elements, like as parallel optical registers, parallel optical memories, optical crossbar switches, and optical I/O un'ts
   - CAD technology for 3-D optical circuit design

3. *Optical Digital Systems*
   - Architecture and design for general/special purpose, optical parallel computers with highly accurate and flexible processing capabilities, based on conspicuous logical algorithms.
   - I/O interface for high-speed data exchange between optical logic circuits and electronic systems
   - Technologies for effecting and integrating various functional optical modules
   - Programming language and compiler for optical parallel digital systems compatible with those for electronic computers, and compilers.

Environment for System Development

Optical computing technologies are based on the presumption of applying newly evolves optical devices, and modularization of opto-electronic devices is also a potent goal in the RWC programme. Optical contributions to the highly parallel and largely distributed systems shall be verified with such modules.

The subjects that require to be investigated are: advanced OEIC processing technology, opto-electronic module technology, and standardization and CAD technology.

Research Organization and Plan

Basic Policy

The important goal of this programme is not to evolve a single computer but to explore the tearsibilites of elemental technologies that are significant and as yet unestablished.

Organization Scheme

MITI selects about a dozen Japanese companies, comprising almost all the major ones in electronics, which form the RWC Partnership. The

RWC Partnership will setup its own central laboratory (RWC Research Centre) near the Electro-technical Laboratory (ETL) in Tsukuba City, expecting close cooperation with the ETL and getting researchers from the laboratories of each company.

The ETL, which belongs to MITI and has been playing an important role in concept formation of the programme, with continue to endorse and lead the programme by sending some researchers into the main position at the RWC Research Center and also carrying out its own fundamental leading research for RWC.

As for the previous Fifth Generation Computer project, MITI will provide a similar amount of total budget (about US $500 million for 10 years). The important part of the budget will be allocated to the RWC Partnership (approximately half to the RWC Research Center and the other half disseminated to laboratories of companies), about 10 per cent to the ETL and domestic universities, and about 15 per cent to foreign research institutes to develop international cooperation.

There is a modality for overseas researchers to participate in the RWC programme. Foreign companies and non-academic organizations will be allowed to directly join the RWC Partnership, while foreign universities will be able to take participation either as subcontractor or by collaborating in joint research with ETL and RWC Research Centre. In the case of joint research fundamentally there is no budget flow except for the information exchange.

Time Schedule

A two-year preliminary study was undertaken in 1989 and 1990 under the research committee on the New Information Processing Technology (NIPT) and several working groups, which comprised the participation of more than 100 researchers in different fields from universities, national institutes like the ETL, and companies. The final report was published in March 1991. FY 1991 was devoted to the possibility study under the new name of Real-world Computing (RWC) and toward making a master plan for the RWC programme in May 1992. Under these activities, we organized three workshops (Dec. 1990 Nov. 1991, and Mar. 1992) and one beginning symposium (Mar. 1991). Which were open to overseas countries.

The RWC programme is beginning in 1992. The RWC partnership will be setup by August, and the RWC Research Centre will open in

October. A call for subcontracts will be announced overseas this autumn, and the deadline will be the end of 1992. The applications will be reviewed and selected in January and contracts will prepared in April of 1993. The chance to join the RWC Partnership or to use for subcontracts will be kept open after this first opportunity.

15

Developing World's Entry in the World of Modern Information Technology

UNU/IIST

The Target

Motivation

The United Nations University, International Institute for Software Technology (UNU/IIST) is mainly related to the software technology needs of the developing countries. It is the first international institute devoted to this subject. It has been set up by the UNU at a time when, although the growth of computer usage in the developing countries is fairly high, most of them urgently require the establishment or expansion of both basic and advanced training, as well as development and research facilities. Therefore, there is at once a lack of available software professionals for industrial growth and a chronic lack of educators and trainers of professionals of the future. Furthermore, most of the developing countries have few software companies and little experience in industrial software development. Local software development is essential not only to establish and strengthen local industry but also to provide software in local languages and with cultural features adapted to the specific needs and conditions of each country.

Even though the knowledge and competence gaps between the developed and developing nations may be substantial, the UNU/IIST can still help professionals to reach state-of-the-art levels in software technology. The discipline is in its infancy.

Master minds vs. Material Technology Transfer

The UNU conducted between 1987 and 1989 two studies into the modalities and the need for an institute like the UNU/IIST. The first basically established the subject areas in which the UNU/IIST, could engage. The second successfully argued the need. The UNU/IIST is deemed a stable body that can carry out the expectations raised in the feasibility study and that can persist in doing so. Since the identified need must be alleviated through international cooperation, and since an important academic component is necessary, the UNU is strongly believed to be the appropriate institution.

The UNU/IIST will exclusively focus on the transfer of knowledge, prototyped products, and awareness of software tools to support intellectual techniques and software. The UNU/IIST is with the important issue of transfer of material technology. The UNU/IIST hopes to be able, with many funding and loan agencies of the UN System (UNDP, World Bank, UNIDO, ADB, IDB, etc.) as the primary agents to assist in secondary role in furthering material technology transfer where needed.

Foundation

The UNU/IIST is the recently established Research and Training Centre (RTC) of the UNU. It formally came into being on 12 March 1991, with the signing in Macau of agreements between the UNU, the Governor of Macau, and the Governments of Portugal and China. It is basically funded by an initial fund of US$20 million contributed to the UNU/IIST Endowment Fund, and it is pledged that this capital fund will be rose to US$30 million through contributions from other sources.

Aims and Objectives

The UNI/IIST intends to assisting the developing world in meeting needs and strengthening capabilities in five activity spheres:

(1) software technology management,

(2) usage of as sophisticated a variety of advanced software as reasonable,

(3) development of its own and exportable software,
(4) university education curriculum development, and
(5) participation in international research.

The UNU/IIST will help fill in the gaps between the industrial and developing countries, theory and practice, university and industry, and consumer and producer.

The UNU/IIST will be a cradle for educating young university computing scientists and industry programmers and software engineers above post-graduate level. The UNU/IIST will be a showroom for demonstrating paradigmatic approaches to needs engineering, programming, software engineering, and software project plus product management techniques and tools. The UNU/IIST will create a bridge for enhancing cooperation between the industrial and the developing countries in the areas of software. The UNU/IIST will be a channel for bringing to international attention the achievement of developing world.

The UNU/IIST Constituency

The UNU/IIST, roughly covering the five areas mentioned above, targets these audiences: public administrations and small businesses and industries in the least developed world, budding software industry management, industry software developers, university lecturers, and research institute scientists.

- *Software users*: National and local government planners and administrators are faced with enhanced demands for computer-supported gathering and evaluation of socio-economic data. Local, national, and regional professionals in, for instance, public health, agriculture, fisheries, and transport are expected to introduce computers in forecasting, planning, and decision-making. Small business and industry management must increasingly introduce computers in day-to-day operations: budgeting, accounting, forecasting, inventory control, order-processing, invoicing, product planning, monitoring and control, marketing, and sales. The UNU/IIST aims at offer such users 2-4 week training courses in software installation, operation, data preparation, and output interpretation. These training courses will typically be intend to the least developed countries—and are expected to be externally funded.
- *Technology management*: Large-scale software users, and software house, utility, and information technology management

require to apply the latest techniques related to technology management. Users require to know techniques for tendering and procuring software, and for managing computing facilities. Developers need to know techniques for bidding for software development contracts, and for managing projects and products. The UNU/IIST intends to offer such managers 2-4 week awareness courses in applicable techniques.

- *Software developers*: The software industry is rapidly increasing the sophistication of its production techniques and tools. To their providers of software, the most advanced of the industrial nations postulates software qualities only attainable through the use of quite advanced development techniques. The UNU/IIST will offer to leading-edge developers, as well as to university lecturers, three-month education courses in software development techniques, and will offer them active participation in 9-15 month possibility, demonstrator, and prototype product development projects.
- *University lecturers*: With the invention of modern techniques for software development, existing computation science and engineering courses are rapidly becoming obsolete. Universities of the developing countries also need to revise their syllabus. Through the three-month software development education courses mentioned above, and through special 2-3 week events, the UNU/IIST will provide the contents of a modern computing systems curriculum and conduct in-depth workshops analysing such curricula.
- *Computing scientists:* The research communities in the industrial countries are becoming increasingly internationalized. They generally have easy access to electronic networks, take participation in internationally sponsored joint research projects, an have reasonable funds for journals, books, and equipment, comprising software tools. These researchers travel regularly, generally in internationally sponsored joint research projects, and have reasonable funds for journals, books, and equipment, comprising software tools. These researchers travel regularly, generally three or four times annually, enabling participation in meetings of various kinds. The UNU/IIST will help towards globalizing the research of developing countries scientists through

joint research, through the Organic UNU/IIST Network, by conducting international workshops and seminars, and thus by communicating developing countries research worldwide.

Programme Activities

The UNU/IIST Programme Activities centre around the organization of projects, training, consultancies, research, distribution and events.

Projects

The UNU/IIST aims at engage in feasibility, demonstrator, and technology transfer projects. All projects develop software utilizing advanced techniques and are expected to last from 9 to 15 months. The UNU/IIST staff, approaching experts, and project fellows will conduct these Macau-based projects, which are expected to be externally financed.

- Feasibility projects formally, but experimentally develop small but difficult subsets of innovative software applications – and may lead to follow-on demonstrator projects. These projects may be prompted by, or lead to, research conducted at the UNU/IIST or within the UNU/IIST Organic Network.
- Demonstrator projects rigorously apply scalable, state-of-the-art techniques to applications that can serve as the ground for software development education courses-and may lead to follow-on technology transfer projects.
- Technology transfer projects systematically develop core, prototype parts of planned products and shall lead to comprehensive plans and technical directions that are then transferred to a developing-world company for concluding full-scale development.

Training: Courses and Seminars

The UNU/IIST provides training through fellows participating in carefully supervised projects and through courses and seminars.

The UNU/IIST will conduct three kinds of courses for training participants from the developing countries.

- Two to four week training courses, usually locate away from the Institute, will instruct software users and computer centre operators to establish and operate large-scale software systems, and to prepare data for and evaluate results of their computations.

- Two to four week awareness courses, usually offered away from the Institute, will reveal management to the intricacies of software technology management—in order to procure software, put out tender or bid for the software products, and computing facilities. Common aspects comprise quality assurance, resource estimation, risk analysis, planning, allocation and scheduling, process modelling and simulation.
- Three-month education courses, based in Macau, will teach software developers to develop application-specific needs, abstract and concrete programs, and the engineering of large-scale software systems, fit for use and purpose, correct, fault tolerant and safety-critical, efficient, maintainable, and portable. Subset education courses may be given, normally away from Macau, as two-week seminars.

Consultancy

The UN system and governmental and non-governmental and non-govenmental agencies today typically employ industrial world consultants to obtain in-depth studies of policy, usage, industry and technical issues of software technology. The UNU/IIST, with its experienced staff of software technology. The UNU/IIST, with its experienced staff of software technologists, comprising visiting experts, offers to perform such studies—thereby bringing them "closer to home", while at the same time training a new generation of developing-countries graduates to themselves perform such work in the future.

Research

Leading information technology countries and regions of the industrial world have long been and are still engaged in coordinated multi-billion dollar information technology research and pre-competitive projects involving sizable software technology components. Several years of research have brought these countries up to a very sophisticated level of software technology techniques that increasingly are being applied industrially under controlled supervision. The UNU/IIST will bring out comes of this research to scientists of the developing countries through frequent research seminars, usually offered away from Macau. The UNU/IIST will itself do research, this research being done by UNU/IIST staff, visiting experts, and research fellows. The UNU/IIST will also co-sponsor joint research collaboration elsewhere.

Dissemination

To reach growing software technology segments of the developing countries, the UNU/IIST plans to continuously issue a Software Technology Monitor free of cost to managers, programmers, and software engineers of the developing world. The monitor will track international public domain and commercial software products, events, and developments—in both the industrial and the developing countries. Eventually it is planned to establish an electronically accessible Software Catalogue that provides technical details on prerequisites, functions and operating characteristics of software products of interest to the developing countries. A low-cost UNU/IIST News Letter additionally will provide survey, technical, and research articles on software technology issues and otherwise inform of UNU/IIST and developing countries activities. Lastly, the UNU/IIST plans to publish low-cost case-study books that record actual development of advanced, application-specific software.

Events

Besides projects, courses and seminars, consultancy, research, and physical and electronic document dissemination, the UNU/IIST will arrange or co-sponsor task forces, panels, workshops, and symposia. Task forces and workshops may find out such issues as university curricula, professional accreditation, and software product and process standards. Task forces will start out by recognizing issues worthy of study at panel events, will work in decentralized fashion over extended periods, offer workshops at regular intervals, and will present their findings at final panel events. These events will include middle to low-level management staff from the developing world, together with the UNU/IIST staff and visiting experts. Additionally, scientific and technical workshops, intended to leading-edge scientists and developers from the developing world, will explore new research directions and software development techniques. ImaS2T – The International Macau Symposium on Software Technology – is to be held continuously. It will typically feature two days of tutorials, three days of keynote lectures by internationally reputed experts, by invited and contributed-paper presentations, poster sessions and tool exhibits, and demonstrations-all within the area of the software technology profession as outlined in 1.6.

Fellowship Programme

The main objective of the UNU/IIST fellowship programme is intellectual and technological redistribution. The UNU/IIST will focus on the best and the brightest, seeking out new talent in young people.

The Profession

In this section I shall discuss one technical approach to software development. Another approach – together with a comparative analysis – will be sketched in the interlude section, "Two Worlds of Computing."

To develop software involves various disciplines: requirements development, programming, software engineering, management, and the support of resident computation scientists. Although the UNU/IIST is also engaged in other, non-developmental issues, the above disciplines will be a major focus.

The UNU/IIST is devoted to the professionalization of software development.

Requirements Development

With a view to ensure that the customer, the user, gets software adapted to its intended purpose, a careful study must be made of the domain to which the software is to be introduced. Thus, requirements development may involve the mathematical modelling of concepts of facilities of the problem domain, and of functional and behavioural characteristics; together these form the conceptual model. Additionally, the physical model involves modelling interfaces between components implementing the conceptual model, and safety critically, dependability, performance, and human-computer interface facets. Finally, simulation models may permit experimental model executions before final needs are captured—and in preparation for the programming and engineering of the software.

Programming

With a view to secure efficiency and correctness of implementations, the latter regarding requirements, programming now traditionally employs the precise, logical techniques that allow objective validation and the controlled, carefully motivated design decision introduction of efficiency. Typically programming thus comprises abstract functional and behavioural specifications, their stepwise design transformation into efficient implementation, followed ultimately by the coding in some executable programming language. Proofs of properties of individual stages and correctness of stage transformations intersperse this somewhat simplified process picture.

Software Engineering

With a view to insure conformable, maintainable, and portable software systems, software engineering employs such subsidiary techniques as ongoing-in the field-conformance testing; version control and configuration management; change request recognition; monitoring and control; test-case generation and validation; needs and design decision tracking; and hypermedia-supported documentation.

Computation Science

Software developments usually make necessary new application domains, new functions and behaviours, and new software designs—for which state-of-the-art development techniques only partially introduce. A resident computation scientist is hence a person who can check the case-by-case recognition of the techniques applied and, in cases, provide justification for the use of novel techniques. The UNU/IIST will exemplify, in its projects and its education courses, examples of such problems and instances of their remedy.

Management

With a view to secure timely, economic, and manageable development projects, managers must introduce resource planning: estimation, risk analysis, allocation and scheduling, resource monitoring and control techniques, and total quality assurance: planning, monitoring, and control. The UNU/IIST will, in its projects and courses, propagate state-of-the-art management techniques.

Organic Network

An Organic Network will be connected to the UNU/IIST. It will be an expanding circle of affiliated, cooperating software technology development centres, university computation science and engineering departments and research institutes. The network will focus on the developing countries, but industrial world centres are expected to help secure the objectives of the network.

Objectives of the network are to strengthen identify, stability, quality, and productivity in developing countries centres, regarding development projects, university education, and research in the areas covered by the UNU/IIST.

The UNU/IIST will assist affiliated centres in becoming connected to an electronic mail service. This electronic aspect of the Organic Network shall ultimately include ability for general file transfer, log-in to remote computers, and general access to international academic and technological (commercial) e-mail networks. This form of on-line connection will form the backbone of the UNU/IIST Organic Network. The UNU/IIST will attempt to secure uniform electronic network access so as to avoid a degradation into "first" and "second" class affiliates.

Network Projects

Organic Network institutions are expected to be involved in projects in two ways: 9-15 month secondment of project fellows from affiliated software development centres to Macau, and by some of these centres ultimately technology transferring prototyped products for final completion. Only by real hands-on experience under careful supervision can newest methodologies and technologies be efficiently transferred into industry.

Professional Accreditation

The UNU/IIST assumes a heretofore unprecedented high level of professionalism to be achieved in its projects, to be conveyed in its courses, to be introduced in its consultancy, and to otherwise be further developed in its research. In cooperation, typically with professional (computer science and information technology) societies—also associated with the Organic Network—the UNU/IIST intends to develop criteria and standards for industry-oriented professional accreditation.

Curriculum Development

The UNU/IIST is applying the latest, but proven "didactics" and techniques in its course programme and projects. In cooperation with Organic Network-affiliated national and regional universities, the UNU/IIST intends to help these upgrade local computation science and engineering course curicula.

Network Research

The UNU/IIST software development model represents a rich, multifaceted picture—for which not all aspects are yet in a state where matured courses can be taught or techniques applied using conventional management principles. The UNU/IIST projects will illuminate particular methodological and technological facets in requirement of further research. The UNU/IIST intends to cooperate WITH Organic Network-affiliated research centres in pursuing this research-thereby bringing several of the positive aspects encountered in advanced university industry projects (within for instance the European ESPRIT programme) to bear also on universities and industries of the developing world.

The UNU/IIST offers suggestion to information technology agencies of regions of the developing world regarding possible multilateral research and pre-competitive development programmes.

The UNU/IIST: Novel Facets

The UNU/IIST will reach its task by novel compositions of actual, live feasibility, demonstrator, and prototype product technology transfer projects with on-the-job training in the shape of advanced education courses. The UNU/IIST is to be geared explicitly to narrowing gaps between theory and practice, and thus between universities and industries. The UNU/IIST will thus differ meaningfully from most conventional university, educational, and research systems, including those in the industrial world.

Funding and Donation

The UNU/IIST depends, in carrying out a number of its programme activities (notably projects and courses), on funding primarily from the UN system: the UNDP, Unesco, UNIDO, World Bank (WB), and regional banks like the Asian, African, and Inter-American Development Banks. All such funding requests will be coordinated by the UNU Centre in Tokyo, Japan.

Low cost or even free, dissemination shall additionally want operational donations thereby making endowment income available for fellowships. Donations will thus be sought to cover such day-to-day base facets as library, soft and hard computing, and networking. Lastly the UNU/IIST invites private companies to establish Distinguished UNU/IIST Research Chairs in their names.

UNU/IIST Interfaces

The diagram endeavours to illustrate operational interfaces between components of the UNU/IIST and Organic Network.

Two Worlds of Computing

In preparation for parts 2 and 3 of this paper, I discuss issues concerned with so called "intelligent access"—mentioned in the Announcement of this Kyoto Symposium.

Part 2 assumes some familiarity with the field of computing science. It is applied in order to make reasonably qualified statements on one of the roles that the UNU/IIST might play. This role concerns those topics of the Kyoto Symposium that are depended on advances in Computer-Human Interfaces (CHI), Cognition, and Natural Language Interfaces (Computational Linguistics). (These terms were found in the Symposium Announcement).

I have outlined one view to software development. For technical problems and facets, see [5,6,2,3]. That approach is currently the predominant one, but probably not the best. The approach outlined with a few terminological changes, be brought to cover also the next one.

This at times and in particular circles somewhat controversial approach is represented by so-called knowledge-based systems (KBS) Engineering (KE). Derivative terms are as: Artificial Intelligence (AI), Heuristic or Expert System (ES) approaches.

Novel applications, as we shall see, are generally "advertised" as being of the latter kind (KBS, AI, ES).

Algorithmics and KBS

The KBS/AI/ES approach, precisely characterized here, is based on the Lisp and Prolog tradition of programming. In this style of programming, one endeavours to represent knowledge about the problem domain in such a way that it is this representation that forms the ground for execution time interpretation.

Algorithmic vs. KBS Development

We call the "classical" programming style "algorithmic" (and by ALG we mean Algorithmic Software Development), while the other style is known as "knowledge engineered" (and by KBS we mean Knoweldgebased Systems Development). The choice of terms is not rather pragmatic-as will be argued below.

Let us contrast the two styles of programming and programmes in order better to recognise differences and complementarities.

A.a. In ALG program computations, all reasoning has been very "compiled" (away) into efficient, but not very general, not very adaptable, code.

K.a. In KBS programs,-computations take the shape of reasoning based on often adaptable knowledge representations.

A.b. In ALG specification, we experiment logic at the specification level,

A.c. In ALG development, we refine by steps,

K.c. versus remaining faithful to the problemdomain in KBS.

A.d. In ALG, we intend to efficiency through specialization.

K.d. versus through general methods in KBS.

A.e. In ALG, our units of specification are functions in extenso.

K.e. versus rules or facts in KBS.

A.f. The composition principle in ALG is functional composition.

K.f. versus catenation of assertions and object classification with multiple inheritance-however comprising non-monotonicity in KBS.

A.g. In ALG, we speak of computation

K.g. while in KBS we mention deduction, induction, and abduction.

A.h. In ALG, we operate with partial evaluation.

K.h. versus partial deduction in KBS.

A.i. We mention of compilation in ALG.

K.i. versus intelligent backtracking in KBS.

For a more thorough analysis, see [4].

Part 2: Advanced Applications

Advanced Applications imply computing systems that introduce state-of-the-art information technology to novel end-user problems. In this part, I will review state-of-the-art applications, while part 3 reviews state-of-the-art technology.

Background

The UNU/IIST seeks to be a bridge between the industrial and the developing countries for new applications. Several presentations at the

Kyoto Symposium have outlined specific application technological means like: databases, data banks, communications networks, electronic libraries, information retrieval, multi-media, cognitive (expert) systems, natural language processing, etc.

It can be foreseen that the UNU/IIST will endeavour to organize advanced courses on: Database and information Retrieval Systems; Knowledge- and Expert-based Systems and Data Engineering; Visualization of Data, Hypermedia, Data Communication Networks as well as ISDBN, etc.

Specific Application Disciplines

Each of the following subsections addresses one of the topics covered by our colleague speakers. From these you may get the erroneous impression that the UNU/IIST will help in transfer of material technology. The UNU/IIST will not be so occupied. The UNU/IIST will not advise the developing countries on which hard, material technologies to adopt. Instead, the UNU/IIST will consult on the software technological results of most such hard technologies, will conduct technology management awareness courses, will train in their software components, will support develop these, and will educate in their development.

Database Knowledge Systems

We describe here a spectrum: from conventional "old-fashioned" databases—in which data ("knowledge") are represented in a form that does not readily permit the kind of reasoning generally experienced in deductive, inductive, and "adductive" systems—to knowledge bases where such reasoning is readily provided for. In creating a database, one often imperceptibly transforms the knowledge gained, when analysing the introduction, into some efficient physical storage representation—thereby "compiling" away those knowledge facets that might be useful in heretofore unforeseen contexts. In generating a knowledge base, such generally adaptable knowledge is preserved. Execution time is longer, but the time is longer, but the time it takes for humans to formulate a new application and get it "running" is often very short.

In either case (of information-base creation), the requirements developer takes a very long time analyzing the domain of interest. In the former case, the knowledge gained is specialized with reference to the specific, usually narrow, foreseen application—and thus most is lost with reference to unforeseen, future, related applications.

Communication Networks and division Systems

Techniques for implementing secure and fault-tolerant communication net-works and distributed systems include cryptographic and verified protocol designs. It appears inescapable to have any computing system being developed today involve networking and distribution. Typical networks are either Local Area Networks (LANs) or mainly based on fiber optics whereas WANs typically includes radio telescope communication via satellites. There is a tendency to vastly over-sophisticate, especially the WAN networks. Too many optional features and too general communication capabilities, for instance between any two ground stations involves only one intermediate satellite call usually take such systems economically out of the reach of most nations.

The National Informatics Centre (NIC), part of the Indian Government's Department of Electronics, has developed a low-cast WAN called NIC-NET. Claims to connect about 500 computer centres across India. There has been central, "expensive " computer centre in New Delhi, and each of some 500 ground stations communicate via one satellite (India-Sat) directly with this centre.

If the communication is wished for some other ground station, then the centre passes it on. NIC-NET then combines this network communication with seemingly reasonably homogeneous, conventional databases at each ground site. Together the network communication plus the databases form a typical distributed system. It appears that NIC-NET offers a very interesting solution to a global problem, one that is generally frowned upon in the industrial world for being "too simple" (industrialist would claim,) but one that might appeal to countries and regions of the developing countries by being low cost.

The tendency to over-design networked, distributed systems is a typical result of engineering-of electronic engineers putting too much stress on getting maximum functionality and flexibility out of the hardware. The result is oftentimes that the software part of these systems is hard to get right and that the end user is offered several options.

Electronic Libraries and ISDN

Here we are talking about a particular application area within information base systems-and hence the question arises as to whether such systems should be database or knowledge oriented. ISDN stands for "integrated services digital network," With the ISDN the feasibility exists of freely mixing structured (tables) and unstructured (text) data, structured (drawing, diagrams) and unstructured (photos), still and live (video) pictures, and voice in any one communication. Whereas the "narrower" issue of electronic databases may primarily be application driven, ISDN is a classical case of a technology-and monopoly driven development. There still appears to be some international uncertainty with respect to the introduction and spread of ISDN.

The focus that the UNU/IIST could stress is that of software implications of the ISDN would not be economically feasible. Again I remind the reader that the UNU/IIST eventually would like to establish a form of electronically accessible database in relation to its Software Catalogue Establishing such a facility could ultimately become a "carrier" for a UNU/IIST engagement in the ISDN.

Higher Education Management Information Systems

There appears to be a demand, voiced through Unesco, that the UN system help, specifically African universities, in jointly developing and installing Management Information Systems (MISs) for Higher Education (colleges and universities). The introduction is a typical (LAN, and possibly WAN-based) distributed information planning, control and base system. Typically such kind say systems can primarily be databased, rather than knowledge based, with no loss in generality.

The UNU/IIST is currently in the process of formulating for Unesco a proposal for the requirements development and software development of such a system. The UNU/IIST will propose that it coordinate a possibility study, to be followed by a demonstrator project, and hopefully a prototype technology transfer product development project. A university MIS usually enables these functions. (I) budgeting (planning and approval) and accounting; (ii) personnel; (iii) student registration; (iv) course/class planning, scheduling and registration; (iv) examination planning, monitoring, and control consisting of student and grade registration; external reviewer liaison, etc.); (v) research project planning, monitoring, and control; (vi) central and distributed library database; (vii) services management (buying invoicing, facilities management, etc.); and so forth.

A computerized university management system thus needs software that helps in planning, regulatory control, and information dissemination-hence it may contain both classically, i.e., formally developed as well as conceptually developed components-all integrated.

The ambitious is to create, in one or more developing world on each of two or three continents (Africa, Asia, Latin America), specialized software houses whose expertise is exactly in such college and university MIS. The long-range hope is that such software houses, by being specialists in a very application-specific domain, can become competitive in the global market.

Education Technology

Much is being said about computing system learning and instruction technology: primary and secondary schools, high school education, trade school training, profession-oriented instruction, etc.

Here we are dealing, in general, with systems that need computing components that reflect national language translation and cognition and hence will typically be knowledge based. Generally it is believed that the computer-human interfaces should additionally include multimedia technology.

It is not explicit to me- I am not an "expert" in the field-whether there requirements issues are well understood:

- There are about four "players" in any such educational technology system: (I) there is the computer system with all its "gadgets"; (ii) there is the student; (iii) there is the teacher; and (iv) there is the subject-the topic is taught or learned.

The sequence in which I listed these four "actors" is generally reflected in many proposals and actual products. That is: often the multimedia components of the computer hardware "swamp" the intellectual content of the subject field. It also appears that we do not always expose, let alone exploit, all the possible interfaces between the four "players" consistently.

- In this connection, there are different stress to be made; either the teacher is supported in the education process vis-à-vis the students, or the students are helped in their learning process. Thus there are times in an expert system like educational technology when it is unclear who is being the expert.

- When an educational technology system is provided it naturally appears that definitive means of "didactic" and "pedagogic" nature are being provided. But it is that the case? Do there exist generally accepted criteria for good "didactics" and good "pedagogics" at the operational level needed by educational technology?

  Thus the role of cognition appears far from settled.
- The few systems that we have seen demonstrated have usually been developed by one person. Most often this results in less than professionally engineered and programmed systems, which in addition stress only one of the four cornerstones of the educational technology-based teaching/learning process. By less than professionally engineered systems I mean for instance obvious, generally adaptable knowledge-based techniques are generally omitted in favour of standard, "hard-wired," non-flexible coding tricks.

The UNU/IIST is not interested for becoming involved in controversial issues, but the UNU/IIST is potentially interested in establishing, probably as a UNESCO-sponsored project, a series of increasingly ambitious possibility demonstrator, and technology transfer product development software projects, combined with training course about existing technology.

It is most probably an over-ambitious aim that such studies can bring together, on a global scale, the best expertise in order that some "standardizable" consensus can be obtained and such that this pedagogic, didactics and cognition consensus could form the basis for a distributed software "village" industry in the developing countries where each "cottage" specializes in some field and subject. To wit: secondary school mathematics University biochemistry, trade school auto mechanics, etc.

The UNU/IIST is interested in evaluates its good offices in an international, cooperative effort that critically providing the problem of educational technology and proposes portable structures for implementation.

Multimedia Technology

It has been implied that multimedia technology may divert the developer and the user from the "real thing" namely, that of reflecting, respectively utilizing, through computer software deep knowledge about the problem domain. The UNU/IIST will try not to forget issues of multimedia technology and will be ready to undertake projects and train in multimedia issues. Should be UNU/IIST be so involved, then it is likely that it will stress (i) how to choose such technology based on proper requirements studies. (ii) how to let its functions be conditioned by considered use of cognition, (iii) how such technology influences technical solutions, and (iv) techniques for their programming.

It appears that many small software houses could potentially base their project services or their marketable products on specialization in the use of special media in specific application areas. It appears that one does not need vast armies of programmers with a view to develop appropriate software.

Material versus Intellectual IT Worlds

It is normally the material quantities, the physical components comprising the "smart, gimmickly, colourful" user-interface equipment), the high-speed execution, the large-volume storage, and the low price that enable ergonomically and economically feasible access to IT.

And generally that is naively all that IT journalists see and report on!

The real advances in our improved understanding of problems and in our alogorithmic or deductive ability to solve this problem utilising computers are harder to communicate and digest.

The UNU/IIST will attempt to present a balanced picture.

Part 3: Advance Technologies

In the final part of the talk I express the will of the UNU/IIST to become a showroom for demonstrating advanced computer-based technologies.

In addition to the "soft technologies" of methodologies and the 'less soft' applications (Parts 1-2) the UNU/IIST also intends to featuring, as an integral part of its operations, some of the underlying technologies implied by the presentations at the Kyoto Symposium. Thus, the UNU/IIST is expected to become a showroom where awareness courses and "hands-on" experience an illustrate front-of the wave technology in a context not readily available elsewhere in the developing countries.

This then represents the third axis through which the UNU/IIST hopes to able to help the developing countries improve access to information technology.

Specific Material Technologies and Tools

From the next subsections you may get the erroneous impression that the UNU/IIST will help in the transfer of material technology. The UNU/IIST, however, may, in Macau, feature some of the hard, material technologies some of which are now desired.

Supercomputing

This subsection is some what speculative! The UN system has a great requirement for collecting and evaluating socio-economic data-but lacks facilities for the kind of supercomputing seldom called for when performing extensive regional and global modelling and simulation (based on such data and with large-scale mathematical operations research analytic and statistical models). The developing countries itself has no such well-identified supercomputer centre. Modern technology now provides dramatically new, and, in some cases, quite lower priced supercomputers than heretofore experienced. The industrial world-the United States. Japan, and Europe—now has several such supercomputer centre could be a combined effort with a supercomputer manufacturer (XXX) and be announced as the 'XXX/UN Supercomputer centre.

That centre could be the place where the entire UN system could satisfy its demand for supercomputing. Its presence in a developing country and close to several other developing countries could stimulate local build-up of expertise in supercomputing. The centre could also be a place where universities of the developing countries fill their demand for supercomputing facilities. Its presence in one of their countries should offer a more sensitive affinity to the requirements of the developing world. It is envisaged that each user of the global (or Asia-Pacific regional) centre link up with that centre via satellite communication-much like the NIG-NET.

The UNU/IIST can train users in establishing operating, and applying existing software for the modelling and simulation of large-scale models, and for visualization of socio-economic and scientific data. The UNU/IIST can make policy planners and university administrators aware of the various possibilities supercomputing offers. The UNU/IIST can finally coordinate regional and global attempt in large-scale modelling and simulation.

The above are "loose" plans, "dreams" perhaps "in the eyes of the beholder"!

Multimedia Laboratory

The UNU/IIST is interested in establishing, and many clients of the UNU/IIST expect it to setup a Multimedia Laboratory-a showroom featuring the latest multimedia technology: hardware plus software, comprising tools and applications. Different condition in the developing world prevent the ready availability of such technology. The UNU/IIST could repair such a situation. The UNU/IIST can then, notion multimedia laboratory, give training awareness, and education courses, in usage, product management, and actual software development of applications that are based on multimedia technology. The noting is to have easy access to this technology, provide a means for software companies of the developing countries to skip a product generation or two and step right into one of the commercially most appropriate forefronts.

Other Technologies

It might be useful to feature many other technologies at the UNU/IIST Telematics, CIM (Computer Integrated Manufacturing, incl. Robotics), etc.

Conclusion

There is prominent danger that in focusing on the "hard" technologies, applications often become artificially technology motivated and driven. On the other hand, the newest versions of these technology often enable applications that were previously not possible.

4. Conclusion

In part 1 I stressed the methodology aspects: techniques for achieving applications. In part 2, I emphasized developing-world requirements applications that solve problems. And in part 3, I have stressed the hard technology: ultimate "carriers" of such applications-carriers often needing special development techniques, novel technologies that often remove constraints on previous usage.

I have thus sketched three axes of feasible UNU/IIST offering- each intend to at helping developing countries improves their access to information (including computing) science and technology. The first axis exphasised "soft –soft methodologies, the second stressed "soft" applications and the third stressed "hard" technologies. The UNU/IIST stressed intellectual possibilities afforded through any of these axes.

Obviously the UNU/IIST cannot feature a total range of access provisions-as outlined in parts 1, 2 and 3 of this paper. Which will actually be pursued relies on policy priorities within the UNU/IIST and on funding opportunities originating outside the UNU/IIST will try to see the establishment, if required of similar institutes perhaps specializing in countries IT (including software technology) programmes, regions of the developing countries should they wish to embark on similarly successful R&D programmes.

16

Information Technology and International Cooperation

Introduction

Information Technologies is an object of international cooperation as paper stresses. The paper Abstract information technologies as an object of international cooperation. The activities conducted by a lot of international organizations active in this area are outlined. Reflections follow on the identification of appropriate thrusts for international education and training activities concerned with new information technology in particular regarding to the developing countries. It is not feasible to work together without exchanging information. In this respect, information technology may be considered as basic instruments for cooperation.

But when we discuss the potential of information technologies for international cooperation, it is charge to distinguish two different aspects: (1) information technologies as a tool for, and (2) information technologies as an object of international cooperation. In this paper I emphasize the latter.

When keeping in view the information technologies as an object (and objective) of international cooperation, I shall briefly discuss the idea of "information" as a substance to be processed through these technologies.

As instances of successful ongoing international cooperation in information technologies. I review some activities of the International Federation for Information Processing (IFIP) the Intergovernmental Informatics Programme (IIP) of Unesco, the Committee on Data for Scientific Unions (ICSU) and the project of the International Council of Scientific Unions (IAU) called the "University-based Critical Mass System for Information Technology " (USIT) This selection is based on my personal relation with these organizations. There are a number of other governmental and non-governmental, international and regional organizations active in information technology that it would be difficult even to list their names.

Education is an important objective for international cooperation in information technologies. There are various important problems in devising strategies of education for the information age that concern all countries. I will discuss some of these problems with emphasis on requirements for radical change. Collecting and using various types of information (in the form of data) are also important problems of international cooperation, especially in science.

Among the areas requiring attention are standardization, accessibility, reliability, and last but not least, the cost of getting and processing different types of scientific data.

1. The New Technologies

When speaking about "new technologies" we usually imply information technologies. From the vantage point of the approach to information, the history and foreseeable future of mankind can be viewed as consisting of the following eras [7, 19]:

(1) Neolithic era. Man acted on the ground of learning how to make use of the potential provided by Nature to have food available in sufficient amount and whenever required.

(2) Industrial era. Man acted on the ground of learning how to use the laws of Nature to have energy available in sufficient amount and whenever needed.

(3) Information era. Man acts and will act on the ground of how to use Nature and its laws to have information available in sufficient amount and whenever required.

The technologies of the industrial era, or the old technologies are based on the transformation (processing) of energy. More generally speaking, the technologies of the industrial era concerning to the transformation of physical matter. The technologies of the information era, or the new technologies, are based on the processing (transformation) of intellectual product.

The information technologies include basically the storage, processing, and transmission of information. These branches of information technology have roots in the history of knowledge and learning. The book, for instance, represents an accumulation of knowledge and culture. Instruments for the automatization of arithmetic operation have been used for centuries. But only after information technologies were based on electronics and new physical principles were the new information technologies born.

These three sorts of information technologies have their specifics. Historically, they were created as independent technologies. The electronic computer became the integration medium for these three branches of information technology. Today it is not possible to imagine communications without computers. But while the computer has a vital role in the new information technologies, these are not to be identified with computers only.

2. Information and Knowledge

When using information, very often we talk about the information as knowledge. But it would be wrong to equalize them. According to the Random House Dictionary of the English language (1971), "information" is:

1. Knowledge communicated or received concerning a special fact or circumstance.
2. Information, knowledge, wisdom are terms for human acquirements through reading, study, and practical experience. Information applies to facts told, read, or communicated which may be not organized and even unrelated........Knowledge is an organized body of information: or the comprehension and understanding consequent on having obtained and organized a body of facts.....Wisdom is a knowledge of people, life, and conduct, with the facts so thoroughly assimilated as to have produced sagacity, judgement, and insight.

In the first approximation there is no substantial difference between information and knowledge. It is accepted that knowledge is "structured information". Today, the information industry is producing so-called "knowledge based systems." A point I would like to make here is the distinction between "knowledge" stored in a computer and "knowledge" possessed by a human being. The "knowledge" in a computer is information structured according to given rules that are briefly defined and well known. The "knowledge" possessed by a human being is information structured through the learning process, and the rules for this structuring are not known. It is obvious to expect that the learning process, or the rules for structuring that transform obtained information into human "knowledge" stored in the memory of a computer [14]. The first may be called simply knowledge (or natural knowledge), and the second artificial knowledge.

On the other hand, the idea of knowledge is correlated to the notion of "intelligence", which means the capacity for reasoning, understanding and for similar forms of mental activity. Knowledge is a necessary condition for every manifestation of intelligence. I have to emphasis intelligence has been considered as a unique characterstic of a human being. That is why when the notion of imitating man's intelligence was born, the term "Artificial intelligence was accepted as the most correct description.

The successes and shortcoming of Artificial Intelligence are well-known. Critics like Hubert Dreyfus {4} several years ago called attention to its difficulties and restrictions. But in one aspect the enthusiast of Artificial Intelligence are on the safe side. They have addressed the fundamental task of imitating intelligence, and this imitation, good or bad, they called Artificial Intelligence. Their objective is not to create intelligence artificially, but to something different from natural intelligence. Let us mention that in the material world we are happy with host of artificial materials such as artificial wool, artificial silk, artificial caviar etc.

3. Activities of Some International Bodies in Information Technologies Cooperation

The International Federation for Information Processing (IFIP)

The IFIP came into official existence in January 1960. It was established under the auspices of Unesco to meet a requirement identified at the first International Conference on Information Processing convenced in Paris in June 1959 under the sponsorship of this UN organization.

The IFIP is a non-profit organization with the following basic aims.

- To promote information science and technology;
- To advance international cooperation in the sphere of information processing;
- To stimulate research, development, and the application of information in science and in practical activity;
- To further the distribution an exchange of information on information processing;
- To encourage education in information processing.

The IFIP is devoted to improving worldwide communication and increased understanding among practitioners of all nations about the role information processing can play in different walks life.

Information, science, and technology, together with informatics, are important instruments in today's world and affect people lives, in everything from their education and work to their leisure and their homes. They are powerful instrument in science and engineering, in commerce and industry, in education and administration. They are truly international in scope and offer an important opportunity for the developing nation. The IFIP helps to bring together professionals in all areas of practice research, and education to share their knowledge and experience and acts as a catalyst to advance the state of the art.

The IFIP's mission is to be the leading, truly international, apolitical organization that encourages and helps in the development, exploitation, and application of information technology for the benefit of all people.

The IFIP intends to assist developing countries in their application of information processing and cooperates with Unesco achieve this. Liability for planning and overseeing the work rests with the Developing Countries Support Committee (DCSC).

The aim of the DCSC is to develops the cooperation of the IFIP with the developing countries through the sharing of IFIP experience, technical information, and knowledge and to help developing countries and areas with their particular and request. The DCSC's programme includes distribution of IFIP publications, regional activities, and training courses and seminars. Support has also been provide to the developing countries to participate in IFIP conferences.

The Intergovernmental Informatics Programme (HP) of UNESCO

The IIP is the youngest intergovernmental programme of Unesco {5}. The first meeting of the Committee took place in October 1986 in

Sofia, Bulgaria, and the activities began in 1987. In the short intervening time, the IIP made considerable progress.

The programme for action of the IIP is depended on the following priorities:

- Training of specialists, researchers, instructors, users, and maintenance technicians:
- Information exchange networks between institutions specialized in informatics in order to carrying out joint or complementary activities;
- Production of software for informatics and computer-assisted teaching, and for the management of education systems or other applications in different fields of activity;
- Studies on the implementation of integrated policies and strategies for sectorial computerization.
- Research and development in informatics with a view to making the best use of the human resources available (so as to create, innovate, or adapt in the sphres of theoretical and applied informatics).

These priorities, which concern in varying degrees both the industrialized and the developing countries form a good basis for regional and international cooperation.

Committee considered that training should extend beyond the training of specialists in informatics. It was realiseds a priority matter to train instructor users, and maintenance technicians, and also to train researchers so that they could use informatic techniques to fasten their research and improve economic performance in their countries.

The Committee on Data for Science and Technology (CODAT) of the International Council of Scientific Unions (ICSU).

CODATA is an interdisciplinary ICSU body founded in 1966 {10} CODATA is related to all types of quantitative data resulting from experimental measurement or observations in the physical, biological, geological, and astronomical sciences. Particular stress is given to data management problems common to different scientific disciplines and to data used outside the field in which they were generated.

The general objectives are the improvement of the quality and accessibility of data, and the methods by which data are obtained managed and analysed; facilitation of international cooperation among those accumulating organizing, and using data; and the promotion of an increased awareness in the scientific and technical communities of the importance of these activities. The activities of CODATA are extremely important for international scientific cooperation in astronomy geology, ecology, biology, and many other sceinces, where a huge amount of data has to be used in a standardized way.

Factual data constitute the essence of scientific knowledge. Easy access to data is a fundamental condition of the evolution of science. The huge increase in the generation and collection of the data poses major financial, technical, and ethical problems to the potential user. The gap between producers and consumers of data is expected to widen across the world in the future.

There are two more interdisciplinary groups in the ICSU that deal in separate ways with data activities. They are: GAGS, the Federation of Astronomical and Geophysical Data Analysis, and the WDC Panel, of World Data Centres Panel.

University-based Critical Mass System for Information Technology (USIT) of the International Association of Universities (IAU)

In cooperation with the International Association of Universities has introduced the University based critical mass system for Information Technology (USIT). The purpose of the USIT is to improve and unify the access, adaptation, and use of computer technology in higher education on a world sale. The USIT provides a detail strategy for higher education on a world scale. The USIT provides a detail strategy for higher education on a world scale the particular economic, social and cultural conditions in different national settings.

The USIT approach is based on the these assumptions.

- Higher educational institutions, as agents of change, are the best vehicles for creating a critical mass in the utilization of a new information technology-a "critical mass" including of levels of knowledge and usage that allow the activity to be self-sustained.
- The critical mass is crucial because, in industrialized and developing countries, the availability of computers and the utilization of information technology is neither uniform nor sufficient to allow the creation of effective knowledge and consumer bases.

- The higher education system, with its various types of institutions, should be a major developer and dispenser of technology. These institutions are in a peculiar position to lead in informatics development and to work as partners with the governmental and private sectors. By stressing on higher education, the USIT addresses an indispensable component of the larger national informatics effort.
- Optimization of informatics development and utilization within available resources is badly needed.

The USIT intends to promote optimization by assisting in such matters as original purchase and delivery, assuring hardware and software compatibility, and constant upgrading to meet changing needs and conditions.

Central to the rationale for the "critical mass" is the fact that the utilization of information technologies tends to be dispersed, of low intensity, and lacking support structures that allow either optimal or efficient applications. The critical mass system is designed to achieve long-term goals by promoting the self-sufficiency of users. Educational human resource development, and support programmes are developed with of reducing the involvement of outside personnel and the need for outside assistance.

The implementation of the USIT started in Africa. A Research Committee, comprising of 20 persons who indicated an interest, was organized. Six specialists with a particular expertise in informatics will serve on a Project Steering Committee. A proposal to support the UIST was submitted to the International Development Research Centre and a grant to fund data collection was received. The study sample will be drawn from the 62 IAU member universities in Africa.

4. Educational Strategies

From an analysis of the activities of the international organizations just reviewed, it is natural that the problems of education and training dominate. That is only natural, and a very explicit of concepts and strategies for education in the information age is essential.

If one connections the computer as an extension of the human mind, it follows that the purpose of education in the future should be to educate human beings with an extended mind.

At analysis of the character of computer use in education [12 13, 16] exhibits three main tendencies:

(1) the computer a training device;

(2) the computer a an object of study;

(3) the computer a an extension of the human mind.

All three have their place in education, but the last will lead to the most profound and essential, since it changes the very object of education.

It is natural to expect changes in the methodology, and in the content, of education.

The change in school curricula is especially significant. But this change cannot be carried out easily because of the traditional conservatism of educational systems, and the fairly rapid improvement of computer of computers. I do not mean that the object of education has already changed; it is still undergoing a change. A proper school training model will develop and crystallize only a the outcome of a long and difficult process.

The expected changes in the contents of education are measured against Bloom's taxonomy concerning the hierarchic aims of education [6]. These can be grouped in three main domains:

(1) the cognitive domain, concerned with knowledge and its use;

(2) the affective domain, associated with emotional responses and values that are taught;

(3) the psychomotor domain, associated with physical and manipulative skills.

The changes in education will affect most substantially the first domain of Bloom's taxonomy. The second and third domains will undergo minor changes. Manipulative skills will perhaps change considerably.

Education Curricula and Knowledge Structure

I shall share my view of some principles for education in the information era that have been introduced in an educational project in Bulgaria during the last decade [13, 15, 16, 17,18]. The fundamental principle is the integrity of knowledge. The principle of integrity, or the wholeness of education, is not a new one. The idea of studying objects and phenomena from different standpoint and combining knowledge of various school subjects, is a well-known approach, particularly in primary education. The very integrity of knowledge itself can have different characteristics. Specialization is possible within the different subjects, while at the same time examining and stressing their interconnections remains the focus of the learning objectives.

Another approach is integration on the ground of fundamental ideas from many fields of knowledge. Methods using projects are well-known, and achieved great popularity in the 1920s and 1930s in the United States.

The integrated approach for the information era is of a particular nature and differs in principle from other methods of education defined as integral. The fundamental difference lies in the emphasis placed on the need for integration of knowledge as a result of a qualitatively new situation—the development of new information technologies. This new situation can be characterized by the following embroilments:

- the school will no longer be the sole nor the most attractive source of knowledge;
- quick and unhindered acquisition of knowledge in a pleasant atmosphere will be transmitted through TV, radio, and computer networks.

These sources therefore provide tough competition for the school. However, thee is one aspect of school education that cannot be rivaled by other sources of information. This is the peculiar commitment and capacity of the school to provide systematized and well-structured knowledge. Hence, in the stress of highly advanced information technologies, the main preoccupation of the school should be the systematization and structuring of knowledge, whereby stress is laid on fundamental and universally valid principles. In this sense, the integration of knowledge acquires a special significance. The objective of the integrated approach to education in the information era is not to limit the learning in different spheres to a certain body of facts required to carry out a definite practical job, or to develop a project. What I have in mind is just the opposite. It is to concentrate the attention of the student on the fundamental and valid principles from the viewpoint of a large number of scientific subjects. That will encourage further independent study and the utilization of specific information through information technologies.

It is easy enough to formulate this requirement in principle, of course, but it is quite more difficult to implement it as a particular learning process incorporating curricula, textbooks, and study aids. The school, even the university, is not in a position to give sufficient knowledge for the entire range of human working life. It can be said that man's life-span will continue to increase in the future, if by this we mean the degree of change man will experience and skills to serve for a lifetime. No doubt citizens will be compelled to study all their lives. So the chief task facing the school of today is to teach pupils how to learn. In this regard, the integrated approach has indisputable benefits; it enables the student to observe natural and social phenomena from different angles and stimulates the requirement for a constant search for new relationships and facts.

5. Developing Countries

Particular attention in the area of international cooperation in information technology is provided to the developing nations, a shown in the activities of Unesco [3] and its International Informatics Programme (HP), and the International Federation for Information Processing (IFIP) and the International Council of Scientific Unions (ICSU). The importance of information technologies for developing countries is emphasized first of all in the sphere of education. To prepare for the coming new technologies, it is natural first to educate the new users.

Strategies for education in the information era may vary in different countries, but the chief principles are more or less universal. The main difficulties in the developing countries are related to the lack of hardware and communication.

It is very important for the developing nations to set their priorities in information technologies [8, 11]. It is strongly advised to develop first powerful communication facilities, even if this slows down, in the starting, the general process of development. Investing in communications are important for effective international cooperation in all spheres and for using international information services.

6. Negative Tendencies and Illusions

Some have said that in an information era, with powerful computers, excellent communications, and access to knowledge bases, the pupil will require less education. If we use the analogy between energy and information, the argument may go as follows: In the industrial era, men learned how to make use of the laws of Nature to have energy available in adequate amount and whenever required. That made human beings physically very powerful, having at hand energy from various different processors (transformers) of energy. The natural human physically powerful men and women in the industrial era generally found their vocations in sports and entertainment, but not in industry. In the information era, man will learn how to use Nature and its laws to have information available in adequate amount and whenever available. Because of the analogy, we may expect that in the information era, natural human knowledge as capacity to produce information will lose its value. It is difficult to deny this feasibility. But it would be wrong to conclude that because of this, in the information era we shall require less education. It is completely true, though, that we shall require a different type of education.

The supposition, that in the information era we need less education, is wrong. On the contrary, education will become much more important and a lifelong process. International cooperation in education at all levels is very important to eliminate this dangerous illusion.

The encouragement born of the first use of computers, for processing highly structured information, or for processing of knowledge, as it is usually called, creates another illusion. It is believed that it will be feasible to use knowledge processing and Artificial Intelligence to build fully automatic factories and eliminate human beings from participation in industry and industrialized agriculture. The opinion in this respect of Coy and Bonsiepen [2] is a follows:

> The general idea of the "fully automatic" factory which is backed by artificial intelligence products like expert systems is wrong and leads to the wreckage of different Computer Aided Manifacturing projects. It is dangerously wrong because of its consequences for all participants in this adventure........The use of expert systems in risky environments—where quick decisions are demanded, must be viewed irresponsible. The control of nuclear, chemical or petrochemical factories by expert systems leads to irresponsible actions and must therefore be inhibited......Though we probably cannot avoid the transfer of responsibility from humans to machine systems, it should be clear that this responsibility transfer must stay transparent to the users.

It is potent to realize the difference between knowledge as structured information in a human brain and that in a computer. The difference is in the rules defining the structure. We still do not know how the educational process structures the acquired information. This structure, as explained above, is perhaps individualized and dynamic. The obvious difference between the rules producing these two kinds of knowledge has to convince us that they are different breeds of knowledge. To distinguish them, we use the ideas "natural knowledge" and "artificial knowledge". The illusion that these two types of knowledge are similar and mutually exchangeable is wrong and may be dangerous.

17

Basic Structure

The Information System Security Policy Statement

Instructions

- The information systems policy statement must be issued by the head of the organization.
- The policy statement should offer a framework for the detailed security programme. It should be short and, as it contains only matters of principle, be infrequently revised.
- The policy statement should deal with information system security management, liability, accountability, and cost.

Discussion

A statement of policy is a description of the principles and ends established by those in authority to guide the conduct of some activity. A statement of information security policy must comprise the reasons for issuing it, the goals, and the basic principles which will guide the conduct of the information security programme.

The ends of an information security programme include the confidentiality, integrity and availability of information which is sufficiently complete, accurate, and timely to meet the requirements of users.

Information security policy should be issued from a level in the organization with effective control over all of the activities important to the successful conduct of an information security programme. Usually this is the head of agency of chief executive officer.

The Need for an Information Systems Security Policy

The conduct of a successful information security programme includes the coordinated participation of many people in many different activities. The policy statement can play an important role in achieving the co-ordination needed. It makes employees aware of the importance which senior management places on information security and assigns particular responsibilities.

It is difficult to achieve cost effective security without considering the overall security architecture and the interdependence of the organizational components which must support it. These comprise :

- topology of the organization: headquarters only, or few or various field offices in few or many countries? Also, is the headquarters site one building, or a multi-building environment distributed over many city blocks?
- Information systems staff;
- Users of systems;
- Personnel department;
- Internal and external audit;
- Physical security;
- Building and facilities;
- Legal;
- Employee training

Senior management and middle managers of functional areas must be aware of their roles in information security and be assigned liability for the confidentiality, integrity and availability of their data. If functional area managers do not accept their liability for the security of their information, the result can be the implementation of expensive and inappropriate controls which leave systems vulnerable to threats which have not been identified.

Developing the Policy Statement

The information security policy statement must be signed by the person to whom all those people who are expected to abide by the policy ultimately report. Although an information security policy statement represents positive direction from the top of the organization, it is not generally prepared by the head of the organization. The policy statement is generally written by a group comprising representatives of senior managers of functional areas, information systems management, auditors and security officers. At least one team members should have had prior experience in preparing and implementing an information system security policy. The presence of functional area managers should make sure that the team keeps in mind the sensitivities of the key people who will be responsible for the implementation of the information security programme.

The preparation of the policy statement should be guided by these considerations:

(a) It is rare to find a good policy statement that is longer than three pages and two page policies are quite common. This reflects the value of keeping the policy general in nature to avoid early obsolescence.

(b) It should not contain references to specific people by name, nor to specific job titles.

(c) The policy should assign primary responsibility for the security of information to the manager of the functional area which most depends upon it or contributes to it.

(d) A person who has primary liability for the security of a group of data is often referred to as the owner. The term "owner" implies both rights and liabilities. Owners are responsible for maintaining their information and have the right to limit the access of others to it.

(e) It is not uncommon to see various major functional areas supported by the same data. This makes it impracticable for any one of them to assume primary liability for the security of the data. Joint ownership works well in these circumstances.

(f) Users are assigned access rights by owners. Users have an obligation to abide by the security constraints imposed by the owners.

(g) Information systems staff have custodial responsibility for the security of data. The custodians are liable for maintaining the infrastructure which enables owners and users to use the information. Custodians should be assigned specific rights and responsibilities by the owners. They should provide all the security needed by the owners. The owners are less likely to ask for unnecessary countermeasures if they have to pay for the security that they require.

(h) An information security competence centre should be mandated by the policy statement. It may need only one member of staff in small organizations, or many staff in very large ones. This group should help the owners to detects threats and vulnerabilities, gain awareness of the effectiveness of different approaches to security, identify the critical workload for the purposes of contingency planning, and stay abreast of changes in information systems, information security technology and the threat environment.

(i) The policy statement should assign primary liability for contingency planning to the information systems division. The contingency plan must reflect the requirements of the users for emergency response, backup and recovery as identified by the owners. The competence centre will usually be best able to work out a contingency plan. This is especially true where there are different relatively autonomous information systems organizations which must cooperate in agreeing on a contingency plan.

(j) The role of the internal audit function is evaluating security controls must be stated explicitly. This should include evaluating the owners' assessments of threats and vulnerabilities and in specifying proper safeguards in response to them.

(k) When preparing the policy statement consider the advantages of making a single senior manager liable for the oversight of physical security, risk management, the competence centre and contingency planning.

(l) Care should be taken to exclude particular requirements, standards, guidelines, procedures and practices from the policy statement. The more detailed instructions contained in procedures and practices manuals are quite voluminous and require frequent modification due to changes in the organization. The policy statement should be aimed at such a high level that changes are rarely required.

After the statement of purpose and the list of guiding principles, it is often best to describe the key elements of the security strategy. These comprise matters such as the assignments of liability, the criteria for selecting security measures, and any major organizational changes accompanying the publication of the policy statement. Items which should be considered for inclusion in the policy include the following:

(a) The cost of security measures must be according to the value of the protection provided.
(b) The assignment of primary liability for the security of each group of information to the owner(s).
(c) Users and custodians must follow any security restrictions imposed by the owners.
(d) The management of information systems facilities have custodial liability for the provision of such data safeguards as have been agreed upon by the owners.
(e) The information security competence centre is the focal point for all support and guidance on information systems security.
(f) The security programme must be conducted in compliance with all laws, rules, and regulations protecting the rights, priveleges, and advantages of persons operating, using and affected by the information being protected.
(g) The security objectives must be achieved without compromising the rights of employees and others.

Responsibility, Assignment and Managing Information System Security

Instructions

- Managers of functional areas should specify, and pay for, security requirements concerned their own information.
- An information system security competence centre should be set up to advise, educate and co-ordinate staff.

Discussion

Concern about information systems security mainly in the late 1960s. Initially most people assumed that information security problems were mainly technical and, for that reason, should e the responsibility of information systems support. This was not a good decision in a batch environment and has become even less appropriate as data-entry has moved further and further away from systems support.

Principle Liability

In most organizations, information systems staff are not the best choice to be given principal liability for information security, for the following reasons:

(a) Information systems management is generally assessed in terms of system performance and functionality. As a result the primary concern of information systems staff will be system optimization rather than security.

(b) Systems staff generally have little access to, or interest in, information on threats to security. This makes them poor judges of the measures required to counter those threats.

(c) Information systems staff are rarely in a position to accurately assess the results of loss of the confidentiality, integrity, or availability of the data held on their systems. As a consequence they have difficulty providing an economic justification for the implementation of the measures needed.

(d) Users are liable for most breaches of information system security. Information systems staff have no direct management control over users of their systems.

(e) Information systems staff are generally more geographically centralized and are not well aware of the security concerns of field offices abroad.

The managers of the functional areas which control changes to the data are known as "owners". The owners are in the best position to assess the value of their data. Where organizations have assigned primary liability for the security of data to the owners, the results have been good.

Some managers of functional areas may not know how to assess the consequences of a security incident involving their data. It may be that they have never been particularly charged with the protection of the data on which they are dependent. They may not have given much thought to the threats to their data, the vulnerability of the data to threats or the results of one of the threats occurring. Nevertheless, it is they who are in the best position to learn how to do this and take on the responsibility for protecting their data.

Major files or databases generally support more than one functional area. For example, a personnel system may be used by the department preparing the payroll, the personnel department, and the line managers. In this condition a committee approach is appropriate because no one manager will be aware of the concerns of all of the others.

Deciding who should pay for the security programme and motivating them to do so is often a major problem. Once functional area managers are liable for determining their own level of security it makes sense for them to pay for any of their needs which exceed the baseline set by the information systems organization. If a user manager requests too little protection and suffers a loss, then a negative senior management reaction should be expected. On the other hand, user managers will be not interested to specify excessive protection if they have to pay for it.

Internal audit should review the levels of security set by the functional area managers to make certain that the managers have properly assessed risks, have responded properly to those which can be contained by controls and have not unwisely accepted risks for which containment is economically possible.

Secondary Liability

People who are permitted the use of data but are not responsible for maintaining it are called "users". Users, who are allowed access to data by the owners, have a secondary responsibility to comply with the restrictions set by the owners. The owner should specify the user's rights and liabilities in writing. Copies of agreements between owners and users should be held by the data administrator in organizations that have appointed one.

Custodial Liability

Operations staff maintain information systems containing data which does not belong to them. They have a "custodial" responsibility to protect the data to the extent specified, and preferably paid for, by the owners who have principal responsibility for the safety of the data.

There will be some measures, which are provided whether the owner specifies them or not. These are called the "baseline" measures. The custodians must make sure that owners appreciate which measures fall within this category.

The Information Systems Security Competence Centre

The information systems security competence centre should include people who embrace the full array of skills, talents, disciplines, and experience required to provide advice and guidance in computer security. Many organizations have found that centres of competence work very well as a source of guidance and a focal point for information security activities.

The size of the competence centre can vary from one person to many people relying on the size of the organization and the problems it faces. It is not important for all of the members of the competence centre to be full-time. Specialist staff can be seconded to the centre as needed. The centres which are most successful have a mixture of full-and part-time people with the majority being part-time. It is necessary that all members attend regular meetings to keep the whole group informed of developments in the information system security environment.

Building a balanced security programme is difficult. A well balanced programme reflects the interdependence of elements like physical security, employee awareness, employee discipline, logical access control and several others. The programme must cover each element adequately and none to excess.

A balanced security programme requires contributions from different groups of staff such as each major user group, each applications programming group, a systems programming representative, the computer operations staff, the communications and/or network function, the personnel department staff, the physical security staff, the builders and facilities staff, the internal audit function, and the legal department. The competence centre offers an appropriate forum for representatives of each group to meet.

The competence centre is in a position to know about security requirements which, although above the baseline, are common to several data owners. The centre can bring together the owners and suggest a joint solution. In this way it may be possible to employ a countermeasure which no individual owner could justify. It may also be feasible to make savings by introducing a high level control which avoids the necessity to build in controls at the application level.

A major role for the competence centre is the establishment and maintenance of adequate security procedures and practices. They are often either the instigators or authors of several of the items in the security procedures manuals.

18

Risk Analysis

Threats and Vulnerabilities Analysis

Instructions

- The big majority of information systems losses are the result of errors or omissions by staff. Countermeasures which address this area should be given a high priority.
- Countermeasures which ensure early identification and individual accountability should be employed and publicized because the fear of detection and public humiliation plays an important part in the reduction of misconduct.
- Organizational change is a major cause of staff grievances. Staff should get training in the management of change. In addition a procedure should be in place to rapidly enhance grievances before disgruntled staff seek revenge.
- Trained staff to deal with emergencies before they become catastrophes. Various losses of information systems infrastructure due to fire or flood could have been avoided if staff had been provided with less expensive equipment and trained to use it.
- Keep the threat posed by infiltration or sabotage by outsiders in perspective.

Discussion

A complete list of the threats to data integrity would be very long and not very useful. It makes sense to consider threats in broad categories as security measures are generally applicable to broad ranges of threats.

An ACCIS consultant analysed information systems losses in 2,000 organizations over a period of 12 years. Demonstrates the proportion of the total monetary loss attributable to each threat category. The results show that most security problems were attributable to errors, omissions, malice, or avarice. Even the loss of information systems due to acts of God, like flood and hurricanes, can often be attributed to people who located computing facilities in places where such problems should have been anticipated.

Errors and Omissions

The percentage of losses attributable to errors and omissions showed a remarkable consistency with widely varying organization sizes and in both public and private sectors. The particular nature of the mistakes varied widely.

In smaller organizations operational errors, errors in programming, and failures to establish or use good physical security measures causing a large proportion of the losses. In larger organizations, data entry and file maintenance errors caused a far higher proportion of the losses.

The detection and attribution of errors and omissions is important for these reasons:

(a) It is better to correct mistakes before suffering significant results. This can only be achieved if strong detective controls are in place.

(b) Flaws in personnel selection and training, systems design, and procedures and practices cannot be assessed and rectified unless the problems are identified and attributed to specific individuals or groups.

(c) People perform better if they can be held individually and particularly accountable for their mistakes.

(d) Undetected mistakes support dishonesty. If people make accidental mistakes which go undetected, they will soon see the potential for deliberate errors which operate to their own benefit.

It is sensible to concentrate on measures which minimize errors and omissions because the same measures tend to reduce losses due to other causes. In a very secure environment total losses will be minimized but errors and omissions are likely to be the major cause of losses that are incurred. Because errors and omissions cost so much it is easy to justify countermeasures to reduce them. When other threats are considered at a later stage, it should be found that many of the measures needed have already been justified by the effect that they will have on errors and omissions.

Dishonest Employees

A distinction is made here between dishonest and disgruntled employees. "Dishonest" employees are those whose primary motivation in committing security violations is economic. The primary motivation of "disgruntled" employees is retaliation against an individual or the organization as a whole.

The ACCIS consultant analysed data on computer concerned theft by employees in a large number of organizations and found that:

(a) There is little useful relation between the tendency to the dishonest and the level of the employee in the organization.

(b) The largest thefts by individual employees are generally committed by clerical employees in the bottom 20% of the wage scale.

(c) Although collusion is important to the commission of some thefts, computer related theft requiring collusion is rare.

(d) People who work in small groups are just as likely to be dishonest as those working in larger groups.

(e) The data cannot be used to create profiles of the employees most likely to be dishonest.

(f) The possibility that any one employee will behave dishonestly enhances with time on the job for about the first yea to fifteen months. This reflects the learning curve. It is hard for anyone to steal from an information system until they have learned how to manipulate it.

(g) In most of the cases of computer related employee dishonestly, neither the employer nor the employee had any reason, at the time of hire, to anticipate theft. Many of these cases result from unanticipated emphasis on the employee's personal integrity well after the date of hire.

(h) Unlike most other forms of employee dishonesty, those using the computer in support of their misconduct tend to have no prior history of dishonesty.

(i) The threat of humiliation before family, fellow employees, and friends is a more important deterrent than prosecution.

(j) Information systems staff are in the very good position to steal without being caught but they seldom do so. Information systems staff have caused serious damage but usually for revenge rather than profit.

(k) The most speedy growth in theft by computer is by persons on very high salaries. The total amount taken by people in the top 20% is quite small when compared with the thefts by those in the bottom 40%, but the growth in that category has been rather rapid in recent years as the use of on line microcomputers by senior staff has become more common.

These findings suggest that early detection and individual responsibility are key control areas and that particular attention should be paid to disgruntled information systems staff.

Disgruntled Employees

Management actions which threaten to disturb the working environment, professional status or prerogatives of valuable, dedicated employees and professionals can sometimes trigger surprisingly strong resentment. Sometimes the resentment results in efforts to retaliate against the organization, and these can be very damaging.

It is rare for dissatisfaction to mature within a single day to an extent great enough to provoke revenge. One or more fellow employees and the next one or two levels of management above the disgruntled employee are almost always aware of the unhappiness and have sufficient opportunity to take corrective action.

Training staff in change management can contribute towards solving the problem but some changes will be both important distasteful to some staff. The procedure for dealing with disgruntled staff should ensure rapid escalation. If they can see that their grievances have been considered at a high level a number of staff will be satisfied whether a solution is found or not. Where a solution cannot be found and the employee remains disgruntled then damage limitation should be used. The employee should be reallocated to a job where little damage can be done while awaiting an improvement in attitude or dismissal.

Infrastructure Damage

Many events can cause important damage to the infrastructure that supports information systems. Water damage is singled out in Figure 1 as it is the most common cause. Other causes, such as electrical failure, can occur with greater frequency, but the service is usually restored before significant damage occurs.

Most large information systems have suffered substantial losses due to water damage. In most cases the water came from leaking roofs, overflowing lavatories, defective humidifiers in the air conditioning systems and inadvertent discharges or sprinkler systems rather than floods or water used to extinguish fires. A big proportion of the damage could have been avoided if a supply of plastic sheeting had been readily available to cover up sensitive equipment.

Many major disruptions to information systems are directly attributable to situations which were initially no more than an inconvenience but which became a catastrophe as nobody was prepared to cope with them. Major information centres have been destroyed by fire as no one was properly instructed in the use of hand held fire extinguishers. Minor fires have become major ones as no one was prepared to properly direct professional firemen to the correct location. Employees have been killed due to not proper or thoughtless installation of carbon dioxide fire quenching equipment. This demonstrates the importance of training staff to deal with emergencies before they become catastrophes.

Outsiders

"Outsiders" refer to people who have not been employees for at least six weeks. There is a very strong predisposition, especially among technical people, to blame outsiders. This prejudice is not supported by, which demonstrates that only three percent of losses are caused by outsiders. The threat of infiltration and sabotage by outsiders can not be ignored but must be kept in perspective to get a balanced security programme.

The Economics of Information System Security

Instructions

- Countermeasures should address particular threats to certain information systems. Expenditure on countermeasures should be justified by the degree to which they are expected to minimize the frequency or impact of threats.
- When seeking to justify a countermeasure, it is advisable to begin by quantifying the effect on errors and omissions.
- Advantages should not continue to be quantified once they exceed the cost of the countermeasure under consideration.

Discussion

In information security thee are various problems, which are less costly to tolerate than to solve. If the expected loss from a security problem is less than the costs of solving it, the risk should be accepted.

Demonstrates the relationship between security-related losses and the cost of protection against those losses. As security measures are implemented, assuming proper selection of measures and their application in the proper sequence, security losses are reduced. This is shown by the curve sloping downward to the right. The cost of security increases with the level of security provided, which is shown by the curve increasing to the right. The cost of security increases with the level of security provided, which is shown by the curve increasing to the right. There is a crossover point beyond which the cost of further security exceeds the value of the advantages. The objective is to introduce countermeasures until the crossover point is reached.

In practice the curves are never nearly so smooth as they seem here. The losses displaced are in fairly large increments and control costs are incurred in increments of widely varying sizes. The curves are made still more irregular by the interdependence of various security controls.

Although it is rather clear that we should not spend more resources solving a problem than it costs to tolerate it, it is not always easy to make the cost benefit comparison. It can be difficult to assess the advantages and costs of security measures, particularly procedural ones.

Losses due to errors and omissions are comparatively easy to quantify and are large in magnitude. It is common practice to justify measures, particularly procedural ones.

Losses due to errors and omissions are comparatively easy to quantify and are large in magnitude. It is common practice to justify measures on the ground of the effect that they have on errors and omissions without quantifying other advantages effects that the measures will have. Individual accountability and both physical and logical access control are frequently justified by their ability to limit the harm caused by mistakes. The same measures have advantages effects on computer related dishonest conduct which it may be more difficult or politically less acceptable to quantify.

Justification of a specific countermeasure should not involve excessive work. Steps that should be taken include finding out what the countermeasure would cost, and assessing the advantages, starting with those that are easiest to quantify. If the advantages appear to be far short of the cost then it is wise to stop. Otherwise the benefits should continue to be assessed until they exceed the cost of the countermeasure.

Risk Analysis

Instructions

5.1 A risk analysis team should be formed which consists of an expert on information systems security and a respected member of the user community. The user representative should lead the team.

5.2 Users' evaluations of the effects of information loss, exposure or modification should be the focus.

5.3 Senior management approval must be sought at each stage of the risk analysis process. Form a risk analysis team which contains an information systems security expert and a respected member of the user community. The user representative should lead the team.

Discussion

It is not feasible to eliminate all risk from an information system. The aim to reduce risk to a tolerable level. Risk analysis involves examining the probabilities and results of undesirable things happening. It prepares the ground for risk management by identifying the most important threats. Risk management aims to reduce the frequency of a threat occurring and to reduce the impact when it does occur.

The chapter on the economics of security discussed the importance of selecting security measures that cost less than tolerating the problems they address. Where there are alternative measures which both meet the security requirement, the least costly measures should be chosen. Both of these decisions need information on:

- the occurrence of the threat;
- the impact when a threat occurs;
- the costs of countermeasures;
- the effect of countermeasures on the frequency and impact of threats.

It is generally argued that a qualitative approach to the risk analysis of information systems is appropriate as there is not sufficient data to support a quantitative approach. Although some risks cannot be quantified, it is still preferable to perform a quantitative risk analysis. Security measures which can be cost-justified by their effect on quantifiable problems generally apply to problems which are more difficult to quantify. If the quantifiable advantages of a measure exceed the cost of implementation, the unquantifiable benefits are no problem.

Qualitative analysis is easier than quantitative analysis. It is comparatively easy to determine, in a range from tolerable to horrible in five steps, the effect of a specific problem. The problem is that it is difficult to select cost effective security measures on the basis of qualitative results. A risk analysis which cannot be used with confidence as guidance in the selection and cost-justification of security measures is not very useful. Quantitative analysis may be more difficult, but it is far more rewarding. The results can be used with greater confidence inspite of the fact that various risks cannot be quantified precisely.

Various measures can only be cost-justified by accumulating their benefits to arrive at their total contribution to loss reduction. In quantitative analysis this can be done by summing the individual loss displacements. Qualitative findings are difficult to amalgamate.

The Risk Analysis Team

The team should contain someone who has experience of risk analysis in the information systems environment. An information system security competence centre, if one is in place, should be able to provide this expertise. Consultants can also be used to provide expertise in information systems security but the consultant should not be entrusted with management of the risk analysis exercise. It is important that he team leader stay with the organization to follow through the risk analysis into the risk management phase.

The results of risk analysis must be supported by senior management and accepted by user managers. At least one influential user should be included in the team, as the user community is more likely to accept the results if they can see that one of their number played an important part in risk analysis. The team leader must be someone who can command the respect of both senior managers and the user community. The user representative often makes a good team leader.

The internal audit department should be approached. However, the auditors generally prefer to remain outside the team so that they can undertake an independent quality control on the results of risk analysis.

There is a place for at least one junior member of the team as risk analysis generates a considerable amount of clerical work, such as filing, data entry, and administration.

When is Risk Analysis Complete

There is no logical end to the risk analysis process. The results of the risk analysis will be changed by each new use of information systems, each incorporation or deletion of a security control and each change in the threat environment. Risk analyses require to be regularly reviewed. Deciding when the changes have been so great that a new risk analysis is needed is a matter of judgement.

The Recommended Approach

Compile a list of all of the information systems in the organization and identify the users of each system. Talk to managers of each group of users and find out the loss that they would expect if the data that they receive was:

Destroyed;
Unavailable;
Modified;
Disclosed.

Some impacts are expressed in non-monetary terms. Some users may concentrate on legal consequences, political embarrassment or the effect on personal safety. Scales will require to be constructed for each kind of impact. The scales should assign a monetary value to the non-monetary consequence. In constructing the scales it may be helpful to consider how much the organization would pay to avoid the result. The scales are important as they provide a consistent basis of assessing the order of magnitude of impacts which are expressed in different terms. Because of their crucial role in valuing information, the scales must be agreed upon by senior management before proceeding.

Eliminate any double counting by looking for cases where different users have detected the same results for the same information system.

At the end of this exercise there will be a list of values for each information system. The next stage is to consider threats that could bring about the results identified by the user. There may be many threats that could each bring about a particular consequence. A good way of documenting this stage is to create a table for each threat to each information system. The table should have columns for the name of the user that detected the consequence, a description of it, and a value in monetary terms.

The next stage is to assess the average number of times that a particular threat will, in any one year, succeed in producing the consequences identified by the user. Where it is rare for the threat to occur or rare for it to succeed in producing the results envisaged by the user then the number of occurrences per year will be between zero and one. Historical or actuarial records can help in this process but there will essentially be a considerable amount of judgement involved. The results will lack credibility unless the judgements are respected. It is a good idea to employ a specialist consultant to review the judgements and to make sure that senior management endorse them.

If the financial value of the consequence is multiplied by the number of times that the threat is expected to succeed in any one year the result is the Annual Loss Expectancy (ALE). All of the ALEs relating to any one threat to any one information system can be added up, providing that it is certain that the results are all independent of each other. The result is an assessment of the maximum amount that it is worth spending countering one particular threat to one certain information system.

Once all of the outcomes have been calculated, the figures can be used to find out the most potent threat and also the information system which is most vulnerable. This is valuable information because it enables limited resources to be targeted on the areas of greatest exposure to risk.

19

Risk Management

The Choosing of Security Measures and Controls

Instructions

- The user community should be involved in the recognition and implementation of suitable countermeasures.
- In identifying security measures it is wrong to ignore "people solutions" or be afraid of high technology ones.
- Security measures should be ideally designed into information systems.
- Countermeasures must be proper to, and justified by, the risks previously analysed and identified.

Discussion

Overview

Preceding chapters have dealt with the recognition of threats and vulnerabilities as well as the impact of threats when they occur. The combination of threat, vulnerability, and impact analyses provided an indication of the level of risk to which an organization's information systems are exposed. This section supplies guidance on the selection of countermeasures to reduce exposure to a tolerable level.

It is unhelpful to think in relation to the functionality and cost of individual components when a whole set of measures must work together to be effective. Implementing an exciting piece of technology accomplishes virtually nothing if proper attention is not given to the mundane tasks of designing and implementing the procedures and practices needed to make it effective.

It is not wise to be so caught up in the desire to implement some technically intriguing innovation, such as smart cards or cryptography, that the ultimate goal - of providing adequate security at the least feasible cost – is lost sight of. Smart cards and cryptography have roles but there should be sound reasons for their selection.

Examinations of security measures often show only the purchase or licensing costs. This is a mistake; the cost of implementation, training, maintenance, and any negative effects on function or performance should be included.

Prevailing information systems will usually have some security measures already in place before the risk analysis is conducted. The effect of these should have been fed into the risk analysis. If prevailing measures are found to be ineffective they should be discontinued.

The cost of the countermeasures selected should be substantially less than the potential losses they displace. They should also be less expensive than appropriate alternatives. In short, it is not good enough to save money by using a particular set of countermeasures; the set that provides the greatest saving is the best option.

Unnecessary Controls

Unfortunately various information systems are burdened by unnecessary security controls which have been installed simply because other organizations used them. Adopting security measures on the ground of their popularity can lead to the proliferation of unnecessary or inadequate controls. For example, file level access control packages are generally used in systems where most of the users share the same data. This is inappropriate since everyone requires the same access rights to the same shared files.

It is necessary to beware of selecting and implementing measures which protect against highly improbable situations. Managers of sites located near major airports often bother excessively about aircraft damage. The threat posed by falling aircraft is negligible when compared to the threat posed by other problems like fire and flooding.

There is a tendency to be oversensitive to technically sophisticated security problems. These are rare and their impact is rather small when compared with the impact of errors, omissions and intentional misconduct on the part of non-technical staff. Special attention should be given to the cost-justification of measures directed at problems such as electronic eavesdropping, viruses, and worms.

If some user areas have especially stringent security requirements, the countermeasures selected to satisfy them must be focused on the area of requirement and not introduced across the board. Otherwise the controls will impose an unnecessary and costly burden on other users.

User Involvement

Users' awareness of security problems can be heightened through their participation in the risk analysis process. The risk analysis team must work with the user community to recognize the need for appropriate countermeasures which are fully cost justified. There are three good reasons for this:

(a) Users know best which countermeasures are acceptable in their working environments. This is especially true for the varying conditions in field offices with their specific economic and cultural concerns.

(b) They are more probably to support the selected countermeasures if they helped choose them.

(c) The most effective scheme for making sure that only cost-justified countermeasures are in place is to need that the user managers pay for the security they require. Users will resist paying for countermeasures if they have taken no part in their selection.

Span of Control

Some countermeasures reduce exposure to more than one risk. The degree to which a countermeasure addresses more than one problem conditions its "Span of control".

For instance, the abuse of data through unauthorized access is often minimized by logical access control software when it could be adequately, and less expensively, controlled by holding people accountable for their actions. A system of personal recognition, activity logs, and log processing can be effective in limiting misconduct because staff know that anything they do can be traced back to them. The use of activity logs usually needs far less logistic support than access control and, more importantly, control a greater array of problems. Be careful to select those measures, which achieve the widest coverage at the lowest cost.

Procedures and Practices

Do not implement expensive technical controls if less expensive, readily implemented, procedures and practices are available. It is especially important to avoid technical controls, which require more complex procedures and practices alone.

Security and System Design

It is essential to design systems which can be adequately secured. If system design proceeds without regard to security, the cost of securing the resulting system may be inhibitive. It is common to encounter the question, "How would you secure a system which has these security problems?" followed by a description of an impossibly difficult situation. The answer most often lies in not having designed the system that way.

It is seldom very difficult to meet the design goals of a system and still satisfy the security requirements, if the two problems are addressed concurrently. Designing a system without security measures is very like building a house without mortar. It is very hard to apply mortar retrospectively but the house will almost definitely fall down without it. Security should be integrated with the system design process.

Personnel Issues

Instructions

- A security awareness programme should be applied and maintained.
- Procedures for the transfer/termination of staff should be set up and maintained.
- It is inevitable to check the background of staff working in key areas.

Discussion

Overview

Most information system security problems are caused by people. Employees currently cause most problems but, as systems become increasingly interconnected, outsiders will pose a more serious threat. Good management procedures and practices can do much to counter threats posed by employees and help to reduce the vulnerability of the organization to threats from outsiders.

If it was feasible to ensure that all employees were immune from the temptation to misconduct then a minimal control environment would be appropriate. Control would depend largely on personal integrity. Technical and non-technical controls to detect and limit misconduct are necessary because personal integrity is not easy to assess and subject to change.

More than 75% of the dishonest employees who are caught have no previous history of misconduct. Some may have been dishonest before but not caught and others may have been caught by previous employers who failed to report the incident. No organization intends to publicize incidents which highlight the ease with which their information systems can be compromised and this has led to under-reporting of crimes in this area.

Personal integrity is not something that people either have or do not have. There is a very truth in the saying that "every man has his price". Although the price does vary greatly from individual to individual, most will succumb to temptation if the rewards are great enough and the perceived risk of identification is low. Factors such as the need to support the family, settle debts, or pay for medical care can strongly influence the point at which an individual may become dishonest is a very truth in the saying that "every man has his price". Although the price does vary greatly from individual to individual, most will succumb to temptation if the rewards are great enough and the perceived risk of identification is low. Factors such as the need to support the family, settle debts, or pay for medical care can strongly influence the point at which an individual may become dishonest.

Prior evidence of arrest, conviction or problems need guarantee that a potential employee will be dishonest but rejecting applicants with a criminal record makes a lot of sense. Information Technology is not an obviously attractive employment area for a criminal; few jobs in the field offer opportunities for abuses and those that do need a long period of learning before the system can be manipulated for personal gain.

The purpose of the measures outlined below is to work within the existing personnel policy framework of the organization to increase current initiatives to:

- Minimize the risk of hiring a dishonest employee;
- Create a culture in which dishonesty is discouraged and therefore less likely to develop:

- Convince employees that the risk of detection and the results outweigh any gain.

Employee Indoctrination

Most organizations have a process for telling new employees about the organization, its culture, rules, regulations, procedures, and practices. Information systems security should be one of the topics covered during induction. New employees should be informed about the organization's security policy and the requirements to protect information from outsiders. Employees could be asked to confirm their assent to the organization's security policy by signing a document embodying the main security needs of the organization; copies of the consent forms should be hold on personnel files.

Employees should be made aware of the requirement for vigilance and encouraged to report instance of dishonesty if they become aware of them. They should be given clear guidance on how such incidents are to be reported.

A number of people who become dishonest do so because of personal problems like gambling or drug dependence. In such cases employees should be advised of the importance of seeking help for themselves or others. Emphasizing the positive results of reporting these problems will make cooperation more likely.

Security Awareness Programme

A security awareness programme is second only in importance to the security policy itself. Achieving a high level of security relies on adopting effective security measures and on employees complying with them. The security programme must be kept up to date and be widely known and respected.

Regular security seminars can be an effective way to maintain a high level of security awareness. They require not be long, but every employee should attend a least one each year. An hour is usually enough to reinforce security awareness and to make employees aware of new developments. Some organizations use a short video followed by discussion to achieve this end.

Brochures, posters, and circulars can also be issued to reinforce the chief elements of the security programme and to keep employees informed of new developments. Some organizations have found it useful to enclose removable cards in security brochures. Employees sign and return the cards as proof that they have read, and will comply with, the security measures in the brochure.

People generally consider security measures to be a nuisance. The security awareness programme should concentrate on demonstrating the purpose of each measure by explaining the possible results of a breach of security. Acceptance will also be enhanced if employees are made to feel that security measures have been introduced as an indication of the significance of their jobs rather than as a hindrance imposed from above.

Background Investigations

The extent to which employees personal history should be researched will depend on the sensitivity of their job. As a minimum, records of employment, education, and qualifications should be verified. Where the job will expose the employee to especially sensitive information or attractive asses further inquiries into social, financial, and criminal background will be necessary.

These attributes, which make people more likely to be dishonest, should be considered.

- susceptibility to blackmail;
- financial problem
- history of dishonesty;
- history of drug or alcohol abuse;
- history of gambling.

Managers may be lulled into a false sense of security by knowing that the background of their staff has been investigated. Circumstances change and the fact that individuals have behaved impeccable in the past does not guarantee that they will continue to do so in the future. The security awareness programme should emphasize the need to be continually vigilant.

In jobs of extreme sensitivity, background checks should be repeated at continuos interval of no more than 5 years.

Notification of Separations and Transfers

Once staff are aware that they are to be moved or lose their job they are much more likely to breach security. Access rights should be revoked promptly once the revised function of an employee renders them unnecessary.

The organization should keep a record of right and privileges given to each employee. The records should be updated whenever new access rights are granted or old ones revoked. Departments issuing keys, password, badges, tokens, equipment of all types books and other documentation and these accountable for maintaing system access profiles should sign the records indicating they have taken the necessary action. The sorts of measures to be taken when as individual change job or leaves the organization might comprise changing locks. Changing locks changing passwords, altering user access profiles an recovering keys. Without a formal method of notifying the appropriate people in the organization of a staff change, employees will get rights inconsistent with their current functions and the security of the organization may be compromised.

If there is any feasibility of resentment of bitterness against individuals or the organization employment should be terminated immediately. It is rarely worthwhile for a disgruntled employee to work out a period of notice; the provision of severance pay in exchange of notice is preferable. Once an employee ha been told that employment is to be terminated, every attempt should be made to ensure that the employee is escorted while on the organizations premises.

Professional counselling should be considered where employees are particularly bitter or highly emotional. There have been various instances where such employees have caused severe physical damage to facilities even after a period of many weeks away from the organization.

Coping with Disgruntled Employees

Coping with employees who are known to be seriously disaffected with their jobs, their managers, one or more fellow employees, or with the whole organization can be difficult. Experience

While it is clearly better to avoid a build up of resentment, where it does arise the manager and the personnel department will require to consult to formulate a plan of action. Changing the individuals role in the organization is one course of action which should be considered. Another alternative is to send the employee away on a course while considering the best way to deal with the problem.

If an employee remains disgruntled despite all appropriate efforts to solve the problem, the best substitute is to move the person to a job where little damage can be done untill employment can be terminated.

Accountability and Access

Instructions

- Information systems require a means of uniquely identifying individuals.
- Passwords should be hard to guess, changed continuously and known only to the authorized user.
- Systems should keep records of actions taken by each individual to facilitate responsibility.

Discussion

Personal accountability underlies various system controls. For individuals to be held personally accountable the system must be able to personally identify them and keep a log of their activity on the system.

Personal Identification

The most common causes for personal identification are:

- To limit user activities;
- To once unauthorized users;
- To be able to hold authorized users individually responsible for their actions;
- To support control of physical access.

Two characteristics are importance for a computer based system to establish the identity of an individual. There is a public "identification" such as name employee serial number, credit card number or bank account number. Then there is a private "authentication" such as password, key or finger print. The objective of the authentication is to prove to the system that the person using the public identification is indeed who he/she claims to be.

There are various ways to identify and authenticate an individual. No single method is best. The question of which method is most suitable for the environment in question will have to be considered. When selecting a means of identification and authentication, the following factors should be considered.

- the amount of effort required to circumvent the authentication proposed.
- The results of successfully pretending to be someone else.
- The likelihood of the system rejecting a genuine user or accepting a fraudulent one;

- The requirement for personal identification to be carried forward into activity logs;
- The possibility of employing different methods of identification and authentication depending on the sensitivity of the function or system;
- The effect of each alternate on system function and performance;
- The flexibility of the approach to respond to future needs.
- The acceptability of the process to the people being identified.
- The expenses of implementation, training and support.
- The cost associated with changing users rights;
- Circumstances in which the method would be impracticable.

The purpose of authentication and the practically of using particular methods should drive the selection process Time –consuming authentication may be acceptable where people log in to the system infrequently and stay for a long time or where a very high level of security is required. A much less arduous method of authentication would be proper for a low system where people log in and out many time each day.

The method of authentication fall into three categories.

- something known, like a password;
- identifying tokens, like badges, magnetic tripe cards smart cards, etc.
- biological characteristic such as physical appearance hand prints, retinal blood vessel patterns, and fingerprints.

Passwords

Passwords are the most common form of personal authentication, Password systems can be very hard to break if they are implemented appropriately It is the poor quality of implementation that has given passwords a bad name. The security provided by password protection can be compromised disclosure, guessing or theft.

Disclosure of Passwords

Passwords are of little use if users independently disclose them. The best way to discourage people from disclosing their passwords is to make it clear that password holders will be held accountable and system of individual accountability and unique passwords. The use of the same password by a whole group of staff seriously compromises individual accountability and should be avoided.

Guessing Passwords

Providing that passwords are drawn from the full charter set and are 6 or more characters long, there is little chance of anyone guessing a password unless they can narrow down the likely candidates. Efforts to break a password are generally made using personal knowledge about the individual or a dictionary of words and name. Even then the process can be very tedious and dangerous especially where the system allows few attempts to get the password right.

Another approach to password guessing is to use inside knowledge of the system default identifications and passwords for the system administrator or engineer. This should be defeated by changing the defaults at the earliest opportunity.

Most systems have a spelling checker and a list of the full names of the authorize users. As a minimum the system can be made to check that passwords opted by users are absent from both the spelling checker dictionary and the list of users names.

System-generated passwords can be very successful providing that people remember the passwords that the system provides them. If the password are very long and cannot be pronounced then people will forget them or write them down. System generated passwords should be pronounceable and not more than 10 characters.

Changing passwords continuously makes password more difficult to guess and reduces the value of attempting to guess them. The frequency with which passwords users choose their down passwords the system should check that they do not revert to a password that they have used before.

Security staff should monitor failed endeavours to log on to the system. If someone is trying to guess a user's password then there should be a series of failed attempts in the system log. If there is evident that special user consistently fails to enter the correct password then security staff should interview the user. If the user cannot explain the entries in the log try changing the users identification of the system.

In the absence of a compelling cause to handle passwords in some other way machine generated, pronounceable passwords which are at least six characters long and do not seem in the system dictionary can be used.

Theft of Passwords

A password cannot be stolen unless it is exposed. Disclosure can take many forms including word of mouth written material VDU screens keyboards and electronic eavesdropping. A good security awareness programme combined with technical measures can defeat all to these forms of disclosure.

The security awareness programme should stress the results of disclosing a password to someone else. Staff should never have to reveal their password to anyone. If a superior of member of the technical support team required to have the same rights as a particular user he should seek the rights from the system administrator rather than by compromising the users password.

Staff do required down. They do this if the supported to hard to remember, too numerous or used infrequently. Users should be help to avoid having to write down their passwords by making them short and pronounceable and reducing the number of different passwords they need to use. If someone uses a password very infrequently there may be a case for reassigning the right granted by that password to someone else.

Some systems produce prints that show unencrypted passwords. If the prints are not necessary they should be disabled. If they are necessary then the prints should be held in a secure cabinet.

Few systems display passwords on the screen but most need the password to be typed. It is easy for someone to work out a password by watching someone type. The security awareness programme should remind users that they should avoid typing their passwords in the presence of other persons.

Electronic eaves dropping can be used to intercept passwords. VDUs keyboards and printers all produce signals which can be decoded to plain text. In extremely sensitive system special shielding may be needed. This involves encasing equipment in materials that are impervious to radio signals.

Communication lines are vulnerable to eavesdropping. If a system is networked it is possible for someone to tap in to the line and record the traffic on it. In various systems the initial log-in will include user identification and passwords. This threat can be addressed in two ways:

- Avoiding reusable passwords. This can be done by issuing users with a devise which can generate a time-dependent password every time the user logs in.
- Physically protecting the communication line or ensuring that all traffic on it is encrypted using a time dependent key.

System-level or application level password files are an important source of passwords for an infiltrator. They should always be held in encrypted form. "One way" encryption is usually used. This means that no-one can decode the password file but the system can regenerate the encrypted password when the user enters the plain text version.

Identifying Tokens

A member of individuals who are authorized to perform a special function carry token such as keys and machine readable cards or devices. Token alone are not adequate as a means of uniquely identifying an individual. Anyone who steals or finds one can use it just as easily as the original owner, many tokens need a password, signature or other confirmation to reduce the chance of misuse. All token require input devices whether it be keyhole or a card reader. This adds to the coast of each workstation where the token can be used.

Biological Characteristics

The most secure means of identifying people is to use a characteristic which cannot be duplicated, and which is inseparable from and totally unique to an individual. The problem lies in finding a means of verifying the characteristic in a way that is economically feasible, socially acceptable, and adequately secure.

Fingerprints are a useful means of identification is some circumstances but are not widely used for information systems. There are devices that can examine and compare fingerprints but the cost per workstation is high. Other schemes to use personal characteristics for authentication have been tried but none have been successful except in high-security systems.

Identifying Terminals

Some terminals have unique codes which cannot be changed but can be read by the system. Unique codes can be applied to limit functions to a particular group of terminals. Electronic funds transfer applications might be limited to terminals in the treasurer's department.

Some systems can limit the facilities available to certain ports, channels or addresses. This facility can be used to limit some powerful facilities to a console situated within the secure computer area. It can also be applied in much the same way as terminal identification codes.

The usefulness of these two methods of control depends on the level of physical security. If it is easy to move terminals around or tap into network cables they offer little protection. Neither should be regarded as alternatives for personal identification or authentication.

Individual Accountability

People will be less likely to make mistakes or be dishonest if they know that they can, and will, be held accountable for their actions. Individual accountability can only be achieved if the system can uniquely identify people and keep a comprehensive record of their actions.

Most systems keep logs of individual activity, but the amount of detail held varies greatly. The level of detail needed depends on the individual definition of a sensitive transaction. Any action which exposes the organization to significant risk should be logged. The level of detail contained in the logs determines their usefulness as a control. Data Base Management Systems (DBMS) can provide logs which are detail enough to hold individuals accountable for all access to, and modification of, the database.

If detailed logs are kept they quickly become voluminous and difficult to use. A strategy will be required for pruning the logs to remove entries that are no longer useful. Powerful interrogation facilities to extract useful information from the unstructured mass of data in the logs will also be required.

User error is a major course of loss in information systems. If the log has been properly enforced it is easy to identify the people making an unacceptably high number of mistakes and take corrective action. It is not always the user's fault when the error rates are high. Poorly designed applications often invite errors. Poorly designed training programmes can result in high error rates. Poor motivation can induce indifference. Whatever the reason of errors it is necessary to identify the source before corrective action can be taken.

It can be useful to examine files or databases and the logs together. Anomalies in the files are often explained by data in the activity logs. Conversely, unusual log entries may be concerned to anomalies in files which might not have been informed without prior examination of the logs.

Once detailed logs are being kept and a good package to extract needed information is in place, the feasibility are endless and not limited to security applications. The information in the log can be used to optimize the allocation of system resources so that the most commonly used facilities run faster.

Data Division and Compartmentation

Instructions

- Division systems should be kept as simple as possible a complex schemes are costly.
- Procedures for controlling the copying of divided material should be examined.
- Procedures for declassifying material should be introduced.

Discussion

Information is divided to restrict access and to ensure that it is handled in an appropriate way by those who have legitimate access. Horizontal divisions like SECRET and MANAGEMENT IN CONFIDENCE limit access to people who are above a particular grade or who have received appropriate security clearance. Vertical divisions such as POLICY DIVISION EYES ONLY limit access to people in a particular division or group irrespective of their security clearance level. Vertical classification is often called compartmentation . Information may be classified both vertically and horizontally depending on the implications of disclosure.

Some information systems cannot support the full range of divisions. Most networked systms can compartmentalize information by keeping like material in a directory to which all, and only, authorized staff have access. Horizontal classification can only be enforced if the system knows both the user's security profile and the information's classification. In addition the system must support a mechanism whereby all copies inherit the division of the original and any printed copies are marked according to division.

Classifying data in information systems is costly. It may involve additional hardware and software and will certainly impose a training, administration and maintenance overhead. The cost and complexity of division schemes limit their use to high security systems.

An alternative to formal division is to allow owners of information to determine who can read or change their information. By default owners alone can manipulate their data but they can give other users rights to see or change it. This can work well but the right to read information usually means the right to copy it. Once there are many copies of the information on the system the owner loses control.

Classification should be avoided if possible. If data requires to be classified, one of the most commonly used procedures provides four levels:

- Undivided, where little impact would result from unauthorized disclosure.
- INTERNAL USE ONLY, where disclosure to people outside the organization would cause embarrassment or inconvenience. This category comprises internal directories and codes of practice.
- CONFIDENTIAL, where disclosure would be harmful but not so harmful as to justify application of the more complex and expensive process of registering documents. This category includes policy papers, specifications to be applied in competitive bidding and unannounced reorganizations.
- REGISTERED CONFIDENTIAL, where disclosure could cause serious harm. This category comprises material supporting litigation, contract bids and pending awards and sensitive personnel actions. REGISTERED CONFIDENTIAL, information is assigned registration numbers, individual responsibility by registration number is maintained and movements are controlled by a registrar for registered confidential materials. No informal direct transfers or loans are allowed.

A single method of classification must be used throughout the organization. Variations cannot be tolerated following the confusion they generate. Detailed procedures, which include arrangements for declassification, should be published before a classification programme is attempted.

Procedures for marking and labelling are much more easily used to hard copy than they are to data in digital form. Databases may be extremely sensitive to disclosure when viewed in their entirely whereas a subset of the databases may be insensitive to disclosure but very sensitive in terms of accuracy or availability.

Hardware Integrity

Instructions

- Obsolete and prototype hardware must be avoided.
- Dual processing should be considered for critical applications.

- It is essential to make sure that the machine's environment is protected form local problems in the power supply, air conditioning or cooled water supply.
- Continuous backups of storage devices must be kept.
- All information systems assets should be inventoried and given a security mark.

Discussion

Hardware is generally reliable providing that it is applied in an environment that meets the manufacturer's specification and maintained regularly. Critical applications can be protected by fault tolerant hardware which will continue to work appropriately even though some components have failed. Prototype and obsolete hardware is not very reliable and should be avoided where possible. It is safer to avoid unusual combinations of hardware and software, because problems are likely to be encountered which no one has yet resolved. Hardware needs to be protected from physical threats such as theft, vandalism and natural calamities.

The Environment

Some machines have exacting environmental needs. The temperature and humidity must be within the specified limits. The amount of dust in the air must be low. Chilled water and power supplies require to be maintained.

The security programme should make provision for the machine's needs by specifying backup chilled water supplies, uninterruptible power supplies, voltage regulators and backup air conditioning units.

Maintenance

The cover provided by maintenance contracts varies widely. Some maintenance contracts have no guaranteed repair time. Such a contract would be of no importance for critical pieces of equipment. Maintenance provision should be examined for each piece of equipment which supports a critical function. Endeavours should be made to establish policies where the guaranteed time to fix or replace the equipment is short enough to avoid disastrous result in the applications supported by the equipment.

Obsolete and Prototype Equipment

At the beginning and end of a product's life cycle it tends to be unreliable. Manufacturers are often intended to establish test-bed sites for prototype equipment. One strategy for doing this is to assure the client that only the latest technology can satisfy their needs. Before the latest technology is accepted, consideration should be given to whether or not it is necessary. New equipment is not only prone to failures but can also take longer to fix because the supply of spare parts has not yet been built up.

Obsolete equipment is more likely to fail and is difficult to maintain due to decreased availability of parts and supplies. Many organizations are not interested to write off old equipment, but keeping it is a false economy since obsolete equipment tends to take up more floor space, consume more power, lack performance and need more stringent environment control. In addition, new software for old equipment costs more because of the diminishing market.

Backup and Fault Tolerance

It is necessary to have a plan for dealing with the failure of each piece of equipment that is critical to the operation of the information system. All equipment with moving parts will wear out in time. Disk drives have bearings with a very fine tolerance. If they wear just a little the heads can crash into the disks destroying the data. Floppy disks wear out as the head is in physical contact with them when they are in use. The best defence against loss of data is to make continuous backups.

Some manufacturers offer equipment that will continue to operate appropriately even if some of its components fail. In some cases al processing is duplicated using separate machines and storage devices. This is a costly option but one that should be considered for applications that must be available all of the time.

Physical Threats

Hardware can be moved, stolen, damaged or destroyed. Good physical security can minimize the risks involved. All information system assets should be indelibly marked and entered on an inventory. Staff should be discouraged from moving equipment around the building. All moves should be organized through information systems support staff. This is especially important when an access control strategy depends upon particular machines being attached to particular points on the network.

The risks posed by natural disasters are very difficult to address, but some protective measures can be taken. Fire extinguishers and staff trained to use them can stop a small fire becoming a disaster. Plastic sheeting can stop water from damaging sensitive equipment if it is available in the right place at the right time. There are also preventive measures, which can be taken. Sites where there is a history of flood, earthquake, or storm should be avoided. Flammable materials should be stored away from critical equipment and smoking banned in their vicinity.

Software Integrity

Instructions

- Established versions of software should be applied.
- "Patching" of system software must be discouraged.
- Strong change control should be established over all of the files that make up the production environment.
- A separate development environment should be set up, and any changes should be thoroughly tested in the development environment before they are moved to the production system.
- It is important to make sure that the system software can support the full range of logging and access controls required.
- The "Orange Book" security rating of the operating system should be considered if the idea is to hold sensitive information on the system.
- A strong quality control system should be set up and maintained, to monitor changes to software.
- Parallel running should be used to test the effect of important changes to application or system software.
- Users should not be provided direct access to the operating system.

Discussion

There are two categories of software on computer systems. "System" software provides services to applications including task management, logging, file handling, communications, network support and database handling. "Application" software makes use of the facilities offered by the operating system to make the computer system satisfy users' needs. System and application software face different threats and are dealt with separately below.

Both systems and applications programmes require to test their work. The best way to do this is to maintain a development system which is a mirror image of the production environment. Software should be tested in the development environment and copied to the live system only when it has passed quality control checks.

System Software

Users perhaps see the operating system directly unless they are working on microcomputers. The system software is fine tuned by specialist staff such as system programmers, network administrators and database administrators. Computer operators supply the day to day requirements of the operating system.

System software, like the machine that it runs on, is necessary for all applications. If the system software fails then all applications will fail too. The first step to ensuring the integrity of the system software is to opt the right operating system. Choose an established operating system if feasible. New operating systems suffer from the same teething problems a new hardware.

Operating systems have different facilities. The operating system chosen must offer all the needed functions. An access control strategy should be worked out, and efforts made to ensure that the operating system can support it. The operating system must also be able to support logs that are detailed enough to satisfy accountability needs.

If process sensitive information is to be processed, the security rating of the operating system should be explored. The US Department of Defense published a "Guide to Trusted Computer Systems" (commonly called the "Orange Book") which specifies a range of facilities needed for secure operating systems. There is an independent testing facility which establishes the security rating. Operating systems that have been tested are awarded a category between D, which is the least secure, to A1, which is the most secure.

One of the functions of an operating system is to permit more than one program to run at the same time. The operating system should make sure that each program is isolated from others. Illicit software often spreads through a machine by writing into disk or memory space which is occupied by another programme. A good operating system should stop this happening.

Once the systems software has been established by the vendor the system staff take over to maintain and optimize it. An air of mystery surrounds systems programming staff. Some people in the organization have or need a comprehensive knowledge of the operating system. The consequences of an error by a systems programmer can be devastating because the error can affect all of the applications running on the system. Information system managers require to have sufficient understanding of systems programming to control it in the same way as application software.

Change control, in association with the supplier of the operating system is the key to ensuring that the operating system continues to function smoothly. Systems staff should make their changes in a development environment that is a mirror image of the production system. All changes should be subject to review by at least one other member of staff with systems programming experience. Given at least two systems programming staff it is feasible to set up a peer review system such that each staff members examines the other's work before it is implemented. Supervisory staff should be liable for authorizing all changes to the software in the production system. One approach to identifying for authorizing all changes to the software in the production system. One approach to identifying unauthorized changes is to store copies of each authorized version on tape. The authorized version can then be compared periodically with the version in the production environment.

Emergency repairs to system software poses a control problem. There is no time for testing, quality control or change control. The solution lies in careful logging of the action taken followed by retrospective examination of the changes that were made.

Systems staff have access to powerful utilities that enable them to by pas normal controls. The vendor should be able to supply the names of utilities that compromise control in this way. These utilities will require to be used sometimes but it is best to keep them away from the production environment. One way of controlling them is to keep them on tape and mark the tape in such a way that the operators will not mount it without authority from the manager of the systems support team. All usage should be logged and cross referred to a comprehensive account of the reasons.

Application Software

Some applications are bought as packages. The guarantee of the integrity of a package lies in the contract with the vendor. The contract is generally voided if any changes ae made to the package code. Systems staff should only make changes to packages if instructed to do so by the vendor. Any changes that are important can be dealt with in the ame way as changes to systems software.

Some applications bypass system controls to improve performance. In the worst cases the user of the application can violate access control and avoid logging. When buying a new application an assurance should be sought from the vendor that these features can, and have, been disabled.

Some packages permit users to access the operating system directly. The vendor should be asked whether this facility is supported and how it can be disabled. If feasible, users should not be allowed access to the operating system. Sometimes users do require a function which the operating system, rather than the package, can perform. It is better to incorporate the function into a menu than to let the user have access to the operating system.

If software is written in-house then a more sophisticated procedure is needed. The life cycle of software comprises specification, development, testing, running and maintenance. All stages of the life cycle with the exception of "running" should take place away from the production environment.

At each stage someone should be accountable for quality control. Users are ultimately responsible for confirming that the software meets their needs. The analyst is responsible for confirming that programs meet the specification. The manager of the programming staff is responsible for ensuring that the programs meet standards and are documented properly. This process should be formalized. A series of documents should follow an application program from starting to end so that the staff responsible for releasing the program to the production environment can see that all of the requisite approvals have been given. Any changes during the life of the program should be subject to the same rigorous quality control as the original application.

Errors and omissions account for more than half of information systems losses. Wherever feasible application programs should:

- give validity to input by checking it with other data held in the information system;

- check that its output is consistent with its input by applying control totals or other checks for completeness and accuracy.

Communications Integrity

Instructions

- Networks must be designed so that they are not sensitive to the failure of any one component.
- Leased lines or dial-back systems should be used in preference to direct links utilising the public telephone network.
- An error-correcting protocol and confirmation messages should be employed to ensure that data is transferred properly.
- Messages should be encrypted to avoid disclosure or modification.
- The requirement to reduce the level of radio signals from VDUs, keyboards and printers or to mask them with noise generating devices, should be considered.
- Feedback should be used so that the orginator can be sure that all, and only, authorized messages have been received.

Discussion

Communications integrity is critical for UN organizations, particularly those with field offices in hard to reach countries. Communications integrity requires that all, and only, authorized messages are transferred promptly and properly. If communication lines are insecure then unauthorized messages may be initiated and authorized ones may be exposed or modified. If communication lines fail then the message will be lost or late. If there is no error checking then corrupted messages may be received. If messages are not encrypted then unauthorised disclosure may occur. If authentication is weak and there is no feedback then unauthorized messages could be began and acted upon.

Resilience

Communication channels require to be fault-tolerant in all but trivial applications. The network should be designed so that any one component can fail without affecting the rest of the network. Duplicate connections may be needed for time critical applications.

Part of the job of a network manager is to keep track of all authorized connections to the information system. The cabling diagrams are a good starting point for diagnosing faults and conditioning critical connections which require to be duplicated.

Disclosure

Public telephone lines are not secure. They can easily be tapped and even diverted. Leased private lines are a little more secure and usually more reliable for high speed communications. Dial-in connections are the main point of entry for "hackers". If dial-in lines are essential, a system should be considered where the computer host hangs up and dials back after an initial log-in sequence. Dial-back systems can be defeated by having kept the line open so that the connection is never broken or using the facilities of digital exchanges to divert calls to another number. Dial back systems present difficulties for staff who do a lot of travelling. They can also be costly to run because they force the host to pay for most of the telecommunications cost.

Corruption of Messages

External electronic mail systems are amongst the least reliable forms of communication. A message is started and then passes out of the local system and starts its journey to the intended recipient. Typically a message will pass through many other systems and may never arrive at all. The sender does not receive any automatic confirmation that the message has arrived or been lost. Furthermore the dearth of error correcting connections can lead to the message being corrupted in transit.

Error correcting protocols offer a high degree of assurance that the message received is the same as that sent. They work by calculating checksums at both the sending and receiving ends. If the checksums do not match then the receiving system asks the sender to attempt again.

Error correction does not affect the risk of disclosure or eliminate the risk of change. If intercepted messages will be able to be read, changed and calculated to a new checksum before sending the message on to the intended recipient.

Encryption is the best method of avoiding both disclosure and modification. The best systems of encryption use long, time-dependent keys. The length of the key conditions how much effort is required to guess it. The short period of the validity of the key is intended to limit the usefulness of guessing any one key.

Authentication

Fraudulent electronic messages can lead to serious financial, political or commercial damage. Error correction and encryption protect against disclosure and modification but do not guarantee the identity of the sender.

Sequentially numbering messages provides some protection. If a fraudulent message is introduced then a duplicate sequence number will arise. If messages are suppressed then a gap in the sequence will come to surface. This system forces the infiltrator to suppress one legitimate message for each illicit one.

Digital signatures are used in some applications. The theory is that no two people can write the same text in exactly the same way. The user writes his/her signature manipulating a special stylus and tablet. The acceleration and direction of the stylus during the signature are captured and attached to a message. The receiver compares the digital signature against copies held locally. Venders claim that it is not possible to forge a digital signature but this is doubtful. A robot could replica a signature if trained to do so. A more possible method of breaking this control is to capture a legitimate message complete with digital signature and copy the signature into any illicit messages.

Confirmation is a good defence against deliberate or accidental corruption of messages. If every message is confirmed then the users should notice that the confirmations do not match either the content or number of messages that they have sent. This makes identification much more likely in that the infiltrator would have to trap all incoming messages as well as inserting illicit outgoing messages.

Microcomputer Security

Instructions

- Diskless workstations should be used if feasible.
- A MicroComputer Support Unit (MCSU) should be set up.
- Procedures should be applied making it a disciplinary offence for anyone outside the MCSU to copy executable files onto the microcomputers.
- Tape backup devices should be provided for microcomputers with big volumes of volatile information stored on hard disks.
- The MCSU should be made liable for all machine maintenance and user support.

- Buying of microcomputers, software and peripherals should be centralized.
- Machines with a lock that not only disables the machine but also disables removal of the cover should be bought.
- All microcomputers and peripherals should be indelibly marked with the MCSU liable for maintaining the inventory.
- Use of exchangeable disks, security shells, and encryption for machines which hold highly sensitive information should be taken into account.
- It must be emphasized that all formatted storage devices are signed into and out of the premises by MCSU staff.
- All formatted storage devices brought onto the site should be virus-checked, comprising those that are "shrink wrapped" and those carried by maintenance engineers.
- Microcomputer security and housekeeping should be inserted in the security awareness programme.

Discussion

Early microcomputers were single user, single task machines with little memory and slow low capacity, storage devices. Although the processing power of microcomputers has improved dramatically, they have retained various of the characteristics from their beginnings. This is reflected in popular operating systems of the eighties such as IBM/ Microsoft DOS. The situation is possibly to continue following the thousands of applications written for the DOS environment. Microsoft Windows and Quarterdeck Desqview have addressed the memory constraints and offered multitasking but neither address security issues. OS2 does address some of the security issues but could not proved popular.

Microcomputer programmes tend to be "dirty" as they by-pass the operating system and address system resources at a very low level. Applications do this to improve work and achieve finer control over individual resources than is feasible using the operating system. The low level interface between applications and the microcomputer is hard to intercept and demands a very high level of compatibility. Any endeavour to place security software between the applications and the hardware tends to lead to compatibility problems.

Microcomputers are outside the controlled environment of the computer centre. Users often act as operators, analysis, programmers and maintenance engineers without proper training to fulfil any of these functions. The machines are vulnerable to abuse and theft. Big hard disks and low capacity floppy disks discourage users from backing up adequately. The presence of floppy disks and serial ports facilitate to transfer data and programmes from machine to machine. This invites piracy of software and the introduction of viruses.

Microcomputers are familiar. Many users have them at home. This can boost productivity if people work in their own time but it also offers users with the opportunity to develop their own applications which could include games and malicious programs. In addition programs written by others are readily available from shops, magazines, bulletin boards and, sometimes, maintenance engineers. Viral infections have been applied to organizations from all of these sources. Even shrink-wrapped software has been found to be infected. All formatted storage devices should be checked for viruses. Security measures are generally concentrated on disks containing executable programs but data disks can contain viruses in the "boot sector" or embedded in spreadsheet macro definitions.

Given all of the problems related to microcomputers the first question to ask is whether the organization requires microcomputers or diskless workstations. If users do not need to copy data to and from floppy disk then the problems posed by microcomputers can be avoided by the simple expedient of providing users with machines without floppy disks. Data can be stored, controlled and backed up centrally whilst applications can reside on local or central hard disks. Before embracing this approach ensure that all applications will run with the chosen network software. Some microcomputer applications will not work if network software is loaded and others require key disks to be inserted in the floppy disk drive.

Micro Computer Support Unit

Microcomputing is a speciality. There is little in common between a multiuser, multitasking mini or mainframe computer and the microcomputer. It makes sense to setup a team of specialists accountable for :

- procurement;
- establishment of new hardware or software;
- awareness seminars, user support and training
- maintenance;

- virus checking;
- developing applications;
- maintaining an inventory of microcomputer assets.

The Microcomputer Support Unit (MCSU) can act as a competence centre for all issues relating to microcomputers including security. Central procurement and support facilitate to introduce standards and enforce regulations. The use of MCSU staff to install, maintain and upgrade users' machines provides MCSU staff an opportunity to check the machines for viral infection and pirated software. A strong MCSU or equivalent function is especially important for smaller field offices, perhaps placed in larger field offices at a regional level. Such a unit can effectively and efficiently handle the specific local support issues which can make or break successful microcomputer applications, comprising their security, in field offices.

Standards can be implemented if applications are developed by the MCSU rather than users. In addition the MCSU may be able to avoid duplication of effort by developing an application which will be of use to various groups of users.

Integrity

The ideal microcomputer would reliably run all the applications that the user needs forever without the requirement for backup, maintenance, upgrade or replacement. Unfortunately, microcomputers are not all "100% compatible", do fail inexplicably, do lose data, do need to be upgraded, do wear out and do require to be maintained. Using a standard range of hardware and software simplifies maintenance and user support and training. Central procurement and establishment is the best means to achieve standardization.

The MCSU and Personnel Department should reinforce standardization by applying procedures which make it a disciplinary offence for anyone other than MCSU staff to install software or hardware. This will give MCSU staff an opportunity to virus check new software and to install it properly.

The most potent asset in a microcomputer is corporate data yet users rarely backup their data adequately. Where floppy disks are the only backup medium this is understandable since it takes some 40 floppy disks to backup a modest hard disk. A host of time and trouble can be saved by setting up a tape streamer on all machines which are used to store large volumes of variable data. Tape streamers are not expensive and make backup quick, reliable and simple. Tape streamers which plug into the printer port can be used to backup portable computers and as a means of sharing the cost of backup between various desktop machines.

Many users keep one copy of their files on a single set of floppy disks. Floppy disks can be damaged easily and do wear out as the disk drive heads touch the floppy disk when it is in use. The security awareness programme should highlight the required backup floppy disks.

Microcomputers are both attractive and portable assets. This makes them principle targets for theft. Marking all microcomputers and peripherals prominently and indelibly discourages theft. If machines are moved infrequently it is worthwhile to chain them to a big piece of furniture.

An inventory is needed as the basis for maintenance contracts, planning for upgrades and holding users responsible for assets in their care. MCSU staff can mark machines at the same time as updating the inventory. The inventory should show the license numbers of any software packages installed on the machine.

Microcomputers do need maintenance. A number of variations of maintenance contracts are available. The main variables are "time to fix" and "time to respond". The shorter the "time to fix", the greater, normally, is the cost. Consider how long it would be feasible to do without a typical machine. If a single range of machines has been accepted as the standard, then it may be feasible to enhance resilience by swapping machines, and to save money by accepting a longer time to fix. If some machines are dedicated to performing critical functions, it may be important to arrange a short "time to fix" for them.

Privacy

There is often no access control on microcomputers. The file structure used by DOS makes no provision for data division or compartmentation. This may be acceptable if the machine is used by a single person and locked away when that person leaves the room. In most of the organizations microcomputers are scattered throughout the building and rarely locked away. Under these circumstances access control does become an issue.

There are some programmes which can password protect machines or achieve access control by trapping users in a menu system, but many can be disabled by starting the machine from a system floppy disk. Packages which disable use of the floppy disk drive can cause problems if the hard disk becomes corrupted as the user is deprived of an alternative means of starting up the machine. Menu systems have the disadvantage of a high maintenance overhead if user needs are volatile. They can also be trivially defeated if the applications driven by the menu have a "shell to DOS" option or even a text editor. In spite of these problems they can be effective where the user need is fairly stable and the user population is not too sophisticated.

Buying machines which can be disabled using a key is a simple measure which is adequate for most purposes. Make sure that the cover cannot be removed when the machine is locked since the lock can be disabled once the cover is open. Two keys are usually supplied. If both keys are lost, it is not feasible to get a replacement unless the key number is known, and even then it can take months to arrive. The MCSU should enter the key number on the microcomputer inventory and keep one key.

Locking the microcomputer saves the contents of the hard disk but does little to avoid disclosure of data if floppy disks and backup tapes ae left lying around They should be locked away when not in use.

If very sensitive data is held on microcomputers, then extra measures are necessary. Magnetic media and prints which contain sensitive information will require to be security-marked. Magnetic media will haave to be security erased or destroyed before leaving the site. Simply erasing a file is not enough since DOS just destroys the directory entry leaving the data intact. Security erasure involves frequently overwriting the space occupied by the file with a fixed pattern to obliterate any trace of the sensitive information.

Small quantities of highly sensitive information can be stored on floopy disks which can then be treated in the same way as divided documents. If this approach is adopted, steps will have to be taken to ensure that none of the applications that process the infromation copy it to he hard disk. Print spoolers, word processors and spreadsheets and create adhoc file on the had disk. It is usually possible to disable the production of the temporary files or cause them to be created on the floopy disk.

If big amounts of highly sensitive material need to be stored. It may be important to consider exchangeable disks, security shells and encryption. All of these measures introduce some degree of incompatibility, cost increase and performance penalty.

Exchangeable hard disks are the least intrusive privacy measure. If users have their own exchangeable hard disks they can secure their data by locking their disks away. This approach has the added benefits that users can alter their own setting for applications without affecting those of anyone else. The disadvantages lie in coast, compatibility an performance. Exchangeable hard disk tend to be slower than fixed disk equivalent and incompatible with some applications. Security marking and erasure can be dealt with in the same way as floppy disks.

The quality of encryption provided by general purpose microcomputer generally poor but encryption programme are available which conform to US Department of Defense standard. Encryption programs can be used to encrypt particularly sensitive files but this is not worthwhile if the files are ever stored in unencrypted form on the hard disk because fragments of the unenecrypted information will be scattered around the hard disk. Print spoolers generally lead to this problem. Encryption can itself expose the organization to the risk of data loss due to users forgetting their passwords or leaving the organization.

Some sequrity programs take over the microcomputer and enerty the whole hard disk as well as any floppy disks that are used. The program intercepts are endeavours to read or write disks and encrypts or decrypts the information as required. The main problems with this approach are performance degradation compatibility. The encryption and decryption process takes time which slows down applications and uses some memory which may lead large applicable to all. Some fail as the information is still encrypted or defeat the object by writing the unencrypted version to the hard disk.

Local Area Network Security

Instructions

- Local Area Networks (LANs) should be designed as part of an integrated information systems strategy. They should not be permitted to grow in an unplanned fashion.
- A LAN administrator should be appointed, who reports to information systems staff rather functional areas managers.
- It is important to use LAN hardware and software which has a

proven record of running the applications needed.

- It should be made sure that the application needed by the LAN can handle contention for access to files or devices.
- It should be ensured that the LAN software can handle data compartmentation and classification needs.
- The enviornmental needs of network file servers should be considered, and strong physical control over access to them established.
- Programmes should not be transferred from local disks to servers.
- The fault-tolerance of the network should be taken and a backup strategy established.
- Users should be given the minimum require rights consistent with the applicable that they require.

Disscussion

LAN are intended to satisfy the requirement to share resources and facilitate communication. The shared resource may be access to expensive device. Gateways to mainframe computers. Information or applications. Electronic mall, electronic diaries and automated meeting scheduling are instances of applications which use the communications facilities of the LAN.

Two groups of staff drive the development of LANs. Microcomputer users intend to share resources and information systems staff want to exploit the communications potential of LANs as a means of delivering applications. Several LAN that applications has failed as they were not integrated properly with the information systems strategy. Poor integration leads to duplication of effort, lack of control, vulnerability to machine or software failure and incompatibility between LANs.

LANs should be planner and administered by information systems staff. Users lack the strategic vision importance to design a LAN that will form an integrated part of the information system and usually lack the skill important to successfully address the technical integrity and access issues involved.

Planning, Design and Implementation

Ensuring that a LAN reliably delivers the services required involves planning design choice of hardware and software implementation and maintenance. Failure of any one aspect can lead to degradation of the service.

If LANs grow in an unplanned way then it will be not easy to integrate the information held on them. This can lead to a situation where incompatible versions of the same information are held in more than one form in more than one place. Another result is the proliferation of cables and terminals. Duplicating connections is not merely wasteful; it makes control much harder.

The choice of a particular LAN should not allowed to drive the design process. It is important to produce a full functional specification of the LAN before beginning to consider the hardware and software that will be used to enforce it. Risk analysis can be used to determine applications where availability privacy and integrity are critical. The specification should comprise needed. It may be required to use a LAN specification and design specification for highlight areas which require to be addressed during implementation and maintenance.

Integrity

The integrity of a LAN can be compromised by hardware failure, communications, failure, software failure, user error or system infiltration. All of these issues have been covered in previous chapters. This chapter concentrates on measures which can taken against threats which are peculiar to the LAN enviornment.

LAN software and hardware is an area of rapid development, problems involving networked hardware and software can be especially difficult to resolve. Networks are volatiie. There state at any one time depend on the independent actions of many individuals. Errors are difficult to diagnose as the circumstances leading to the error cannot be duplicated. The chance of being affected by one of these illusive errors can be reduced by choosing network hardware and software with a proven record of running the applications that are needed.

Various microcomputer applications, written to run under DOS, will run on a LAN. If applications designed for single user mahines are to be used. It is potent to make sure that the application or network software handles contention properly. If neither handle contention it is feasible for two users to gain write access to the same file. Whichever user saves the file last will everwrite the change made by the other user.

The design of a LAN should reflect the risk analysis of the applications which the LAN supports. Risk analysis identifies the critical applications and the components of the LAN that must be in place to support them. The results give an indication of the amount that should be spend on resillience an the best distribution of the resources available. The key components are usually the file servers and the network itself but risk analysis may defect other key components such as a unique output device which is necessary for a critical application.

Duplication is one means of protecting the LAN from the failure or basic components. Some networks use multiple file servers and cabling running in parallel to guarantee continuation of service. An aircraft control system is one instance where the application is considered critical enough to justify triple wiring and triple processing. If one network fails then the work load is switched to another while the fault is corrected. The amount of fault tolerance that is built in should reflect the outcomes of risk analysis. It may be sufficient to duplicate only key components and depend loss is caused by suspension of the applications which depend on them.

Backup of data poses certain problems in a LAN. By the time that the backup has taken place the state of the LAN will have changed. Parallel file servers are an extreme response to the backup problem. Some systems only permit backups to take place when the system is closed down while other can take a "snapshot" of the data on the file server without interfering with the users of the network. Whichever approach is adopted, a procedure for backing up and restoring the file server should be designed and tested.

The physical security and environment needs of the file server deserve particular attention. The file server should be locked away with access controlled by the LAN administrator. As a minimum an uninterruptible power supply and voltage regulator should be fitted. Larger file servers should be designed and tested.

The LAN administrator should control all software which interacts with the LAN. This may include software on workstation disks and the file server depending on the way that the network is configured. Users should have the minimum rights of access consistent with the applications that they require. Users should be unaware of programs and data concerned to other applications.

If users can copy files to the file server there is a risk that they will apply mallicious software. The best defence is to make it not possible to copy files from workstation disks to the file server but this may be impracticable if users require to transfer data to and from the file server on a regular basis. The risk can be reduced on some networks by marking all files which users create on the file server as non-executable.

Most exposures to unauthorized disclosure were covered fully in the chapter on communications integrity but there is one exposure which is peculiar to LANs. Network monitors are used by LAN administrators and by maintenance engineers. Their primary purpose is to diagnose overloads and faults in the network but they can be applied to monitor and record special connections. On an ethernet network it takes less than a minute to setup a network monitor given access to any part of the cabling. This can represent a serious risk of unauthorized exposure if the network traffic is unencrypted. It is good practice to supervise maintenance engineers while on site and this exposure is one more cause to do so. Physical access control is the best way to prevent network monitors being setup surreptitiously. The only effective control is physical examination of the network cabling.

Viruses, Worms, and Trojan Horses

Instructions

- Virus competence centres should be established.
- Information should be contained in the security awareness programme on the threat posed by malicious software. The need for backup and checks on data integrity must be stressed.
- Strong quality and change controls should be applied to prevent employees from inserting time bombs or logic bombs in their programs.
- Key machines must be isolated as much as feasible, and the installation of virus shield programmes on them considered.
- Users should be given access to the minimum set of programs important for their work.
- The competence centre should check all storage devices brought into the organization and test all programs received via communications links.
- At least two independent virus scanners should be applied; it is also necessary to keep up to date by obtaining upgrades to scanning software, and by reading the literature from electronic conferences on viruses and the computer security press.
- An incident register should be started, to record all information

systems failures. Regular meetings should be held between information system administrators and competence centres to know the cause of failures.

Discussion

"Computer viruses" are hidden programs which spread by inserting copies of themselves in other programs. Microcomputer viruses have received most publicity but all computer based systems with writable storage devices can be infected. The effects of virus infection can range from inconvenience to disaster. Any means of programs is a potential means of virus infection. No preventative measures are foolproof, so good detective measures and recovery procedures are essential.

"Trojan horse" programs masquerade as an attractive applications but cause damage to the information system when triggered by some event. The trigger may be a date, time, counter or some other change in system information like the withdrawal of the programmer's name from the payroll. Trojan horse programs are sometimes called "logic bombs: or "time bombs". These names are taken from the nature of the event that triggers the covert action of the programme. A programme may be both a virus and a Trojan horse because it may be delivered as part of an attractive application, replicate itself by infecting other programmes and become destructive when triggered by a predetermined event.

"Worms" are designed to make sure their own survival and use up system resurces. They differ from viruses in that they can exist and replicate in their own right without attaching themselves to host programs. Worms bring a system to a halt by replicating themselves in a geometric progression like a chain letter. Eah copy uses up some system resource and developes more copies until ultimately the whole system is dedicated to copying and executing the worms.

Virus prevention, detection and eradication is a speciality. Controls are more likely to succeed if a centre of competence is established to meet with the problem. This provides staff with a single, readily identifiable, source of advice and support.

Sources

Any storage device can be applied to infect a system. Even the Read Only memory (ROM) of a workstation could have a virus coded into it by the manufacturer. Any formatted disk can carry hidden programmes from one system to another. There have been examples of machines arriving from the manufacturer with viruses present on the hard disk. Viruses have been found on disks from all sorts of sources including magazines, promotional disks mailed direct to users and even "shrink wrapped" applications direct from the vendor.

Any communication channel can be used to introduce viruses. Open networks which permit programmes to be copied from one organization to another and Bulletin Board Services (BBS) are sources of infection. Several BBSs and networks have world wide links for the exchange of news, views and programmes. Every day new files are automatically copied around the network. This system permits malicious, as well as beneficial, programs to become widespread very quickly.

Maintenance staff travel from site to site inserting diagnostic disks in machines. Some maintenance engineers also disseminate utilities and recreational software to the support staff in organizations that they visit. Cases of viral infection have been attributed to engineers.

Viruses frequently trouble field offices due to the smaller environment and interaction with consultants, local suppliers, and other less controlled sources of diskettes. This risk requires to be anticipated in setting up microcomputer operations in field office, and in vetting data entering headquarters from the field.

Viruses are most common in educational and research establishments. Universities and colleges are particularly vulnerable in that machines are shared there is a large and volatile population of users, a number of users have the skills to write malicious programs and there is both the motivation and opportunity for free interchange of programs with other organizations.

Prevention

Good management controls can prevent staff from writing Trojan horse programs. Quality control and change control procedures should include review by staff with sufficient knowledge to follow the logic of the program. This ensures that collusion is important for programmers to embed time bombs or logic bombs in their code. Malicious and inefficient code is more likely to get through management procedures if individuals are allowed to have sole expertise in a particular development environment. Low level programming, obscure languages and systems programming are all environments where this can happen.

The risk of introducing malicious software from outside the organization can be minimized by importing as little software as possible, using merely trusted sources of hardware and software, and thoroughly testing all storage devices on entry to the organization. Every new machine, programme and formatted storage device should be checked even if it is still sealed in the vendor's packaging. Take particular attention to test any disks introduced by engineers or staff who use computers at college and any programs which come from BBSs or open networks.

The competence centre should certify tested storage devices and keep records of the programs tested, tests performed and the user's name. This can be reinforced by introducing procedures which make it a disciplinary offence to use a storage device which has not been certified by the virus competence centre.

There are "shield" utilities which claim to identify attempts to modify programmes. Shields can be set up so that they load automatically when the machine is switched on or rebooted. They are willing to be invisible to the user unless a security violation occurs. Some of the organizations use shield programs on all of their machines; others find that shields cost too much, use too much memory, degrade performance or are incompatible with their applications.

Detection

Most viruses can be detected by a combination of scanning software and a test environment. Scanning programmes search storage devices for characteristic attributes of known viruses. There are several scanning programmes available from commercial suppliers and BBSs. Scanning programmes have to be updated as each new virus is detected. The versions available from BBSs may be more up to date than the ones marketed conventionally. At least two scanning programmes should be used, as thisoffers greater protection and also permits one scanning programme to be used to check the other. Scanning programmes should always be stored, and run from write-protected floppy disks to avoid them from becoming infected.

The competence centre should set up a test environment for scanning. If possible this should consist of a machine which is both physically and logically separate from other machines. Before scanning a new storage device the machine should be loaded from a clean set of write protected system disks. Testing can then proceed by scanning each storage device in turn. Extra assurance can be gained by using a shield program to protect the test machine. Some shield utilities can write protect hard disks. This facility can be used to make sure that an application running on one disk makes no attempt toalter information on other disks.

Checksums are calculated by mathematically manipulating the contents of a file. They are calculated in such a way that changes to the file will give various checksum. Some virus detection programs keep records of the checksums of all executable files on the system. The program can be run at continuous intervals or before and after a suspect programme. If the checksums change there is a good chance that a virus is active but there is a risk of false virus alerts as some programs change themselves as a way of recording user preferences and control information.

A sacrificial machine can be used as a final stage in virus testing. This approach involves establishing the application on a machine that is only used for testing and then running through the full range of functions supported by the application. If the sacrificial machine survives and still passes scanning then the application is cleared for use.

Applications can use checksums to test for changes to data. Checks on data integrity are an important aspect of limiting the damage done by malicious programs. Small damage to data over a long period of time is difficult to detect and makes recover hard because the corruption may be spread over many generations of backups.

Malicious software can be identified by examining the information systems incident log. All information systems failures should be recorded in the log. The log can be used to track errors in applications and hardware but it can also be examined by the virus competence centre to see whether there is any pattern that could be the outcome of a malicious programme.

Eradication and Recovery

Some programs claim to be able to eliminate all trace of detected virus from a disk. Others identify all infected programmes and leave it up to support staff to remove them. The safest course is to security erase the entire disk, reformat it and then reload all of the programs and data from a trusted source. It is pointless to restore programmes from a backup in that there is a risk that the backup will be infected too.

There are specialist consultants in virus eradication. If there is any suspicion about the availability of internal expertise to solve the problem then it is better to hire a consultant to undertake the work and train competence centre staff.

The significance of regular checks on the integrity of data and a good backup programme cannot be over emphasized. Programs can be restored from their original disks but, without a reliable source of backup data, recovery can be highly costly.

Physical Security

Instructions

- The security awareness programme should cover avoiding, and dealing with, intruders, fire and flood. Regular drills should be held to make sure that staff understand the procedures to be followed.
- The exact location of sensitive facilities should not be publicized; attempts should be made to make sure that they are visible from public areas.
- Access to sensitive areas must be restricted.
- A contingency plan should be established, maintained and tested.
- Sites where large volumes of water are stored above the height of the computer room should be avoided
- Plastic sheeting, supports and cable blocks should be provided, to minimize the damage done by water.
- Flammable materials should not be stored in the computer room.
- Smoking and cooking should be banned around the computer room.
- The void under raised floors should be cleaned daily.
- Water, smoke and heat detectors should be fitted in the ceilings and floor voids.

Discussion

Intruders, fire and water are the main physical threats. War, civil disobedience, hurricanes and earthquakes may be important physical threats depending on the location of the information system. The measures needed to prevent, identify and deal with these problems depend on the physical location of the site and the sensitivity of the information held.

Good disaster planning and staff training can reduce both the frequency of physical threats and the amount of damage caused. It is a waste of time and money to install countermeasures if they are not helped by procedures and training. Planning and practice are the basic to successfully responding to an emergency. Locating computer facilities in remote, unpublicized sites which are not shared by other organizations makes physical security easier.

Fire

The computer room should be situated away from other fire hazard areas such as boilers, heavy plant, welding equipment, kitchens and fuel storage sites.

Most information systems fires occur in or near paper handling machines. Printers, guilloitines, envelopers and bursters all create static electricity and contribute to the level of paper dust in the atmosphere. Printers which use thermal bonding (including laser printers) increase the risk of fire. The level of dust can be subsided by extraction and filtering units. The risk of combustion can be minimized by regular maintenance of the equipment and fitting static discharge devices to the equipment.

Reducing the amount of flammable material in the computer roomhelps to mnimize the chance of fire. Stores of paper should be well away from the computer room. No more than one day's supply of stationery should be stored within the computer suite. The solvents which are used to clean computer equipment are highly flammable. They should be stored in a locked, flame proof, cupboard. Floor and ceiling voids should be continuously cleaned to avoid a build-up of flammable dust.

Reducing the chance of spark of flame is another aspect of fire prevention. Smoking and cooking should be banned around the computer room. Cable should be supported by travs to avoid shorting due to wear or damp. Machines and cables should be incessantly maintained.

Detection of fire relies on smoke, moisture and heat alarms in both the ceiling and floor cavities. The alarms do wear out and should be included in the planned maintenance programme.

Extinguishing a fire promptly relies on the availability of appropriate fire fighting equipment and staff trained to use it. Poor training can result in staff fatalities and equipment damage. If gas flooding equipment is used then staff will have to be carefully drilled in the procedures to be followed to avoid asphyxiation. Fire extinguishers should be maintained and explicitly marked. The use of a water based extinguisher on the electrical fire can lead to electrocution.

Water

Sites near reservoirs, natural bodies of water (e.g. rivers) and water storage tanks should be avoided. In very cold climates, pipes should be lagged and spaces containing pipes heated. Poorly maintained plumbing systems are an important cause of flooding. Planned maintenance of plumbing systems and the siting of computer equipment away from mains, pipes and cisterns helps to avoid damage.

Moisture alarms can be established to detect flooding quickly. Alarms should be sited in the floor and ceiling voids to avoid shorting of electrical cables due to moisture.

Damage from flooding can be limited by keeping cables raised from the floor in trays. If cable trays are not practicable consider raising cable connectors off the floor. Thin platic sheeting can be used to protect sensitive equipoment from water. Supplies of sheeting should be promptly available in the ocmputer room. Where equipment must be left running the sheeting should be raised above the machines to avoid a build up of heat.

Intruders

The risk of damage by intruders can be reduced by siting the computer room in a remote area away from centres of war or civil disobedience, avoiding publicity and maintaining staff morale. The risk of attempted inflitration is higher if it is widely believed that the system contains valuable information. Outsiders are more likely to try to damage the installation if they believe that the installation performs a sensitive or emotive function. Staff are more likely to damage the installation if they become disgruntled. It is necessary to recognize disgruntled staff quickly and placate or remove them because staff are more likely to be aware of the vulnerable points on the site.

Physical access can be controlled by security guards, card keys, button locks, identity tags, turnstiles, alarms and surveillance. Some site-level security is required even if it is limited to a receptionist who logs in visitors and examines photographic passes held by staff. Security within the installation will depend on the threats and vulnerabilities of certain locations. A layered security system is generally appropriate so that expensive access control measures can be concentrated at the most vulnerable points.

The guidance above applies to larger organizational sites. It should be employed to a proper extent to the information processing environment in smaller offices, especially field offices, to achieve cost-effective protection on information and related resources.

Contingency Planning

Instructions

- A contingency plan, which addresses all of the exposures detected by risk analysis, should be prepared and maintained.
- Change control procedures, which make sure that changes cannot be made without updating the contingency plans, should be setup.
- Security awareness and training programmes should be utilized to keep staff informed of their part in the contingency plan.
- The contingency plan must be tested at least once each year.
- A backup site should be detected, and copies of essential files and documentation maintained at the remote site.

Discussion

Contingency planning, like insurance, involves trading certain costs for uncertain advantages. Many organizations make the mistake of leaving contingency planning until after their first major system failure; some do not survive to make the same mistake again.

Risk analysis must be undertaken before any effort to develop a contingency plan because it identifies:

- Critical applications;
- The losses that justify countermeasures to protect information systems;
- System components necessary to support applications
- Events that threaten applications;

The consequence of risk analysis is a list of exposures sorted by Annual Loss Expectancy (ALE). The ALE reflects the effect that the event would have on critical applications and the probability that the event will happen in anyone year. The ALE is important as it is a measure of the uncertain benefit of contingency planning. It is the ALE which should be used to justify the cost of enforcing the contingency plan. A contingency plan based on risk analysis is much more likely to be accepted by senior management in that every countermeasure can be justified by reference to the critical activities that it protects.

The contingency plan should address all of the exposures detected by risk analysis. Accepting risks is a legitimate management prerogative but the contingency plan should state both that a particular risk is accepted and why it is proposed to accept, rather than address, the risk.

The applications supported by information systems, and the events that threaten them, change over time. The contingency plan and the risk analysis that supports it requires to be maintained to reflect new applications and threats. The information system security competence centre can monitor changes in the nature and importance of threats by keeping up with the literature produced by the computer security press. Changes in applications can be captured by applying a procedure which makes it compulsory for all major information system changes to be signed off by the information system security competence centre.

The competence centre can serve as the contingency planning coordinator. It can monitor the contingency planning endeavours of individual units and report to senior management. The development of contingency plans should be driven by staff rather than consultants as the consultants will not be there when the contingency plans have to be put into operation.

Staff must be aware of the provisions that the contingency plan makes with respect to their applications. Responsibility for each countermeasure should be set out explicitly in the plan and reflected in security awareness and training programmes. The plan should be tested at least once a year to prove that it is not impracticable and that staff both know their role and can perform it.

The aim of a contingency plan is to restore critical applications promptly and to maintain them until normal service can be resumed. The key variables that condition the cost of the contingency plan are the applications covered, time to respond and the period of coverage. The provisions for each application should reflect the time that the application can be unavailable before losses are incurred, the scale of initial losses and the rate at which losses accrue if the service remains unavailable. The provisions for each event should reflect the applications that are affected and the period of the disruption caused by the event.

Backup Provisions

Backup is the key to restoring applications. Risk analysis detects are components of an information system which are critical to each application. This consists of a list of data, equipment, communication lines, manuals, stationary, staff and so on. The level of backup provided should reflect the sensitivity of the dependent applications. A range of responses is feasible from full duplication to acceptance of the risk that a component will fail.

The type of backup essentially depends on the nature of the component which it protects. Duplication is involved in most cases:

- maintaining spare disk drives, modems, terminals;
- duplicating network cables or telephone lines;
- ensuring that no one member of staff is essential;
- copying software, manuals and data.

It is not always important for spare equipment to be held on site. It may be feasible to provide the needed level of resilience by taking out maintenance or standby contracts which guarantee to fix or replace components of the information system within a given time scale.

Data is one of the most difficult components to backup. In an online real time environment, users are continually making changes to data. The only way to avoid the loss of any data is to store changes to more than one device. Where no interruption of service is acceptable it may be important to duplicate all processing so that machines can be switched in the event of failure. At the other extreme, it may be feasible to rely on data stored on paper, microfiche or microfilm to provide a backup service.

At the extreme it is important to consider the destruction of a whole site. As a minimum, up-to-date backups of the contingency plan, data, software and documentation should be kept at a remote site. If it is planned to run the information systems at another site, one will have to be found where the configuration is compatible. It may be feasible to use another site within the organization or come to a mutual backup agreement with another organization. "Hot site" cover can be bought, which guarantees to make a computer establishment, to given specifications, available within a given period and for a specified duration.

Training, maintenance, testing and documented procedures are important parts o any contingency plan. Plans will only work if they are understood by staff. It is especially important that staff have a thorough understanding of contingency plans because they have to be implemented when a crisis occurs.

Security Procedures and Practices

Instructions

- The security policy, security programme and security operating procedures should be cross-referenced.
- The security procedures manual should assign liabilities, explain how to carry them out, explain why each procedure is required and state the consequences of failure to comply.
- Change management procedures should make that every major change in the security policy, security environment or information systems triggers a review of the security programme.
- The security procedures guide should be helped with both general and particular training and awareness programmes.

Discussion

Countermeasures cannot be enforced successfully without clearly defined responsibilities and procedures. A Security Operating Procedures (SOPs) manual should be established and maintained. The manual should contain a preamble explaining the information security policy, security programme and the risk analysis undertaken to assist it.

Procedures should be grouped by responsibility. General procedures affecting all members of staff should be recognized at the beginning. Subsequent sections should relate to specific groups of staff. It is not important to issue the entire guide to everyone. Each member of staff should be given the preamble, general procedures and the specific procedures that apply to their work.

The procedures guide should unambiguously state best practice and persuade, rather than compel, staff to comply with the rules. Staff are much more likely to accept procedures if they have contributed to the security programme and have an overall understanding of it. Procedures cannot cover every eventuality. If staff do not understand the rationale behind each procedure they are likely to make mistakes when faced with situations that are not particularly covered.

Information systems security should form one part of the office procedures manual. The manual should clearly state the procedures that staff are expected to comply with and the consequences of failure to comply. The purpose of the procedures manual is to:

- reduce errors and omissions;
- assign liability, rights and authority;
- educate staff about their role in the organization;
- provide a point of reference if disputes take place;
- develop good practice and discourage bad practice;
- facilitate swift response to emergencies;
- enable staff to stand in for others;
- make sure compliance with legislation;
- reinforce standards and promote consistency.

Procedure guides are likey to be disregarded if staff see them as outdated and meaningless rules imposed from above. Change management procedures should make sure that manuals are kept up-to-date and careful cross referencing will ensure that procedures are meaningful in relation to the security policy. It should be feasible to trace each procedure back to the security programme and through risk analysis to one or more of the objectives in the security policy statement. Every procedure should be justifiable by reference to the impact that particular threats could have on one or more information systems.

The Importance of Standards

Instructions

- It is necessary to buy hardware and software which is tried and tested and conforms to international standards.
- A structured systems analysis and design methodology should be used.
- A strong quality assurance system should be installed and operated at all stages of the System Development Life Cycle (SDLC).
- The requirement for low emission equipment to satisfy security or health and safety regulations should be considered.

Discussion

The objective of standards is to guarantee quality, consistency, compatibility and functionality. The requirement to improve quality control and maintainability led to standards for software development.

Pressure for open competition and interconnectivity has resulted in standards covering the specification and functionality of hardware, systems software and communications equipment. The increasing demand for closer integration of information systems is leading to standards covering the way that applications communicate with each other and with the user. Concern about the security of information systems has led to standards covering encryption and emanations and formal testing procedures for system software.

Development Standards

Methodologies for analysis, design and programming ensure that system development takes place in an orderly fashion and that the software produced can be maintained. Structured methods are essential for large interconnected information systems. Many methodologies have been developed and each have devotees. No one method is proper for all environments. The choice of a specific method is less important than the decision to standardize on one of them. It is the use of a common method for all internal software development which yields dividends in relation to quality control, resilience and maintainability.

There are some salient features which distinguish the better methodologies:

- integration of the information systems and corporate plan;
- availability of a Computer Assisted Software Engineering (CASE) and Integrated Programming System Environment (IPSE) tools;
- use of a data dictionary;
- use of milestones to control project development and provision for essential review at each stage;
- integrated documentation system comprising "user friendly" reports;
- recognition of, and support for, reusable modules;
- provision for system integrity and control checks;
- integration with a computer risk analysis and management method.

Some of the structured methods make quality control easier but none dispense with the requirement for strong procedural quality controls. The application user, systems security staff, and the information systems management should sign off each stage in project development before the next stage begins. Change control procedures should allow the introduction of new software only when the review procedures, testing and documentation have been completed. If some changes have to be made on an emergency basis then the quality control procedures should be introduced retrospectively at the earliest opportunity.

The ability to model the total information system is an important feature. Keeping an up-to-date model of information systems facilitates maintenance, enhancement and error tracking. A change to a single piece of data may affect various processes and derived data. The system model and change control procedures should ensure that the implications of changes are clear and that undesirable.

Compatibility and Compliance

Historically hardware and software vendors used proprietary hardware, operating systems, languages and data structures to stop clients from changing suppliers. This strategy stifled competition and made integration very difficult. Clients pressed for open standards so that they could link information systems from different vendors.

Standards have been issued formally by various bodies comprising the International organization for Standards (ISO), the American National Standards Institute (ANSI), the United Electronic Engineers (IEEE). Formal standards have been issued on all aspects of information systems including encoding characters (ASCII and ANSI), languages (ANSI COBOL), system integration (Open Systems Interconnection), packet switching (X25), data interchange (X400), operating systems (POSIX) and network cabling (IEEE 802.3). Other standards like Berkeley Unix, Hayes modem control language and IBM's PC and AT architecture have emerged due to the leadership of their suppliers in the marketplace.

Choosing equipment and software that complies with recognized standards makes integration easier and should improve the resilience and reliability of the information system. Given the instability of information system vendors it is not wise to become dependant on a single supplier.

Security

There are standards for encryption systems based on the dES and ENIGMA algorithms. Compliance with a recognized standard is necessary but the method of implementation should also be carefully considered. A product that encrypts the body of messages using DES encryption but leaves the key in plain text as part of the header offers little security.

If highly sensitive information is being handled, then the American Department of Defense "Orange Book" standards require to be considered. Operating systems can be submitted for independent testing. Those which have been tested are awarded a security rating ranging from D (negligible security) to A_1 (very high security).

Standards for the emission of radio and sound signals are not well set up. There are standards issued by the Federal Communications Commission (FCC) which dictate maximum levels of radio emissions but there are no particular technical criteria which must be met by equipment which is claimed to be "TEMPEST proof". It is accepted that TEMPEST proof equipment should have very low emanation levels but the precise levels remain to be set. In spite of the imprecision of the standard it may be a useful criterion for the selection of equipment which is to be used to process sensitive information near to a pubic area.

There is increasing concern about he effect of VDU radiation on the health of operators. As a consequence an international standard on emissions appears likely. Sweden has already introduced legislation limiting the permissible radiation levels.

20

Controlling and Maintaining Security Programmes

Controlling Security Measures and Controls

Instructiions

- The information systems security competence centre should monitor organizational or technological change and recognize their impact on the security programme.
- Information system security incidents should be explored by a joint team from the information system security competence centre, system support staff, internal audit and the data ownrs.
- A testing strategy should be established for each control recognized in the security programme.
- Internal audit must test each control on a cyclical basis.
- Statistical sampling should be used to make sure that testing of controls covers the whole period since the last review.

Discussion

The objective of monitoring is to ensure that controls identified in the security programme are appropriate, effective and enforced. This gives rise to three separate activities :

- Monitoring the security environment to make sure that changes are reflected in the security programme and security operating procedures.

- Investigating incidents which affect the confidentiality, integrity, or availability of information systems.
- Testing controls detected in the security programme and operating procedures to ensure that they are implemented and working properly.

Controlling the Security Environment

The controls in the security programme and operating procedures should be based on the outcomes of risk analysis and risk management. If the valuation of the asset protected threats facing the asset or the vulnerability of the asset to threats changes, then the risk analysis will change too. Risk management includes selecting the most cost effective set of countermeasures from the different sets that could protect an asset from a given threat. If organizational or technological transformation affect the relative costs of countermeasures then it may be that a different set of countermeasures should be introduced.

The team which prepared the information system security programme and procedures should monitor both internal and external changes and consider their affect on risk analyses and risk management decisions. The information system security competence centre will generally be best placed to undertake this role. They should review the security programme annually or more repeatedly if major changes take place.

Incident Reporting

An information system security incident register should be maintained by the information system security competence centre. The register should consist of reports from usrs of unavailability and unauthorized disclosure or modification. The incident register should also consist of a record of all emergency amendments to information systems. An emergency amendment is any change which has not been through the normal change control procedures. This will comprise usage of any system programme which can by-pass normal system controls.

All entries in the incident register should be reviewed by a team headed by internal audit. Team members should comprise representatives from the information security competence centre information systems support and the user community. The findings and any remedial action should be filed and cross referenced to the entry in the incident register.

Testing

There is no point introducing a control if it cannot be monitored. A testing strategy should be recognised for every control in the security programme. Tests should be carried out on a cyclical ground. The effort expended on the testing of any one control should reflect the risks that the control displaces. Tests should be designed to give an assurance that the control was operating for the total period under review. If a control is tested once each year then statistical sampling should be used to spread the testing over the year. Any other testing strategy will run the risk of identifying an atypical period when the control was working particularly well or badly.

Testing should be carried out by staff who are independent of those liable for designing or implementing controls. The internal audit department is usually best placed to fulfil these needs. The results of testing should be reviewed by senior management.

Controls may fail as they are inappropriate or because they are not being applied correctly. If the controls do not serve the objective identified in the security programme then the control should be discontinued and the security monitoring team should be alerted.

Staff may fail to implement important controls deliberately or accidentally. If they have compromised controls deliberately then senior management should be informed and disciplinary action considered. Accidental breach of controls may occur if staff are unaware of a control or do not understand how to implement it. In both cases intrnal audit should notify the security monitoring team and the staff responsible for security training and awareness.

Wherever a control breach is found the working papers should be cross referenced to the action taken and kept under review by internal audit until the control environment is restored. Internal audit should follow up control breaches by testing the control area again once any important changes to the training propgramme, security programme and security operating procedures have been made.

Maintenance

Guidelines

- The information system security competence centre should review the information systems security programs every year or sooner if there are big changes in information systems, the threats that they face, or the countermeasures available.

Discussion

The information systems security programme should be based on the results of risk analysis or management results. This will comprise changes in the valuation of information held, vulnerability to threats, magnitude of threats or the cost effectiveness of countermeasures. The security programme must also respond to any weakness detect by internal audit.

The information system security competence centre should be liable for creating and maintaining the security programme and procedures guide. They should monitor changes in the secuirty environment by attending conferences , participating in electronic conferences and reading the journal and books on computer security.

The personnel department should be aware of staff promotions transfers, recruitment, resingnation and dismissal. There should be a procedure which makes sure that the information system security competence centre is notified of any staff changes which affect the security programme or procedures.

Proposals to make changes to information systems should be routed through a change control section. Procedures should make sure that changes will not be authorized until the information system security competence centre has reviiewed them and made any important changes to the security programme.

Incidents which compromise the confidentiality, integrity or availability of information systems should be reported to internal audit. The information system security cometence centre should be represented on the team liable for the review of incidents.

Major changes in information systems should be subject to approval by an information system committee including senior managers of the systems, finance, audit and functional areas. The .information systems security competence centre should either be represented on the committee or receive minutes of each meeting.

It is necessary to keep the risk analysis and management models in step with the security programme and security procedures. Changes in the security programme should be driven by, and cross referenced to, changes in risk analysis or risk management models. Changes in the security programme should drive changes in security procedures and practices.

21

Essence of Guidelines

The Information System Security Policy Statement

- The information systems policy statement should be issued by the head of the organization.
- The policy statement should provide a framework for the detailed security programme. It should be short and, as it consists of only matters of principle, be infrequently revised.
- The policy statement should deal with information system security management liability accountability and cost.

Assigning Responsibility and Managing Information System Security

- Managers of functional areas should specify, and pay for, security needs relating to their own information.
- An information system security competence centre should be setup to advise, educate and co-ordinate staff.

Analyse Threats and Vulnerabilities

- The big majority of information systems losses are the result of errors or omissions by staff. Countermeasures which address this area should be given a high priority.
- Countermeasures which ensure early detection and individual responsibility should be employed and publicized because the fear of detection and public humiliation plays a major part in the reduction of misconduct.
- Organizational change is a major reason of staff grievances. Staff should receive training in the management of change in addition

a procedure should be in place to repidly escalate grievance before disgruntle staff seek revenge.

- Train staff to deal with emergencies before they become catastrophes. Many losses of information systems infrastructure to fire or flood could have been avoided if staff had been provided with less expensive equipment and trained to use it.
- Keep the threat posed by infiltration or sabotage by outsiders in perspective.

The Economics of Information System Security

- Countermeasure should address certain threats to particular information systems. Expenditure on countermeasures should be justified by the degree to which they are expected to wanting the frequency or impact of threats.
- When wanting to justify a countermeasure, it is advisable to begin by quantifying the effect on errors and omissions.
- Advantages should not continue to be quantified once they exceed the cost of the countermeasure under consideration.

Risk Analysis

- A risk analysis team should be formed which comprises an expert on information systems security and a respected member of the user community. The user representative should lead the team.
- Users' evaluations of the effects of information loss, exposure or modification should be the focus.
- Senior management approval must be sought at each stage of the risk analysis process. Form a risk analysis team which comprises an information systems security expert and a respected member of the user community. The user representative should lead the team.

Computer Assisted Risk Analysis

- At the outset, requirements should be conditioned and separated into mandatory and desirable features.
- A package which has good local support, consisting of training, should be chosen.
- It should be emphasised that vendors provide a demonstration of the way that their packages satisfy mandatory requirements.

- The philosophy behind the package should be examined carefully to make sure that the consequences can be defended.
- A package that can do backtracking and "what if" calculations should be chosen.

The Selection of Security Measures and Controls

- The user community should be involved in the recognition and implementation of suitable countermeasures.
- In recognizing security measures it is wrong to ignore "people solutions" or be afraid of high technology ones.
- Security measures should be ideally designed into information systems.
- Countermeasures must be appropriate to, and justified by, the risks previously analysed and recognized.

Personnel Issues

- A security awareness programme should be applied and maintained.
- Procedures for the transfer/termination of staff should be established and maintained.
- It is necessary to check the background of staff working in key areas.

Responsibility and Access

- Information systems require a means of uniquely recognizing individuals.
- Passwords should be hard to guess, changed continuously and known only to the authorized user.
- Systems should keep records of actions taken by each individual to facilitate responsibility.

Data Classification and Compartmentation

- Classification systems should be kept as simple as possible as complex schemes are costly.
- Procedures for controlling the copying of classified material must be examined.
- Procedures for declassifying material should be applied.

Hardware Integrity

- Obsolete and prototype hardware should be avoided.
- Dual processing should be considered for critical introductions.

- It is necessary to ensure that the machine's environment is protected from local problems in the power supply, air conditioning or cooled water supply.
- Regular backups of storage devices should be kept essentially.
- All information systems assets should be inventoried and given a security mark.

Software Integrity

- Established versions of software should be utilized.
- "Patching" of system software should be discouraged essentially.
- Strong change control should be set up over all of the files that make up the production environment.
- A separate development environment should be set up, and any changes thoroughly tested in the development environment before they are moved to the production system.
- It is potent to ensure that the system software can support the full range of logging and access controls needed.
- The "Orange Book" security rating of the operating system should be taken into account if the intention is to hold sensitive information on the system.
- A strong quality control system should be established and maintained to monitor changes to software.
- Parallel running should be used to test the effect of big changes to application or system software.
- Users must not be given direct access to the operating system.

Communications Integrity

- Networks should be designed so that they are insensitive to the failure of any one component.
- Leased lines or dial-back systems should be used in preference to direct connections using the public telephone network.
- An error-correcting protocol and confirmation messages should be employed to ensure that data is transferred properly.
- Messages should be encrypted to avoid exposure or modification.
- The requirement to reduce the level of radio signals from VDUs, keyboards and printers or to mask them with noise generating devices, should be considered.
- Feedback should be utilized so that the originator can be sure that all, and only, authorized messages have been received.

Microcomputer Security

- Diskless workstations should be used if feasible.
- A Microcomputer support Unit (MCSU) should be established.
- Procedures should be applied making it a disciplinary offence for anyone outside the MCSU to copy executable tiles onto the microcomputers.
- Tape backup devices should be given for microcomputers with large volumes of volatile information stored on hard disks.
- The MCSU should be made accountable for all machine maintenance and user support.
- Purchasing of microcomputers, software and peripherals should be centralized.
- Machines with a lock that not merely disables the machine but also disables removal of the cover should be bought.
- All microcomputers and peripherals should be indelibly marked, with the MCSU liable for maintaining the inventory.
- Use of exchangeable disks, security shells, and encryption for machines which hold highly sensitive information should be considered.
- It must be emphasised that all formatted storage devices are signed into and out of the premises by MCSU staff.
- All formatted storage devices brought onto the site should be virus-checked, comprising those that are "shrink wrapped" and those carried by maintenance engineers.
- Microcomputer security and housekeeping should be contained in the security awareness programme.

Local Area Network Security

- Local Area Networks (LANs) should be designed as part of an integrated Information systems strategy. They should not be permitted to grow in an unplanned fashion.
- A LAN administrator should be appointed, who reports to information systems staff rather than functional area managers.
- It is important to use LAN hardware and software which has a proven record of running the applications needed.
- It should be made sure that the applications required by the LAN can handle contention for access to files or devices.
- It should be ensured that the LAN software can handle data compartmentation and classification needs.

- The environmental requirements of network file servers should be taken into account, and strong physical controls over access to them established.
- Programs should not be changed from local disks to servers.
- The fault-tolerance of the network should be taken into account and a backup strategy established.
- Users should be given the minimum access rights consistent with the applications that they require.

Viruses, Worms, and Trojan Horses

- Virus competence centres should be set up.
- Information should be included in the security awareness programme on the threat posed by malicious software. The requirement for backup and checks on data integrity must be stressed.
- Strong quality and change controls should be utilized toprevent employees from inserting time bombs or logic bombs in their programs.
- Key machines must be isolated as much as possible, and the establishing of virus shield programs on them considered.
- Users should be given access to the minimum set of programs important for their work.
- The competence centre should check all storage devices brought into the organization and test all programs received via communications links.
- At least two independent virus scanners should be used; it is also potent to keep up to date by obtaining upgrades to scanning software, and by reading the literature from electronic conferences on viruses and the computer security press.
- An incident register should be started to record all information systems failures. Regular meetings should be organized between information system administrators and competence centres to establish the cause of failures.

Physical Security

- The security awareness programme should cover avoiding, and dealing with, intruders, fire and flood. Regular drills should be held to make sure that staff understand the procedures to be followed.

- The exact location of sensitive facilities should not be publicized; attempts should be made to make sure that they are not visible from public areas.
- Access to sensitive areas should be restricted essentially.
- A contingency plan should be started, maintained and tested.
- That sites should be avoided where large volumes of water are stored above the height of the computer room.
- Plastic sheeting, supports and cable blocks should be provided, to minimize the damage done by water.
- Flammable materials must not be stored in the computer room.
- Smoking and cooking require to be banned in the vicinity of the computer room.
- The void under raised floors should be cleaned.
- Water, smoke and heat detectors should be fitted in the ceilings and floor voids.

Contingency Planning

- A contingency plan, which addresses all of the exposures recognized by risk analysis, should be prepared and maintained.
- Change control procedures, which make sure that changes cannot be made without updating the contingency plans, should be established.
- Security awareness and training programmes should be utilized to keep staff informed of their part in the contingency plan.
- The contingency plan must be tested at least once each year.
- A backup site should be recognized and copies of essential files and documentation maintained at the remote site.

Security Procedures and Practices

- The security policy, security programme and security operating procedures should be cross-referenced.
- The security procedures manual should assign liabilities, explain how to carry them out, explain why each procedure is required and state the results of failure to comply.
- Change management procedures should ensure that every big change in the security policy, security environment or information systems triggers a review of the security programme.
- The security procedures guide should be supported with both general and particular training and awareness programmes.

The importance of Standards

- It is necessary to buy hardware and software which is tried and tested and conforms to international standards.
- A structured systems analysis and design methodology should be utilized.
- A strong quality assurance system should be established, and operated at all stages of the System Development Life Cycle (SDLC).
- The requirement for low emission equipment to satisfy security or health and safety regulations should be considered.

Monitoring Security Measures and Controls

- The information systems security competence centre should monitor organizational or technological change and recognize their impact on the security programme.
- Information system security incidents should be explored by a joint team from the information system security competence centre, system support staff, internal audit and the data owners.
- A testing strategy should be installed for each control identified in the security programme.
- Internal audit should test each control on a cyclical ground.
- Statistical sampling should be used to make sure that testing of controls covers the entire period since the last review.

Maintenance

- The information system security competence centre should review the information systems security programme each year or sooner if there are major transformation in information systems, the threats that they face, or the countermeasures available.

An Approach to Information System Security

Overview

Cost effective information system security makes necessary the coordination of many different countermeasures. Reacting to security problems in a piecemeal fashion leads to fragmentation with too much control in some areas and not adequate control in others. This handbook sets out a methodical approach to developing a sound security programme.

Information system security planning should be an integral part of corporate planning. The corporate plan should identify the chief objectives of the organization. The information system security programme should identify the measures that are necessary to safeguard the part that information systems play in the achievement of corporate objectives. The security policy provides a framework for the security programme which makes that it reflects corporate policy. The security policy should be supported by the results of risk analysis and risk management. Risk analysis of the vulnerability of the information systems. Risk management involves the identification of cost effective measures which reduce to an acceptable level the exposure of information system to risks.

Experience shows that setting up a center of competence and making it liable initiating the security programme leads to better information system security. The staff in the centre should act consultants. Their job is to support and advise the users of information system and not to impose a security programme on them.

Security policy

Sufficient information security programmes rarely evolve from the bottom up. Senior management should worry about the accuracy, timeless, completeness, and confidentiality of the information which they receive and must demonstrate their commitment to the security programme. One of the first consequence of senior management concern should be the establishment of a centre of competence in information systems security.

It is rare for the head of an organization to write the information system security policy statement. However, a security policy will only succeed with the full support of senior management. The policy should be drafted in close relation with senior managers and be signed by the head of organization.

Data Valuation

The valuation of information systems is a key element in the justification of the countermeasures which protect them. Users occupy a central role in data valuation as it is they who can best assess the impact of unavailability, modification or exposure of the information which they receive. A system without users is worthless and should be discontinued rather than protected.

The first stage in documenting the data dependence of an organization is to detect the users of each information system. Support users should be added to the information system security team. This will support to ensure consistent data valuation and facilitate acceptance in the user community.

External users should not be ignored; it may be clients, rather that staff, who place most value on information systems. Where this the case, consider charging out the cost of any additional security measures made important by the clients valuation.

Development plans must be considered. Users of planned systems, and existing ones, require to be identified. It is much easier to design security into a system that to add to it afterwards.

Threats and Vulnerability

The "quality" of data lies in its confidentiality, integrity and availability. For each system threats to the quality of the data received by each user should be identified, and the vulnerability of the information system to each threat considered.

Risk Analysis

The aim of risk analysis is to set up the security requirement of each system by combining the results of data valuation with those from the threat/vulnerability analysis. The result is a statement of Annual Loss Expectancy (ALE). The ALE can be used to rank threats/systems in order of priority for the risk management stage. At the top of the list will be those threats/systems where the threat is possibly to occur, the system is vulnerable to the threat and the users of the system place a high value on the information which they receive from it.

Risk Management

The results of the risk analysis should guide the selection and implementation of countermeasures. It is rarely feasible to implement security measures in exactly the sequence suggested by risk analysis because of interdependence and skill/resource shortages.

The selection of appropriate countermeasures is the first stage in risk management. It is a job which is never completed following changes in the environment and information systems. By the time one security plan has been implemented it is time to review the requirements again.

Despite it major improvements can be made quickly by concentrating on threats/systems where the ALE is high.

In the selection of countermeasures, the following should be kept in mind:

(a) No security measures are inherently good or bad. Each should be considered on its own merits in the light of an in-depth understanding of a specific system.

(b) Security measures should cost less than the value of the information that they project.

(c) A threat/vulnerability analysis of the whole system is important before trying to identify appropriate responses to particular security problems.

(d) Few security problems can be contained by a single security measure in isolation. Most need a set of complementary measures.

(e) Many security measures address more than one problem. The cost effectiveness of a countermeasure depends on its ability to reduce disclosure to a number of threats.

(f) Controls are not inherently good. They cost money and cause user disruption. Controls should only be implemented when the results of their absence outweighs the cost of their presence.

Fortunately many of the steps which are indispensable to information system security are also among the cheapest to implement. Without exception these comprise an organization wide security policy and security awareness programme. These two measures should be implemented as quickly as feasible.

The preparation of Security Operational Procedures (SOPs) should proceed in parallel with the implementation of physical and procedural measures as both require sections in the manual to support them.

Monitoring and Maintenance

The success of the security action plan will depend on careful monitoring and adjustment. Following the rate of change of systems and the threats that face them, a static plan will quickly become useless.

A Security incident Register should be established. The procedures guide should need that all material information system violations be registered. This will help to recognize areas of the security plan that require to be changed.

Continuous testing of security measures is essential. It helps to determine the effectiveness of controls and gives staff a clear indication of management's continuing interest which makes compliance more possibly.

One of the functions of the information security competence centre includes monitor both internal and external developments and assess their impact on the security plan.

22

An Approach to Information System Security Guidelines for the UN Organizations

Summary

Information systems have developed to such an extent that most of the organizations now depend on them for their survival. Unfortunately, protective measures to assure the safety and availability of information systems have not developed at the same pace. Managers are becoming incessantly aware that information system security has to be addressed. This handbook, prepared by the Advisory Committee for the Co-ordination of Information Systems (ACCIS), aims to give help to managers in the United Nations organizations who are looking for adequate and cost effective security for their information systems.

A good security programme offers a level of protection such that the direct and indirect costs of all security measures are less than the direct and indirect losses they displace. In addition, the measures selected should cost less than any others that would displace the same losses. This handbook describes a method of risk analysis and risk management which can be used to start a security programme that meets these objectives.

Senior management should issue a security policy statement which provides a framework for security management, responsibility, accountability and budgetary control. The policy statement should be short and, because it contains matters of principle, need revision only infrequently.

It is not important to be a technical specialist to understand information system security. Managers can specify their needs, in terms of the functionality of the measures needed, without needing to understand the technical details involved in implementing them.

The security of information systems is not something which senior management should leave to systems support staff. The security policy should assign primary responsibility for the security of information to functional area managers. The valuation of information is a basic element in the selection and justification of proper countermeasures. Functional area managers are in the best position to evaluate the impact of loss of confidentiality, integrity, or availability of their information. The managers will require help from information systems staff in understanding some of the technical measures, but this cannot be seen as justification for moving the responsibility for information security to the technical area.

Most computer security problems are caused by non-technical users of information systems who misuse, accidentally or intentionally, the resources to which they are permitted access. Countermeasures which ensure early detection and individual responsibility should be employed and publicized as the fear of detection and public humiliation provides a strong incentive to be honest and avoid errors.

Damage to information systems by infiltrators has received a large publicity, although only around three percent of information system losses are caused by people outside of the organization where the loss occurs. The threat of infiltration by outsiders cannot be ignored but should be kept in perspective.

ACCIS recommends the establishment of a centre of competence in information systems security. The competence centre will develop an expertise in the principles of information system security and their application within an organization. It will act as a focal point for advice and guidance on matters concerned to information system security and make sure that the principles of risk analysis and management are consistently applied to all of the functional areas.

Contingency planning is an important aspect of the information system security programme. An organization should start, test and maintain a contingency plan for information security that covers all of its critical functions. The resources spent on security measures should reflect the impact of the event to which they relate and the likelihood of the event occurring. Contingency planning generally receives too little attention on the basis that the disasters which cause serious disruption happen infrequently. This is a mistake. In consideration of the resources which should be allocated to contingency planning, the enormous impact of a disastrous event should be taken into account. It is necessary to consider the possibility of a disaster occurring rather than the probability of a particular event causing a disaster.

Many countermeasures will not work unless they are supported by policies and procedures. The introduction of a new countermeasure should trigger a revision of the security programme and security procedures guide. Security measures will fail unless employees understand and support them. Staff training and awareness programmes should ensure that staff are kept up to date with changes in the threat environment and the countermeasures introduced to protect the organization.Many countermeasures will not work unless they are supported by policies and procedures. The introduction of a new countermeasure should trigger a revision of the security programme and security procedures guide. Security measures will fail unless employees understand and support them. Staff training and awareness programmes should ensure that staff are kept up to date with changes in the threat environment and the countermeasures introduced to protect the organization.

Index